Police Unionism

Police Unionism

Power and Impact in Public-Sector Bargaining

Hervey A. Juris
Northwestern University

Peter Feuille
University of Oregon

Lexington Books
D.C. Heath and Company
Lexington, Massachusetts
Toronto   London

19729

1972⌣

Library of Congress Cataloging in Publication Data

Juris, Hervey A.
  Police unionism.

    1. Trade-unions—Police—United States.
I. Feuille, Peter, joint author. II. Title.
HV8138.J87   331.88'11'36320973   73-7995
ISBN 0-669-86801-9

Published simultaneously in Canada.

Printed in the United States of America.

International Standard Book Number: 0-669-86801-9

Library of Congress Catalog Card Number: 73-7995

Contents

List of Figures and Tables

Figures

Tables

Preface

This book is an outgrowth of a study of police unions the authors undertook during 1971. The study was made possible by a grant from the National Institute of Law Enforcement and Criminal Justice, Law Enforcement Assistance Administration, U.S. Department of Justice. Without the support of the institute and the understanding guidance of first Sidney Epstein and then Louis Mayo, that study could not have been undertaken or completed.

Additional financial support, which enabled us to complete this manuscript, was received from the University Research Committee of Northwestern University and the Institute of Industrial and Labor Relations at the University of Oregon (from funds provided by the U.S. Department of Labor, Manpower Administration, Grant 31-39-70-09). We are indebted to them for their generous support. The fact that the National Institute, Northwestern University, the University of Oregon, and the U.S. Department of Labor furnished financial support does not, of course, necessarily indicate their concurrence in our statements or conclusions.

We are tremendously indebted to the many police officers, police-union representatives, police-management personnel, city representatives, black-officer association representatives, and others who interrupted their busy schedules to talk with us. Without their generous cooperation we could not have written this book.

Our debt to our colleagues is considerable. Dian Land was involved in the project from its inception and was largely responsible for the transformation of the data from interview transcripts to forms more amenable to analysis. We are indebted to Arvid Anderson, Herman Goldstein, Robert Igleburger, and George O'Connor (members of our advisory committee) for their guidance during the course of the research and writing efforts and for their invaluable assistance in gaining entry into various police agencies and city governments. Arvid Anderson and Herman Goldstein are, in addition, responsible for significant improvements in the quality of the manuscript. We have profited greatly from the work and criticism of Thomas Kochan. George Strauss offered valuable suggestions throughout the course of our research and writing efforts. We are grateful to Donald Berney and Philip Kienast for making available their material on police organizations. Several other individuals, too numerous to mention, gave us constructive feedback on various portions of the manuscript. We gratefully acknowledge the contributions of all these people to whatever strengths this book may have and take full responsibility ourselves for any errors of commission or omission which remain.

We are also grateful for the expert secretarial assistance provided by Sandra Hennessy, Francine Krasno, Marcella Kreiter, Laura Wolf, Joanne McGovern, and Carol McMillan (who became Carol Feuille).

A word about division of labor: While both authors contributed substantially to all the material in each chapter, Hervey Juris had the original responsibility for Chapters 6, 7, 8, and 10; Peter Feuille had original responsibility for Chapters 2, 3, 4, 5, and 9; and Chapter 1 was a joint effort. This division reflects the primary research interests of the authors in this project (labor relations process for Feuille, impact for Juris).

In the current social and political climate no one in our society is, or can be, unbiased about the police and police unions. Thus, while we have made every attempt to be objective and to report and interpret the data as we saw it, the reader would best be served if he were aware of the "eyes" through which we saw this data.

During this research and writing effort, the senior author has been Associate Professor of Industrial Relations and Urban Affairs in the Graduate School of Management at Northwestern University, and the junior author has been making the transition from Ph.D. candidate in Industrial Relations-Organizational Behavior at the University of California in Berkeley to Assistant Professor of Management in the College of Business Administration at the University of Oregon. With many of our colleagues in the field of industrial relations, we share a strong commitment to the right of employees to form, join, and assist unions for the purposes of engaging in collective bargaining and other activities in the pursuit of their own self-interest if they so choose.

We recognize and appreciate the need for the police service and the criminal justice system of which it is a part, but we strongly believe that both the larger system and its police component are in need of fundamental change. In particular, we are committed to the establishment of a new definition of the police function, one which explicitly recognizes that policemen spend a minority of their time enforcing the law and fighting crime and a majority engaged in providing a varied package of order maintenance and social services. We are committed to the need for a revaluation of the manpower system in police agencies and to the need for an explicit and widespread recognition of the high degree of intellectual, emotional, and physical skills necessary for effective job performance in the police service (and public acceptance of the high cost of developing and maintaining high quality police forces).

At the same time we are committed to the right of policemen to form, join, and assist unions, if they so choose, in order to participate via bargaining and other political processes in the decisions which affect their work lives. We recognize that in the short run such participation might increase the social, political, and economic costs of implementing needed changes, but we believe that in the long run participation in these decisions by those affected can be beneficial to all concerned. For thirty-eight years the bedrock principle of our national labor policy has been that private-sector employees have the right to participate in an organized manner in the decisions which affect their work lives. We have yet to encounter any compelling reasons why policemen (and other public employees) should not also enjoy similar rights.

Our main concern in this book has been to chronicle and interpret as objectively as possible the activities and impact of police unions in twenty-two cities. In writing this book we have presented material as we saw it. Operationally, this means that the book contains something with which everyone can disagree.

Finally, we owe a special debt to our wives, Toni and Carol, both of whom drastically altered their lifestyles so that we could be free to travel and write. Had the shoe been on the other foot, we are not sure we would have been as tolerant.

Police Unionism

1 Introduction

The rise of militant police unionism in the decade of the 1960s caused a lot of comment and concern among police executives, the press, and the public. Some of this concern was based on firsthand experience, much of it was based on misinformation and fear of the unknown. The purpose of this book is to attempt to place the police-union movement in perspective, relying primarily on a field study of the practice of police unionism in twenty-two urban jurisdictions across the country.

Police Unionism and the Information Gap

It is not our intention to suggest that the concerns expressed by officials, the press, and elements of the public were unfounded. "Blue flu" and other job actions by police employee organizations clearly raised the spectre of the 1919 Boston police strike. The 1969 strike by police and firefighters in Montreal with its toll of looting and property destruction seemed to indicate that the doomsayers were if anything understating the potential harm that could come from the police-union movement. It is not the events, however, which concern us so much as it is the interpretation and reporting of those events and the conclusions drawn from these reports as to the implications of police unionism for police managers and the public.

The Concerns of the Chiefs

In 1972, Police Commissioner John Nichols of Detroit made the following comments to an audience composed of police chiefs, police personnel administrators, and some police-union leaders:

In closing, let me sound the "certain trumpet" of dangers of "It can't happen to me-ism." Police unionism is on the move—power struggles are forming, and I would fully expect the rise of police unions almost across the country to closely follow the patterns of ascendancy of other labor unions, which resulted in attempts to immobilize equipment, harassment of nonparticipating employees, work slowdowns, control of organizations by a well indoctrinated, vociferous few, a diversion of loyalty from organizational goals to union goals, and ultimately, as expressed to a public seminar on community relations by two of

1

our most outspoken union leaders—one from New York and the other from Detroit—who said, "Chiefs, Superintendents, and Commissioners are temporal. They'll change. The Union is the only permanency in the Department. It is us with whom you will deal, we will make the policy!"

So for those of you who feel that unionism has no designs on management prerogatives, no desire for power, no intentions to covertly or overtly control the organization, forget it.

Many issues are raised in this statement. Is police unionism the wave of the future? What kind of power struggles are forming? Are work slowdowns and strikes a natural consequence of unionization? Are police unions controlled by a well-indoctrinated vociferous few? Do police employee organizations divert loyalty from the department to the union? It is true that the union has greater permanency in the department than the commissioner, but what are the implications of this diverse tenure? Finally, what are the intentions of the union toward management prerogatives, and power and control within the organization? It is our purpose to investigate all of these questions in the remainder of this book.

There are other questions that concern chiefs of police to which we also hope to be responsive. What is the proper role of a police administrator vis-à-vis police unions? What happens if my men go on strike? Does it make any difference if I face a union steward or an FOP delegate—is AFL-CIO unionism different from independent union membership? What happened to my local police association—a few minutes ago it was a social and fraternal organization; now it's a union! Can a chief do only what the consensus of his department allows? Is it possible to make unions a positive force in good police administration?

The Concerns of the Public

In a widely circulated series originally appearing in the *Cleveland Plain Dealer*, Joseph Eszterhas concluded on the basis of a "national" study of patrolmen's associations that the police-union movement "is challenging and in some cases curbing the power of the chief of police to function as he has traditionally." Other "basic conclusions: within a police department unionization can lead to the edge of chaos in management of the department; a powerful police union can completely frustrate the goals of a city administration; police unions have waged particularly bitter direct battle against liberal mayoral administrations."[1]

Sociologist Jerome Skolnick, author of *Justice Without Trial*, writes in the widely read *The Politics of Protest:*

The police have become more militant in their views and demands and have recently begun to act out this militancy, sometimes by violence but also by threatening illegal strikes, lobbying, and organizing politically. These organizations ... originally devoted to increasing police pay and benefits, have grown stronger. . . . Moreover these organizations have begun to challenge and disobey the authority of police commanders, the civic government, and the courts to enter the political arena as an organized militant constituency.[2]

Skolnick cites examples primarily from Boston, New York, Cleveland and Detroit, the same cities which formed the basis for Eszterhas' conclusions.

Unfortunately, Eszterhas and Skolnick chose to focus on the more militant examples of labor-management relations in the police service, ignoring at least ninety other jurisdictions over 50,000 in population where police unions were negotiating over wages, hours, and conditions of work.[3] However, the questions raised by Eszterhas, Skolnick, and others are not to be overlooked merely because of the sensationalistic way in which they are presented. Indeed, they are a reminder that the evolution of police unions into strong economic and political institutions has occurred largely unobserved and virtually unstudied.[4]

Objectives of the Study

In part to test the validity of Eszterhas and Skolnick's observations, and in part to seek answers to some of the concerns expressed by chiefs, the authors set out to systematically collect information in six areas: the nature of police employee organizations, the structure, scope and process of collective bargaining in the police service, the impact of police unions on law-enforcement policy formulation, their impact on the chief's ability to manage, the impact of police unions on the potential for professionalization, and the relationship between police unions and the black officers' organizations which have sprung up in many urban areas. Each of these is discussed in more detail below:

— *The nature of police employee organizations.* Their evolution, structure, and government; the factors, if any which might distinguish their behavior from the behavior of other unions in the public and private sectors.
— *The structure, scope, and process of collective bargaining in the police serivce.* Here we were particularly concerned with who bargained for the city, the role of the chief in bargaining, and the impact of structure on results; we were also concerned with impasse resolution, arbitration, and the use of power in police bargaining.
— *The impact of police unions on law-enforcement policy formulation in the community.* Skolnick and Eszterhas were both quite concerned with the political activity of police employee organizations, so we were quite conscious of this aspect of the unions' operations. Particularly, to what extent is the political activity of police unionism oriented toward influencing law-enforcement policy. Are the observations by Skolnick and Eszterhas in the four pathological examples valid and if so, do they carry over to other urban jurisdictions?

— *The impact of police unions on the potential for professionalization of the police service.* The IACP especially has been concerned that police unionism is inconsistent with professionalization of the police service. In our field work, we were particularly interested in examples of behavior which might be construed as retarding or accelerating professionalization.

— *The impact of police unions on the ability of the chief of police to manage* (and implicitly to maintain control and direction of his department). In this case, we attempted to gather as much information as possible on the subjects in which the union had even attempted to gain a voice. In addition, we asked department personnel to give their assessment of the impact of each request as it related to their ability to manage.

— *The relationship between police unions and black officers' organizations* (where they exist). We were particularly concerned with whether these were groups competing for collective-bargaining rights, whether each was adversary toward management but not toward one another, or whether each was adversary to management and to one another. We were also interested in the nature of the issues raised by black caucuses and the strategies and techniques followed in achieving their goals.

Methodology

Our information was obtained primarily through a field study conducted in twenty-two urban areas. The sample selected was not random; it was important for a study of impact that there be some history of labor-management relations in each city studied. The chief sample selection criterion was the existence of systematic interaction among the police union, the police department, and the city. Because our interviews would be based on discussions of critical incidents in the bargaining relationship, we were primarily looking for cities with a collective-bargaining history, some kind of job action or at least a well-publicized conflict between the union, the department, and the city.

Initially a detailed questionnaire was sent to the police chief, the police union(s), and the chief labor-relations executive in the thirty largest cities and thirty-five additional cities selected from among the respondents to the 1968 Juris and Hutchison survey.[5] It was felt that this mixture would give us a good representation from large cities and also a large number of cities where we knew collective bargaining was taking place. While a few cities flatly refused to participate, we received at least one response from fifty-five of the sixty-five cities and responses from forty-nine of the sixty-five police chiefs. Some of the unions were unwilling to fill out a long questionnaire and many of the cities, it turns out, did not have a chief labor-relations executive.[6]

On the basis of the returned questionnaires, twenty-two cities were selected for field study. During these field visits (which were usually of four to five days' duration each) information was collected via interviews with city labor-relations representatives, the police chief or his representatives, police-union leaders (elected officers, business agents, and union attorneys), and black officer organization leaders (where such a black organization existed). The number of interviewees per city ranged from three to fourteen, with a norm of four to six. All interviews were conducted by one or the other of the authors, or both. This interview information was supplemented by extensive consultation of newspaper files and other published sources in each city. The field visits yielded most of the information reported in the following pages.

In conducting the interviews a critical incident technique was used. The field investigator would familiarize himself with the broad outlines of police labor-management relations in that city (usually through archival research in local newspaper libraries and questionnaire data), frame questions relative to specific issues, and then pursue each party's relationship to these issues in subsequent interviews. This approach was used first because it enabled us to investigate the parties' actual conduct toward one another and to look at the process of the relationship and second because the substance of union-management interaction deals with specific issues (e.g., a pay raise, a pension improvement) rather than with abstract principles.

Some Strong Disclaimers

First, we acknowledge that readers may find errors of fact and/or interpretation as they read through this report. This is inevitable when one is dealing with such a large amount of data, almost all of which reflects the interpretations of particular interviewees and the responses of the interviewers who may not always have "heard" what was actually being "said." The generalizations that do emerge, however, are not of the type to be severely affected by what we believe are random errors.

Second, we promised anonymity to our interviewees in return for their cooperation. Most of our respondents are continuing in their roles and we have no intention of embarrassing them. While such phrases as "in five cities we found . . . " may frustrate those who want to know *which* cities, we ask the reader's indulgence in honoring these commitments. We have attributed many issues or disputes to particular cities if they had already been recorded in the public press, but doubts were resolved in favor of anonymity.

Third, we were not able to ask identical sets of questions of people in identical positions in each city. We talked with those respondents who were willing to see us, and we tailored our questions to fit the local situation. Thus we are not able to present our findings in a series of tables, charts, or graphs showing numerical breakdowns of respondents' answers to general questions.

Finally, extreme care and caution must be exercised in generalizing from the information in this book. The fact that this is an exploratory study means that many of the conclusions we present are suggested by our data but not proved. Moreover, as we stated above, the sample was not meant to be representative of the nation's 40,000 plus police jurisdictions: half of our sample consists of cities over 500,000 population; only two cities had less than 100,000 citizens; none were from the South. These findings do, however, tell us something about the particular activities police unions undertake to achieve their goals, something about the relationship between particular issues and the union's use of power, and something about the impact of aggressive police unions on the agency and the public. Our purpose is to present our findings in such a manner that others in similar situations may use this information to further their own understanding of the process of labor-management relations in the police service by testing our findings against their situations.

The Background: American Trade Unionism

We anticipate that two distinct audiences will be interested in this book—those whose role involves engaging in or studying the process of collective bargaining and those whose primary background is law enforcement. For this latter group we include the following historical overview of the trade-union movement in America and the Glossary which appears at the end of the study. Our other readers may find it more useful to proceed directly to Chapter 2.

One of the strongest findings to emerge from our research is that the twenty-two police unions we studied are solidly within the mainstream of American trade unionism. They emphasize traditional union goals of higher wages and fringe benefits, shorter hours, and improved working conditions, and they employ the same pressure tactics to achieve their goals as are used by other unions in the public sector. Subsequent chapters will present information which will substantiate this sweeping assertion. However, to maximize the value of the following chapters, it is necessary to describe briefly the main features of the labor movement of which police unions are a part.

The Legal Base of Trade Unionism

Police unionism has its roots in a U.S. tradition which goes back to the post-Revolutionary War period. Workers in the skilled, apprenticeable trades (carpentry, shoemaking, printing) formed self-help organizations which were patterned after the European guilds. These organizations of the late eighteenth and nineteenth centuries maintained a precarious existence, becoming skeletons or disappearing entirely during periods of economic depression and making modest improvements in wages, hours, and working conditions during prosperous times. Under early common law, however, these associations were considered criminal conspiracies "in restraint of trade" and an employer who did not choose to voluntarily deal with an employee organization could have it dissolved by the courts.

An 1842 court decision removed the onus of criminal conspiracy from organizations; however, the courts continued to prohibit, primarily via injunction, union self-help activities including strikes and boycotts. Thus, until the 1930s, while union organization was not unlawful in and of itself, most employers could and did obtain injunctions against employee collective self-help activities. While collective bargaining took place prior to the 1930s, it was on a relatively limited scale and was not legally protected activity.

This changed drastically during the following decade, in large part because of legislation introduced during the period 1932-35, when the federal government established the legality of private sector employees' right to form unions and to bargain collectively. In 1932 the Norris-LaGuardia Act outlawed federal injunctions in labor disputes. In 1933 Section 7(a) of the National Industrial Recovery Act affirmed that workers had a right to organize and bargain collectively and forbade employer interference in the process of choosing union representatives; however, there was no provision in NIRA for enforcement of these rights if an employer should refuse to cooperate. Experience under NIRA showed that collective-bargaining rights were of limited value unless the government sought to protect and enforce these employee rights. In 1935 the Supreme Court struck down NIRA.

The *protected* right to organize and to bargain collectively came in 1935 with the passage of the National Labor Relations Act (known as the Wagner Act after its chief Senate sponsor). The act specified certain unfair labor practices which prohibited employers from interfering with employee rights to freely choose a majority representative and prohibited employers from refusing to bargain collectively. The act also created the National Labor Relations Board to enforce these prohibitions. In addition to its judicial function, the board maintains machinery for the orderly selection of majority representatives.

The act did facilitate organization and collective bargaining; however, a decade or so of experience (including the immediate postwar period) showed that in redressing the imbalance between private sector employees and employers, the government had underestimated the strength some unions might achieve. Consequently, in 1947 Congress adopted the Taft-Hartley Act. While Taft-Hartley continued the organizing and bargaining guarantees of the Wagner Act, it added an employee right to refrain from union activity, it specified union unfair labor practices which prohibited union activities that might interfere with the exercise of employee free choice, and it compelled unions also to bargain in good faith. In general, Taft-Hartley imposed restrictions on unions where none had existed previously. Further restrictions were contained in the 1959 Landrum-Griffin Act which established a union member "Bill of Rights" and imposed federal reporting requirements on unions (similar to the requirements imposed on public corporations). The significant fact to remember, though, is that the 1947 and 1959 acts did not diminish the federal government's support for the basic protected right to organize and bargain collectively for employees in the private sector, and this is still the policy of the U.S. government today.

The Growth of Unionism

As we discussed earlier, private-sector trade unions have existed in this country since the latter eighteenth century; however, they have achieved their current levels of social, economic, and political significance in our society only in the last thirty-five years. While the change in the legal climate discussed above was an important factor in this rise to prominence, other factors had also changed since that time: the continuous pre-1920 flow of immigrants had slowed considerably, economic recessions were less recurrent, and consequently there was a significant period during which tighter labor markets prevailed.

In this century, private-sector unions grew fastest during the periods 1917-20, 1933-37, and 1941-45. The World War I period growth was primarily a result of employee desires to combat the very severe inflation of that period. The depression-era growth appeared to be a result of a vast stock of labor grievances (reflecting the managerial practices and antiunion efforts of the period), the general "social unrest," the favorable political climate as reflected in the Wagner Act, and the sharp institutional rivalry between the established American Federation of Labor (craft union-oriented) and the emergent Congress of Industrial Organizations (mass industrial union-oriented). Union growth continued at a high rate through the World War II period, and this growth can be explained by the extremely tight labor market, rising prices, a continuing favorable political climate, a continuing stock of depression-era grievances, and the spread of union security provisions which required union membership.[7] In general, American unions have attracted most of their members during prosperous periods of tight labor markets and rising prices or during periods of social and political unrest. As we shall see in Chapter 2, these conditions prevailed during the period of police union expansion in the 1960s.

Structure of the Labor Movement

There are some 20 million members of trade unions in this country organized into 185 national and international unions.[8] Approximately 15 million are in national or international unions affiliated with the American Federal of Labor and Congress of Industrial Organizations (AFL-CIO). The remainder are considered "independent" or unaffiliated unions.[9]

National Unions. National unions are the key structural units in the labor movement. The local unions to which individual employees belong are chartered by the various nationals. The AFL-CIO expressly guarantees its national affiliates almost total control over their own affairs, especially the all-important decisions regarding the bargaining function. Since most nationals have locals scattered throughout the United States, groups of locals usually are organized into regional and functional bodies for improved internal administrative functioning. For example, the Teamsters have metropolitan region Joint Councils and multistate Area Conferences. The Auto Workers have skilled-trades and white-collar councils to represent the interests of these particular member groups.

The main function of the national union and its subordinate bodies is collective bargaining—the negotiation and administration of the collective-bargaining agreement. The tremendous variety that exists in the practice of bargaining is evidenced by the approximately 140,000 collective-bargaining agreements extant. The organizational level at which the most important bargaining occurs varies widely from industry to industry. For example, in the construction industry, bargaining generally occurs between one local craft union and the relevant local contractors' association in a local market. In contrast, the most important bargaining in the auto, steel, airline, and electrical equipment industries, for example, takes place at the national level and may involve one national union dealing with one employer or a group of companies or a coalition of unions dealing with various companies in a national market. While a variety of factors determine bargaining structure, including government policies (as expressed by the National Labor Relations Board), power considerations, representational considerations, and the bargaining issues, probably the most important factors are the economic influences of the relevant product markets.

Because many organized firms, particularly manufacturing companies, compete in large regional or national product markets, the unions representing their employees need to bargain on a basis coextensive with the firm's product markets. A single local union could not effectively bargain with a multiplant corporation, for in most cases the firm could easily take a strike in this single plant and make up the lost production elsewhere. Furthermore, in most multiplant firms the decisions regarding economic issues are made at the headquarters level (or at some organizational level higher than the local plant), and many national union officers try to establish and enforce national or regional wage-fringe patterns in all the plants in one firm and all the firms in an industry in order to "take wages out of competition." In contrast, in the construction industry where bargaining generally occurs between one craft local and the relevant local contractors' association, local bargaining is a function of the fact that the product market and the labor market are local: local contractors build locally using local labor. When a national builder enters the market, he meets local market conditions.

Whatever the shape of the bargaining structure, U.S. trade unions have jealously guarded their bargaining autonomy.

The Functions of the Federation. Typically, all the AFL-CIO affiliated locals in one metropolitan area (city or county) are members of the local labor federation or city central body. These locals and city central bodies, in turn, are usually affiliated with the state AFL-CIO, and the city centrals and state federations are, in turn, part of the national administrative structure of the AFL-CIO. The city centrals have a twofold purpose—to represent labor's political interests at the local level and to coordinate relations among the various local unions in the area. The state AFL-CIO represents labor's political interests in the state capitol, while the national AFL-CIO represents labor's interests to the federal government. The national AFL-CIO, and to a lesser extent the state and local bodies, also engage in public relations and dissemination of information to their constituencies. While the independent unions are not formally affiliated with these AFL-CIO bodies, there tends to be a lot of informal cooperation among the affiliated and nonaffiliated unions with respect to both political and bargaining issues.

The relative importance of the various union bodies and federations and their functions is reflected in the distribution of members' dues payments. Of the $5 to $7 monthly dues collected by the typical local union, the lion's share is divided among the local, regional, and national levels of the union, with the local and the national receiving the largest amounts. Perhaps 15 cents will be forwarded to the city central, 10 cents to the state body, and the national will forward several cents to the national AFL-CIO. Thus national unions and their regional bodies and local unions retain the vast majority of trade-union income, most of which is used to finance negotiations and contract administration with only a small fraction of regular union income going to the bodies whose primary purpose is political activity (however, union political expenses are supplemented by member contributions to separate political funds modeled after the AFL-CIO Committee for Political Education [COPE]). This distribution of dues income is also an approximate representation of the importance of the various union bodies and their functions to the members' self-interests.

The foregoing discussion is briefly summarized in Figure 1-1.

The Emergence of Public-Sector Unionism

The material in this section of the chapter has so far focused on the private sector trade unionism. As we shall see, public-sector unionism functions in a different legal, political, and economic environment, and includes many employee organizations which have historically not functioned as, nor been considered, unions but which recently have begun to act like trade unions.

Public-sector unions have their origins in the same conditions that cause private employees to unionize. The severe inflation of the World War I period caused policemen, firefighters, teachers, and other government employee groups

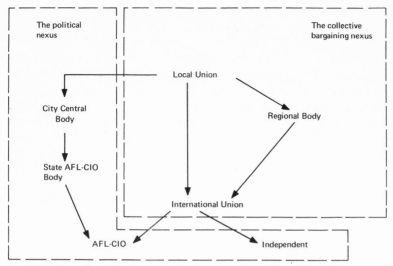

Figure 1-1. A Functional Diagram of the U.S. Labor Movement

to form self-help associations. The American Federation of State, County, and Municipal Employees (the second largest public-sector union) had its birth during the depression. However, public-sector unions grew very slowly during the 1920s, 1930s, 1940s, and even into the 1950s. The history of public-sector unionism suggests four primary reasons for such slow growth. First, public employees enjoyed a high degree of job security, which was especially prized during the 1930s. Second, public employees generally enjoyed better fringe benefits and working conditions than private-sector employees (though public wages were lower). Third, public employers staunchly resisted public-sector unions and, fourth, until the end of the 1950s public employees had no protected right to organize and bargain collectively. The first two factors caused a lack of interest in unions among many employees; the second two factors posed formidable obstacles to employees expressing such interests.

Employer resistance to public unionization has been phrased in many ways, but it reflects the same desires among public-sector employers to avoid sharing managerial authority and to keep labor costs down that are historically found in the private sector. One set of responses invoked the protection afforded by civil service and the paternalistic concern of management for its employees. Another argument held that the government is the supreme authority in the land and that the sovereign cannot be bound by (labor) contracts. While the principle has little legal protection today, it once was widely accepted. A third set of arguments revolved around the idea that the strike was an essential part of unionization and bargaining and since the strike was illegal, so were unionization and bargaining. The argument is made that public services are a monopoly and that to deprive the public of its government supply of these services would be injurious to the public health and safety. This point of view is reflected in the illegality of public-sector strikes in most jurisdictions.

This deprivation of services argument has been an especially crucial one in the resistance to police unions. Police services are viewed as among the most critical and essential of government services and thus cannot be withheld. This argument was empirically reinforced five decades ago in the 1919 Boston police strike violence and more recently during the 1969 Montreal police strike violence. However, the New York and Milwaukee strikes of 1971 showed that under some conditions the argument does not always hold.

As we said earlier, collective bargaining was late in coming to the public sector. The few pre-1960 situations of cities bargaining with their employees are notable primarily as exceptions. However, the protected right to form unions and bargain collectively spread to municipal employees with the passage of legislation in New York City in 1956, Wisconsin in 1959, and then Connecticut, Massachusetts, Michigan, New York, and other states during the mid-1960s. Probably the three greatest spurs to this activity were President Kennedy's 1962 Executive Order 10988,[10] the visible success of the American Federation of Teachers' Local 2 in New York City, and the tight labor markets of the second half of the decade. The first served to undermine many of the arguments about the sovereignty of government preventing agreements with unions, the experience of the second demonstrated to other public employees that there were substantial benefits to be gained from bargaining with the municipal employer, and the third factor reduced the security value of government employment relative to private employment. Twenty-seven states currently provide legislation protecting the right of municipal employees to form unions and to bargain collectively with their employers. Even in the non-South states with no public-sector bargaining legislation, there is a large volume of bargaining activity among teachers, firefighters, nurses, sanitation workers, streets department workers, and others. Examples of police unionism and collective bargaining are found in all of the states where public employees are organized regardless of the legal status of bargaining in the jurisdiction.

This volume of bargaining activity is reflected in public-sector union-membership figures. The number of public-sector members of trade unions increased 100 percent in eight years, from 1,070,000 in 1960 to 2,155,000 in 1968. In addition to those employees who are members of trade unions, hundreds of thousands of others are being actively represented by organizations which have emerged as *de facto* trade unions. The Los Angeles County Employees Association, many of the local affiliates of the National Education Association, and the Detroit Police Officers Association are but a few of the hundreds of examples.

Conclusion

This background information should facilitate the reader's understanding of the police-union material that follows. In Chapter 2 the nature of police employee organizations, their history and growth, and why police officers form unions are discussed. As we shall see, there are many similarities between police unionism and the broader currents of American unionism.

2 Police Employee Organizations

As with unionism elsewhere in the economy, there exists a great deal of diversity of form among police-union organizations. Some locals are affiliated with a variety of national organizations while others are independent; some unions represent patrolmen only while others represent all ranks in a particular department; some unions formally bargain collectively while others have no bargaining rights; and so on. This chapter is intended to provide the reader with an understanding of the variety that exists within the police labor movement. As such, the chapter has a dual focus. The first section will present a brief history of police employee organization development and will examine the emergence of individual and organizational police militancy during the 1960s. The second section will examine police organizations as they exist today, emphasizing the distinctions between the various organizations at the national, state, and local levels.

History of Police Organizations[1]

While there are references to police employee organizations existing as early as the Civil War period, the organizations which have endured to the present were not founded until after civil-service protection had been introduced into the police service. According to Berney, prior to civil service policemen were usually the appointees of the dominant political organization and thus had almost no job tenure beyond the politicians' good will and the politicians' continued tenure in office. Enduring associations could not be founded until civil service provided the men with some protection from managerial retaliation.[2]

Many of these early organizations were formed to provide what we now term fringe benefits (death benefits, welfare insurance), to lobby with the employer for more pay, and to fulfill fraternal-social needs. Policemen in most big-city departments formed one or more of these organizations in the period 1890-1915. Some of these that have endured include: the New York City Patrolmen's Benevolent Association (1892), the Erie Club in Buffalo (1894; now the Police Benevolent Association); the Rochester Police Locust Club (1907; named after the wood used in policemen's nightsticks); the Milwaukee Policemen's Protective Association (1908);[3] an unnamed association in Washington, D.C. (1904); and the Fraternal Order of the Police (FOP) Lodge #1 in Pittsburgh (1915).[4]

The fact that politicians controlled police departments and established the terms and conditions of employment meant that these early organizations had to jump into the political fray and compete with other interest groups for a larger share of the public revenue in order to properly represent their members. Both Berney and Kienast present some interesting examples of early police-union politicking, lobbying, slush funds, and public relations, and a lot can be learned about the period by reading the extensive literature on the early New York City PBA.[5]

Early AFL Unionism

These early organizations also included some who sought formal labor-union affiliation with organized labor. As early as 1897, a police local applied for an American Federation of Labor charter—which was not forthcoming.[6] Twenty years later, policemen again petitioned the AFL for charters. The economic turmoil caused by World War I—rapidly rising prices, rising private-sector wages, relatively fixed public-sector wages—caused the police to become more aggressive in their self-interest activities. Pressure for affiliation during the 1917-1919 period caused the AFL at its June 1919 convention to reverse its earlier position and issue police-union charters. By September, thirty-seven locals had been chartered.[7] Most of these were in small or medium-sized cities, but police in the big cities, including New York and Chicago, watched the emergent police-union movement with keen interest. One of these AFL police locals (No. 16807) was in Boston.

The Boston Police Strike

The details of this initial unionization attempt in Boston have been related in great detail elsewhere.[8] Briefly, the Boston police AFL affiliate asked the city for recognition and bargaining rights over wages, benefits, and working conditions. The city refused; three-fourths of the force went on strike; violence and looting occurred, and the strikers were fired and replaced. Massachusetts Governor Calvin Coolidge emerged as a national hero for his alleged role in ending the strike and was started on the road to the White House.[9]

What is important for our purposes is the considerable negative effect the Boston police strike had on the development of police organizations and police labor relations.[10] The AFL responded to the adverse public reaction to the strike by quickly revoking all its police local charters. Policemen in other cities—including New York—which were considering AFL affiliation, dropped the idea. Even the early FOP, which was attempting to spread out from Pittsburgh, was viewed with great suspicion and did not make significant progress until the 1930s. Municipal management strongly resisted any police organization which attempted to affiliate with organized labor or which aggressively promoted its self-interest. One writer maintains that if the Boston strike had not occurred "the police would have been as well organized within the labor movement as firemen"[11] who were organizing at the same time and for the same reasons as the police.[12] This may or may not be true, but the strike certainly had a chilling effect on police organizational efforts for many decades.[13] As late as 1958, the International Association of Chiefs of Police used the Boston strike for support in its condemnation of police unions.[14]

This negative impact of the Boston strike was strengthened by the antiunion temper of the 1920s and early 1930s. During this period, police organizational efforts were meager. Police employee organizations maintained a "low profile" and generally limited themselves to lobbying for improved benefits. Berney details the New York City PBA's political activities, and Kienast relates the slow growth of the FOP in the Midwest.[15] The 1920s and early 1930s were inauspicious times for trade unionism in general, and police unions were no exception.

The National Unions of the Early Period

AFSCME. During the 1940s and 1950s, police collective activity increased. In 1937 the newly formed American Federation of State, County, and Municipal Employees (AFSCME, affiliated with the AFL) organized its first local of policemen (in Portsmouth, Virginia); by the end of World War II AFSCME claimed forty-nine police locals,[16] and by 1958, sixty-six police locals.[17] However, the AFSCME organizing effort met with substantial managerial resistance and in such cities as Chicago, Los Angeles, St. Louis, and Jackson, Mississippi, AFSCME police locals disappeared under vigorous managerial opposition. In other cities AFSCME locals were tolerated as long as they did not seriously rock the local government boat. On a national scale, these AFSCME police-organizing efforts never did amount to a great deal. AFSCME police membership probably never exceeded 10,000 individual policemen.

FOP. During this same period, the FOP continued its slow but steady growth. In 1941 it called a national meeting of police representatives in Washington, D.C. to successfully lobby against a proposal to extend social security coverage to policemen. By 1943, it had 169 lodges.[18] During World War II, the FOP encountered instances of strong managerial resistance, most notably during Detroit and Lansing organizing efforts. As a result of these Michigan defeats, the national FOP decided not to charter local lodges unless they had prior administrative acceptance and no other organization claimed majority status.[19] Under this restriction, the FOP continued to grow slowly during the 1940s and 1950s; by 1959, there were 194 lodges.[20]

NCPA. In 1953 the National Conference of Police Associations was formed at a meeting in Detroit. The formation resulted from an *ad hoc* gathering of local association representatives in Washington, D.C. the year before to successfully lobby against an impending extension of social security coverage to policemen and firemen. Encouraged by this Washington effort, police representatives met in Detroit in March 1953 to form some kind of permanent structure to facilitate future national cooperation among independent local associations. At this meeting, FOP representatives attempted to control the outcome but the delegates rejected their efforts and founded a competing national organization.[21]

The stated purpose of the NCPA was "to collect, study, standardize, summarize, and to disseminate factual data for the purpose of promoting the professionalization of the police service and to stimulate mutual cooperation between law-enforcement agencies."[22] This professionalization theme apparently cast the NCPA in a nonthreatening manner, for both Kienast and Berney say that the new organization was not opposed by police administrators or the International Association of Chiefs of Police.[23] This acceptance also must have stemmed from the complete absence of any similarity to a union on the part of the NCPA.

Summary

By the 1960s local police employee organizations were widespread.[24] As the level of police employee dissatisfaction with employment conditions rose during the decade, police officers found these employee associations natural vehicles for the expression of their discontent through political and collective-bargaining channels.

It is important to observe that even though many of these organizations chose to affiliate with state or national organizations, they formed historically as local organizations, and it is as local organizations that they functioned almost exclusively. The most salient characteristic of the national organizations— ICPA,[25] FOP, AFSCME, and others—is that they have had very little control over the activities and affairs of their affiliated locals.

The Emergence of Police Militancy

In the late 1960s and early 1970s angry and dissatisfied policemen received substantial public attention. In part this was a result of the public media focusing on the widespread police support for presidential candidate George Wallace;[26] in part it was due to the fact that the loudest ovations at police organization conventions appeared to go to those speakers who roundly condemned such targets as the Black Panthers, Students for a Democratic Society (SDS), and long-haired anarchists;[27] and in part it was due to the high visibility of the mass confrontations between dissident students and blacks on one side and the police on the other. Police spokesmen told the public that policemen were sick and tired of being harassed, cursed, spit on, and shot at.[28] And during this period, literally dozens of police work stoppages occurred, the most publicized being the 1969 strike in Montreal and the 1971 walkouts in New York City and Milwaukee.[29] What has caused the increase in these overt expressions of police dissatisfaction?

The standard explanations for the recent emergence of police militancy tend to focus on the hostile external environment and relatively low economic benefits. The external environment includes such dimensions as the civil-rights revolution and the emergence of black militancy, U.S. Supreme Court decisions which restricted police discretion in favor of individual guarantees of due process, the public clamor by minority groups and white liberals for civilian review boards as watchdogs over police behavior, the emergence of student militancy, increased violence directed at the police, and rising crime rates and the concomitant public clamor for the police to "do something" to control crime. Coupled with these pressures that make the job more difficult is what the police perceived as the low pay they received. While each of these factors has contributed to police discontent, in our research we found four general factors contributing to dissatisfaction (increased public hostility, law-and-order demands on the police, low pay, and poor personnel practices) and three factors contributing to the police willingness to engage in confrontation tactics (the demonstration effect of other public-employee successes, the influx of young policemen, and group cohesion).

Increased Public Hostility

Most of the individual items listed in the previous paragraph are included in this category: black and student militancy, civilian review boards, Supreme Court decisions, and violence directed at the police. In our field interviews, police spokesmen frequently complained that they and their members are "fed up" with being looked down upon, harassed, and assaulted.[30]

Another important element that compounds the hostile external environment is a frequent police perception of a lack of support for police actions among top city officials.[31] Police spokesmen note that the police must continually make important split-second decisions, and they strongly believe that city officials should support their actions rather than criticizing the police for the sake of political expediency.

Law and Order

While the police face increased public hostility, they also face the "law and order" problem.[32] The increasing level of reported crimes involving inter-personal violence has become a national issue. Some segments of the public perceive such crime to have reached epidemic levels.[33] Naturally, the alarmed citizens demand that the "crime problem" be solved. As was observed in one newspaper, the public seems to expect the police to assume the lion's share of the burden in solving the crime problem and restoring law and order rather than sharing these expectations among all the elements of the criminal justice system—courts, convict rehabilitation services, and so on—to do so.[34] Thus many of the same environmental factors that make the policeman's job more difficult also tend to cause louder demands from certain portions of the public for more effective police work.[35] Since it is generally recognized that the police cannot really prevent or control crime, these external factors tend to place the police in a no-win situation.

Low Pay

So far we have talked about the police having to function in an increasingly hostile and demanding external environment. This problem has been com-pounded by the relatively low pay and benefits the police received. During the period 1961-1966, when many of the above-mentioned pressures were beginning to develop, increases in police salaries lagged behind increases for other groups of employees.[36] While police pay in recent years has sharply increased,[37] police still earn less than most private- and public-sector craftsmen, about the same as firemen, and far less than the police think they should be earning considering the increased demands placed on them. The importance of economic rewards is reflected by the fact that most recent police strikes known to the authors were conducted ostensibly over economic benefits.[38] In effect, the hostile environ-ment has increased the police workload and the perceived danger of the job, while our interview information reveals that many policemen feel that their economic rewards have not increased commensurately. Exacerbating this discon-tent have been the sharp increases in the cost-of-living since 1967.

Poor Personnel Practices

Another factor helping to explain employee dissatisfaction is the existence of poor personnel practices in police agencies. During our field visits we heard frequent and intense complaints by police employee spokesmen about poor managerial personnel practices and how these practices contributed to rank-and-file dissatisfaction. Among the practices cited were: the lack of internal civil and constitutional rights for officers being investigated for misfeasance and mal- feasance; lack of a functional grievance procedure; being called to duty and held on standby at no pay; no pay for off-duty court appearances; having to work days off with no pay as penalties for rules infractions; no premium pay for overtime work; being transferred from one shift or job to another with little or no advance warning; and (for patrolmen) being subjected to demeaning treat- ment (abusive and degrading language, physical intimidation) by superior officers. As will be discussed in Chapter 7, police-union efforts in many departments have resulted in the elimination of most of the above practices, and several police managers told us that the unions' efforts in their departments have resulted in a definite improvement in personnel policies and practices. However, according to police-union spokesmen, some of these poor personnel practices still exist, and their existence contributes to dissatisfaction.

While these four general factors—a more hostile external work environment, greater demands on the police to control crime, relatively low economic rewards, and a poor internal work environment—offer a possible explanation for the increase in police job dissatisfaction in recent years, they do not explain the increase in militancy. Three other factors are important in contributing to the emergence of overt expressions of police militancy.

A Demonstration Effect

During the 1960s the confrontation tactics of students, black militants, and other groups of organized public and private employees brought both attention and results. For example, teachers, transit workers, and sanitation employees struck and received benefits that previously had not been forthcoming. On campuses, students have achieved participation in university governance as a result of campus turmoil. The auto companies sought out and employed thousands of ghetto blacks after the 1967 Detroit riot. And in our study, a black policeman told us that a previous riot in his city had produced and was still producing tangible gains (increased black hiring, promotions, and favorable assignments) for the black police there. The fact that confrontation politics—the threatened or actual use of coercion—achieves results is not lost on the police, especially since the police are usually on the scene to regulate the confronta- tionist groups.[39]

The Influx of Young Policemen

The large group of men hired during and after World War II began retiring in large numbers in 1965, while concurrently many police departments were creating additional positions in response to increased urban tensions. These two factors made possible a large influx of young men into the police service during the middle and late 1960s. These are the young men who grew up during the 1960s and were accustomed to the existence of confrontation politics. In addition to this "cultural" heritage, these younger men who by definition have few years of police service, are relatively unsocialized into the paramilitary mentality of obedience. Many of our police management interviewees mentioned (or lamented) that their under-30-with-less-than-five-years-of-service policemen—which in a few departments accounted for more than half the force—are much less socialized into the militaristic atmosphere of police work than the older policemen. On a day-to-day level, they are more critical and less accepting of orders from superior officers than older police. They are more inclined to challenge orders that appear unjustified. When an employment dispute or impasse develops, they are more willing than older police to take some kind of organized overt action. For example, the January 1971 New York City wildcat strike was pushed by the younger officers who put great pressure on the older officers to join them, including physical intimidation.[40] Some of our management interviewees went so far as to predict that many of these younger policemen would never become completely socialized into the obedience mentality.

Group Cohesion

The third factor contributing to the emergence of over militancy is internal group cohesion. As will be explained in more detail in Chapter 4, the police tend to be very cohesive in their quest for group goals, especially when they face a common external challenge. Our interview information reveals that this cohesiveness has resulted in a propensity for the police to be more aggressive in pressing for the attainment of their goals than are other city employees (with the exception of the firefighters). In addition, this generally high degree of group cohesion may be positively correlated with the level of shared dissatisfaction. That is, group members may be more willing to undertake group action if a large percentage of group members share a high level of common dissatisfaction.

Summary

Material in this section is summarized in diagrammatic form in Figure 2-1. The four environmental factors—increased external hostility, increased law-and-order demands, low economic rewards, and poor personnel practices—have contributed to the sharp increases in police dissatisfaction in recent years. The transformation of this dissatisfaction into militant statements and actions has been aided by the demonstration effect of confrontation tactics by other groups, by young policemen who are more willing to actively seek redress of their perceived grievances, and by the high degree of occupational cohesion among policemen.

Few of the above observations are new or startling. The militant police response to a more difficult and demanding environment is consistent with the knowledge we have of norms of equity, job dissatisfaction, and reasons for employee unionization.

Research findings on equity theory reveal that when a person sees that his efforts are not as well rewarded as the efforts of someone else expending the same or even less effort, he will be dissatisfied and take overt steps to correct the perceived inequity.[41] These findings suggest that the police, who appear to perceive themselves as doing a difficult job for relatively low economic rewards compared to civilians, will take steps to increase their rewards or reduce their efforts.

Unionization is but one of the possible responses to increased job-related dissatisfaction (absenteeism, quitting, sabotage, or punching the boss are a few of the other possible responses). As was pointed out in Chapter 1, the largest increases in private and public sector trade-union membership in the United States have occurred during periods of rising prices and wages and during periods of social or political unrest (World War I and the immediate postwar period; the late 1930s; World War II and the immediate postwar period; and the middle and

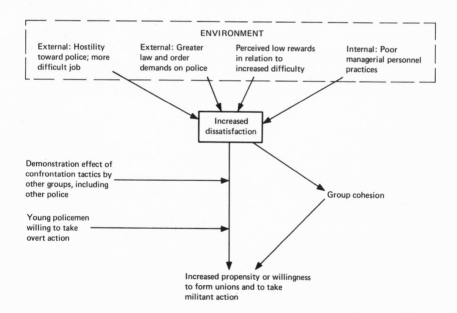

Figure 2-1. Factors Affecting Recent Police Propensity to Form Unions

late 1960s). These wage and price changes threaten the employee's economic status, while societal unrest threatens the employee's desire for psychological security. Employees join unions primarily to obtain improved economic benefits and to feel stronger in their relationship vis-à-vis the employer.[42] Research on group cohesion suggests that the police are more likely to act as a unified group when their expectations are violated than many other employee groups because of the greater degree of group unity or cohesion among policemen.

Thus existing knowledge tells us that when a cohesive, established group encounters a more difficult and threatening environment, which results in increased dissatisfaction and violation of its norms of equity, this group will engage in some kind of self-interest activities to improve its situation. The recent emergence of militant police attitudes and behavior for the purpose of advancing police self-interest is no exception. Instead, it appears as a natural or predictable response to the environmental conditions in which the police service functions.

Organizational Militancy

This emergence of militant feelings among individual policemen may take many forms: some policemen may quit the police service; a few may "take out" their dissatisfactions and frustrations on handy targets; others may reduce their efforts; and some police spokesmen may issue public statements decrying the "permissiveness" that many police appear to see as the cause of much of the social unrest which in turn makes their jobs more difficult. The most visible and widespread response has been the emergence of police employee organizational militancy, either via the formation of new, aggressive organizations or through the transformation of relatively complacent existing associations into more active organizations.

New Organizations

While the numerically dominant organizational response has been the transformation of existing organizations, a very noticeable response has been the formation of new organizations. For example, in 1965, a group of Boston patrolmen formed the Boston Police Patrolmen's Association in the face of four quiescent organizations that already existed in the department. After an uphill organizing struggle in the face of strong managerial resistance, the BPPA in 1967 defeated a federation of these other organizations by a two to one vote in a bargaining unit representation election. After it became the official bargaining agent for the patrolmen, the BPPA became one of the country's most aggressive police unions. Another new union is the Cleveland Police Patrolmen's Association formed in 1968. The CPPA has been challenging the more staid and long established FOP for departmental supremacy.[43] While Cleveland has no official collective bargaining for police unions, the FOP and the CPPA compete for the right to be called "the voice of the patrolmen."

A second category of new organizations consists of pressure groups that formed within existing majority organizations for the purpose of inducing changes in the posture and activities of the larger group. This category would include the Silver Shield Club in Buffalo, which formed to put pressure on the majority Police Benevolent Association to be more cognizant of the patrolmen's interests, and the Law Enforcement Group, a politically hyperconservative group of New York City policemen founded in 1968 to combat "coddling" of criminals by judges, to seek abolition of the New York City Police Department's Civilian Complaint Review Board, and to eliminate civilian employees from stationhouses, among other things.[44] While the Law Enforcement Group did not appear to have any intention of replacing the certified Patrolmen's Benevolent Association as the majority representative, it did result in the PBA's public rightward shift, including the famous "100 percent enforcement of the law" verbal controversy between PBA President John Cassesse and Mayor John Lindsay.[45]

At the national level, 1969-70 were the formative years for John Cassesse's International Brotherhood of Police Officers.[46] The IBPO's founders intended that the organization become the national union representing U.S. policemen. After a promising and well-publicized start, the IBPO never really took off and it presently has less than 4,000 members. In 1970 the fledgling Rhode Island International Brotherhood of Police Officers (no relation to the Cassesse IBPO)[47] affiliated with the National Association of Government Employees and began an organizing drive in Connecticut and Massachusetts. In Rhode Island the IBPO has been challenging established FOP lodges; in Connecticut, it has challenged several AFSCME locals and has captured Hartford (the largest municipal department in the state) away from AFSCME.

Transformation of Existing Organizations

In most cities the emergence of militancy was expressed through existing organizations becoming more aggressive in their representation efforts, frequently after the election of militant leaders.[48] The most noticeable examples of this phenomenon occurred in Detroit, San Francisco, Pittsburgh, Oakland, and Seattle. In 1965 Detroit patrolmen elected a leadership slate which transformed the Detroit Police Officers Association from a "beer drinking social club" into a full-fledged trade union, and which has since conducted a ticket strike and "blue flu," has lobbied extensively, been involved in political campaigns, and has vigorously administered its collective-bargaining agreements. In Pittsburgh, the FOP lodge elected a more militant president in early 1970 and the organization has since become publicly more aggressive in its activities. In early 1971 the so-called Blue-coat faction electorally won control of the San Francisco Police Officers Association and the POA has since assumed a more aggressive posture, especially in its dealings with police management. The Oakland Police Officers Association has adopted a more union-like appearance, including picketing of City Hall and threatening to strike, after a 1968 membership vote strongly in favor of direct union affiliation (which was immediately blocked by the city council). During 1968-70 the Seattle Police Guild emerged as a strong voice in local politics and departmental operation as it vigorously asserted its members' interests.

There also have been significant organizational developments at higher levels. At its 1969 convention the Peace Officers Research Association of California (PORAC) reorganized itself from a low key, research and information-dissemination organization to a much better financed and more union-like organization for the purpose of assisting affiliated local groups with employee relations and lobbying for benefits in the state legislature.

The more established national police organizations have also been moving in a more activist direction: at its 1969 convention the International Conference of Police Associations responded to potential unionization challenges by levying a five cents per month per capita tax on member associations to finance an expanded national staff;[49] at its 1972 convention the organization elected a full-time president (former New York City PBA President Edward Kiernan) and doubled its per capita tax to finance an increased package of activities, including a more comprehensive congressional lobbying program. The FOP, at its 1971 convention, deleted its constitutional provision prohibiting political activity; earlier the national lodge had endorsed collective bargaining as an FOP policy after decades of rejecting the concept.

The recent emergence of *de facto* police unions—whether via the creation of new organizations or the transformation of existing social-fraternal-insurance associations, which actively bargain, engage in political activity, and speak out on behalf of their members' interests—is a logical outcome of increased police dissatisfaction. With this historical-developmental discussion as background, we now proceed to examine the current state of police unions.

Structure of the Police Labor Movement

The discussion of American trade unionism in Chapter 1 focused on the private sector. As we mentioned at the end of that chapter and as we saw in this chapter, most policemen are members of employee organizations which are not officially known as trade unions but which do act *as if* they are unions. In this section we examine the organizational structure of the police labor movement.

By the end of this chapter it should be clear that local police unions are the most important organizational unit in the police labor movement, for it is at the local level that the most important decisions are made regarding employment conditions. After examining local unions, we will look at the national and state organizations with which many of them are affiliated.

Local Organizations

Our research has revealed that national and state bodies do not play major roles in police employee relations; that police unionism is primarily a local phenomenon. This local emphasis is due to two main factors. The first is the inability or unwillingness of the national organization to become integrally involved in local affairs, frequently because a low income financially precludes playing such a role. Much more important is the localized and monopolistic nature of the municipal police industry. For example, New York City police deliver their services in New York City, and do not compete in the product market with police in any other city. In effect the relevant product market for any particular local union has the city limits for its boundaries. In addition to local product markets, the police labor market also tends to be local in character. The majority of patrolmen are recruited from the local metropolitan area, and there is virtually no intercity mobility in the police industry except at the levels of patrolman and chief. The terms and conditions of municipal police employment are primarily determined by interactions among local city officials, local police management, and local police-union leaders. This local locus of control means there is no pressing need for the national or regional representation and bargaining arrangements that exist in many private-sector industries with national or regional product markets (e.g., autos, steel, electrical equipment, coal mining, airlines).[50] While it is true that there are regional and national "orbits of coercive comparison" (i.e., a large wage increase in an important city such as New York becomes a target for other unions to shoot for), these outside forces are not strong enough to override the local control that municipalities have over the determination of their employees' employment conditions.

This local locus of control of the employment relationship not only helps explain why the local union is so important in the structure of the police labor movement, it also helps explain why the relatively centralized national police organizations (AFSCME, SEIU, NAGE) have failed to enroll large numbers of policemen as members. Basically the answer is a function of economics: why would a local union pay a significant per capita tax to a regional and national labor organization, a city central body, a state AFL-CIO body and the national AFL-CIO when the essential functions will be performed solely by local union leaders interacting with local officials in a local political and collective-bargaining arena in which the union exercises a great deal of power. As we shall see, the dominant state and national organizations consist of sworn police officers and their functions are tailored to the lobbying and information needs peculiar to police local unions.[51]

National Organizations

Earlier we briefly discussed the history of some of the national organizations. In this section we examine their current status.

The largest of the national police employee organizations is the International Conference of Police Associations. In 1972 the ICPA claimed as members more than 100 local and state organizations representing a total of 158,000 policemen.[52] As its name implies, the ICPA issues memberships to organizations rather than to individuals. Its membership is concentrated in California, New York, Illinois, and New Jersey. Many of the largest city unions are members, including the New York PBA, the Detroit DPOA, San Francisco, Washington, D.C., Chicago, St. Louis, Milwaukee, Buffalo, and Seattle. The organization historically has had only one full-time staff employee—the executive director, located in Washington, D.C., although as indicated earlier the ICPA has expanded its paid staff. The organization puts out a monthly newsletter and quarterly magazine, and disseminates information of interest to member associations. It conducts and disseminates wage-fringe benefit surveys, and it also handles local and state requests for specific information.

The ICPA and the other national organizations have taken on a more activist appearance in recent years. In addition to the strong public statements made at recent conventions, ICPA has expanded its activities to include a regular lobbying program in Congress.[53] While the ICPA has very little control over the affairs of its affiliates, these expanded activities at the national level reflect an increasing willingness of police to gravitate toward a more traditional union structure in employment matters and to attempt to emerge as a more potent political force.

The next largest national group is the Fraternal Order of Police. In 1969 the national FOP lodge claimed 733 affiliated lodges with 80,000 members.[54] Its membership is concentrated in Pennsylvania with Ohio, Florida, Illinois, and Indiana having sizeable representation.

The FOP presents a more homogeneous appearance than does the ICPA. While the ICPA was formed by a group of existing state and local associations and admits other associations who apply for membership, all the local, state, and national units of the FOP have the same name, and the national lodge of the FOP issues charters to local lodges in much the same manner as national unions do for local unions in the private sector. There are twenty state lodges in those states with several local lodges and individual policemen may have membership in the national FOP lodge as well as his local lodge (whereas a policeman may not belong directly to the ICPA).

While there appears to be closer ties between the national FOP and local lodges than between the ICPA and its affiliates, the local lodges do have considerable autonomy in the conduct of their affairs. Historically the national lodge has played a limited service role. Its important regular function has been the publication of an annual salary and working conditions survey, and a quarterly magazine. On occasion the national has given financial assistance to local lodges who have undertaken expensive actions to defend national lodge policies, such as the Philadelphia lodge's fight against the city's civilian review board. More recently the national FOP has become a more active organization. In 1969 the national organization put a Washington, D.C. public relations firm on an annual retainer, and at the 1971 convention the delegates voted to delete the constitutional prohibition on political activity. In contrast to its earlier efforts to be completely disassociated from an image even remotely related to organized labor, the FOP and its local lodges in recent years have begun to warmly embrace collective bargaining for policemen.

The FOP and the ICPA represent far more policemen than any of the remaining national organizations—AFSCME, NUPO-SEIU, and IBPO-NAGE. Of these other national organizations, the American Federation of State, County, and Municipal Employees, AFL-CIO, has the most police members. While AFSCME's total membership is in excess of 500,000, it has less than 8,000 police members in police locals scattered about the country. The largest concentration is in Connecticut, with twenty-four locals and 2,500 members, and the largest local is in Baltimore with 1,500 members.

AFSCME has not become a dominant figure among police organizations. It is apparently difficult for the organization to minister to policemen's needs and thus police members see little return on their heavy per capita tax.[55] Policemen have been such a small minority in the organization that they have not been able to make their voice heard. Because of its general inability to appear attractive to police members, AFSCME in recent years has lost police members to both of the rival police-only SEIU and NAGE affiliates.

The National Union of Police Officers has several locals in small and medium-sized cities, some of which were formerly AFSCME locals (including Portland, Denver, St. Paul, Salt Lake City, and Omaha). Its total membership is less than 4,000, and it is beginning to suffer a problem similar to AFSCME's— some police members can see little or no return on the hefty per capita tax ($1.00 per month) and have decided to leave the organization. This was the reason given for the Omaha local going independent at the end of 1971 and the Portland, Oregon local in 1972. For a while NUPO looked as if it would blossom into a national police union and it received a great deal of publicity during its gestation period, enough to cause the ICPA and FOP to consider combining in opposition. However, a variety of factors, the most important of which appears to be a "wait-and-see" attitude among potential local affiliates, sharply limited its growth rate. Early in 1972, NUPO affiliated with the Service Employees International Union, AFL-CIO, a private sector based union which in recent years has been aggressively organizing public employees.

The International Brotherhood of Police Officers exists primarily in Rhode Island and has recently engaged in substantial organizing efforts in Connecticut and Massachusetts. It claims about 2,000 members and its largest local is in Hartford (which was formerly an AFSCME local). In 1970 it affiliated with the independent National Association of Government Employees, and the 250,000 civilian member parent organization has been providing substantial organizing and negotiating assistance to its police subsidiary.

State Organizations. With the exception of a few isolated police locals affiliated with such organizations as the Teamsters, the Service Employees (independent of NUPO), and the Operating Engineers, the above five organizations (ICPA, FOP, AFSCME, NUPO-SEIU, and IBPO-NAGE) account for just about all the police locals that have some kind of national affiliation. Many locals, however, are affiliated with state associations as well as, or in lieu of affiliating with, national organizations. Some the larger ICPA-affiliated state groups are the Police Conference of New York, the New Jersey State Patrolmen's Benevolent Association, the Police Officers Association of Michigan, and the Wisconsin Professional Policemen's Association. The Peace Officers Research Association of California, the California Alliance of Police Associations, and the Massachusetts Police Association are examples of state organizations not affiliated with a larger body.

Some local organizations are members of state organizations and national organizations. FOP local lodges belong to both the state and national lodges (if a state lodge exists in their state), and AFSCME locals either belong to a state police council (as in Connecticut or Maryland) or to a state council that includes nonpolice AFSCME locals (as in Illinois), as well as the AFSCME international union. The San Francisco Police Officers Association belongs to the California Alliance of Police Associations and to the ICPA, as does the Los Angeles Fire and Police Protective League. Similar state and national membership exists for local unions in Detroit, Buffalo, and Rochester. On the other hand, the Milwaukee union belongs to the ICPA but not to any state association, while the Oakland union used to belong to PORAC but not to the ICPA or any other national group.[56] Some local unions are not affiliated with any larger body. The two independent locals in our study were the Boston Police Patrolmen's Association (formerly affiliated with the ICPA) and the Omaha Police Union Local 1 (formerly affiliated with AFSCME and then Cassesse's IBPO).

These state federations of local unions usually do not directly represent policemen for collective-bargaining purposes. Rather, as collections of local associations in their respective states, they lobby in state capitols, document and disseminate wage surveys, and provide legal, financial, and informational assistance to member associations. For example, PORAC has lobbied for compulsory arbitration and retirement benefit bills and has provided legal and financial assistance to local groups engaged in disputes with their employers. These services cost member associations a per capita of $1.00 per member per month. FOP representatives in Pennsylvania and the Police Officers Association of Michigan have successfully lobbied for legislation providing for compulsory arbitration of public safety labor disputes in their states (both efforts were conducted jointly with the firefighters). The Wisconsin Professional Policemen's Association, in addition to active lobbying, conducts an annual wage survey and sends local leaders to an annual WPPA-sponsored collective-bargaining institute at the University of Wisconsin. The Connecticut Council of Police, AFSCME District Council Number 15, in 1971 had three full-time staff representatives (all former policemen) to assist Connecticut AFSCME police locals in their representation activities. In return the Connecticut locals pay a $2.00 monthly per capita tax to Council 15.

Black Officer Organizations

A special category of employee organizations we investigated were associations of black officers. We found these organizations to exist in most of the departments we studied that have twenty-five to thirty or more black policemen. These groups have been formed, or have evolved from preexisting social-fraternal organizations, to combat racial discrimination against their members and to agitate for better police services to, and police treatment of, the black community. They usually do not compete with the majority union for representational rights; indeed, most of their members are also union members. A detailed analysis and discussion of these groups and their behaviors will be presented in Chapter 9.

Distinctions Among Organizational Levels

The foregoing descriptions are brief and somewhat incomplete. Our purposes in presenting this information are to show that there is a wide variety of organizational arrangements among police groups and to note that national affiliations are not overly meaningful when trying to explain and analyze police-union behavior. Both the ICPA and the FOP explicitly state that they grant a great deal of autonomy to their affiliates, and AFSCME has a long tradition of local autonomy. Interview information in all twenty-two cities in our sample revealed that local leaders and their hired aides (mostly attorneys) made the decisions about the use of organizational resources. As this and other chapters will show, there are no sharp patterns of behavior that distinguish the ICPA affiliates from FOP lodges or from AFSCME, NUPO-SEIU or IBPO-NAGE locals. On the other hand, this is not to say that these national organizations do nothing and that affiliations with them are meaningless. The assistance rendered to local groups via lobbying, public relations, and dissemination of useful information can be very valuable.[57]

State organizations may play a more important role in representational efforts than do national organizations. As indicated earlier, some state capitols have been the scenes of extensive lobbying by state organizations. This state lobbying can be largely explained by the fact that some state legislation frequently may have tremendous impact upon the local unions in the state. For example, unions and management in some of the cities we visited have been directly affected by state laws regarding collective bargaining and compulsory arbitration systems, retirement programs and benefits, administration of discipline within the department, shift scheduling, residency requirements, and of course, the amount of state financial aid received by certain cities. On the other hand, most of the state lobbying we were told about was done by local union leaders, and many of their legislative efforts were devoted to securing benefits specific to their own city.

Distinctions among Local Unions

Functional Identification

Our previous discussion should make it obvious that it would be more useful to identify the police unions we examined by a set of functional criteria rather than by national or state affiliations. These functional criteria include: the ranks the organization represents, percentage of eligible officers as members, whether or not the organization has exclusive representation status, the presence or absence of state bargaining legislation, and the type of union-management relationship. As Table 2-1 indicates, there is a wide variety of representational arrangements among the local police unions we studied. For example, some organizations are exclusively certified to represent patrolmen only, and they do so in a bargaining relationship, while other organizations represent several ranks in a lobbying relationship with no exclusive representation status.

Table 2-1 includes approximations of the numbers of eligible and actual members in each organization. As can be seen, police unions with exclusive representation status generally count 80 to 100 percent of their constituency as members. Four unions in our sample had agency shop provisions, but a dozen or so other unions report member-to-eligible ratios of 95 percent or higher. The ranks included in each organization also tell whether or not there are two or more organizations in a department competing for the same ranks. As would be expected, where this occurs the ratio of actual to eligible members is generally lower than among exclusive representatives.

Enabling Legislation

Enabling legislation is a crucial determinant of the nature of union-management relations in any context, including the municipal sector. The key distinction is between bargaining legislation which *requires* cities to bargain with police unions and other legislation which is not mandatory (including the absence of any bargaining legislation). As will be discussed in Chapter 4, the existence of mandatory bargaining legislation is an important source of union power, for such a statute requires the city to deal with the union as an equal participant in determining the conditions of employment within an institutionalized adversary framework.

Column 5 in Table 2-1 lists the statutory requirement *as it pertains to the police* in the various states during 1971. A "mandatory" listing means that the city must bargain collectively with a police union, and "silent" means that no state bargaining law exists to regulate the union-management relationship (though city ordinances may fill this regulatory vacuum).[58] As indicated in the table, the vast majority (eighteen of twenty-two cities) selected for field visits were in states with mandatory bargaining legislation.

Type of Relationship

Column 6 cites the nature of union-management relationship. Respondents chose from among four alternatives presented in our survey questionnaire. The four alternatives are:

1. Individual officers make their desires and options known through normal administrative channels. The police employee organization does not actively attempt to represent the officers in the department on questions of salaries and/or working conditions. However, there may be occasional informal meetings between leaders of the organization and the chief of police for the purpose of discussing matters of mutual interest. In the following tables this is referred to as an "informal" relationship.

2. The police employee organization actively undertakes to present officer views on questions of salaries and/or working conditions through appearances at city council meetings. Appearances before the city council may be supplemented by occasional meetings between the police chief and organization representatives, but these meetings are not for the purpose of negotiating mutually acceptable recommendations to be taken to the city council but are generally only exploratory in nature. This alternative is labeled "lobbying."

Table 2-1
Police Organizations Surveyed

City (1970 Population) / Organizations and National Affiliations (1)	Ranks Represented by the Organizations (2)	Approximate Numbers of Members and Eligibles (3)	Certified Exclusive Representative Status (4)	State Collective-Bargaining Legislation (5)	Type of Union-Management Relationship (6)
Baltimore (905,759)					
Local 1195, AFSCME	P,D,S	1,416 of 3,300	No	Silent	Lobbying
Lodge 3, FOP	All ranks	977 of 3,500	No		Lobbying
Boston (641,071)					
Boston Police Patrolmen's Assn., Ind.	P,D	2,300 of 2,370[a]	Yes	Mandatory	Bargaining
Superior Officers Federation, Ind.	S,L,C	393 of 397	Yes		Bargaining
Buffalo (462,768)					
Police Benevolent Assn., ICPA	P,D,S,L,C,I	1,365 of 1,405	Yes	Mandatory	Bargaining
Silver Shield Club, Ind.	P	650 of 950	No		N.A.
Cincinnati (452,524)					
Lodge 69, FOP	P,S,L,C	960 of 981	Yes	Silent	Bargaining
Cleveland (750,879)					
Lodge 8, FOP	All ranks	2,257 of 2,320	No	Silent	Lobbying
Cleveland Police Patrolmen's Assn., ICPA	P	1,750 of 2,100	No		Lobbying
Cranston, R.I. (74,287)					
Local 1, IBPO-NAGE	All ranks	70 of 105	Yes	Mandatory (arbitration)	Bargaining
Lodge 20, FOP	All ranks	30 of 105	No		Lobbying
Dayton (243,601)					
Lodge 44, FOP	P,S,L,C	426 of 426	Yes	Silent	Bargaining
Detroit (1,513,601)					
Detroit Police Officers Assn., ICPA	P	4,081 of 4,081[a]	Yes	Mandatory (arbitration)	Bargaining
Detroit Police Sgts. and Lts. Assn., ICPA	D,S,L	1,172 of 1,172	Yes		Bargaining
Hartford (158,017)					
Local 308, IBPO-NAGE	P,D,S	437 of 465	Yes	Mandatory	Bargaining

City (population)	Organization	Ranks	Members		Type	Activity
Los Angeles (2,816,061)	L.A. Fire and Police Protective League, ICPA	All ranks	6,877 of 7,000	No	Mandatory	Lobbying
Milwaukee (717,372)	Milwaukee Professional Policemen's Protective Assn., ICPA	P,D,S	2,042 of 2,097	Yes	Mandatory	Bargaining
New Haven (137,707)	Local 530, AFSCME	P,D,S,L,C	380 of 408	Yes	Mandatory	Bargaining
New York City (7,895,563)	Patrolmen's Benevolent Assn., ICPA	P	24,000 of 25,000	Yes	Mandatory	Bargaining
	Sergeant's Benevolent Assn., Ind.	S	2,600 of 2,646	Yes		Bargaining
	Lieutenant's Benevolent Assn., Ind.	L	1,000 of 1,097	Yes		Bargaining
	Captain's Endowment Assn., Ind.	C,DI,I,DCI	500 of 532	Yes		Bargaining
	Detective's Endowment Assn., Ind.	D	2,700 of 2,800	Yes		Bargaining
Oakland (361,561)	Oakland Police Officers Assn., Ind.	P,D,S,L,C	710 of 720	Yes	Mandatory	Bargaining
Omaha (346,929)	Local 1, Omaha Police Union Ind.	P,D,S,L[b]	500 of 520	Yes	Mandatory	Bargaining
Philadelphia (1,948,609)	Lodge 5, FOP	All ranks	7,154 of 7,972	Yes	Mandatory (arbitration)	Bargaining
Pittsburgh (520,117)	Lodge 1, FOP	All ranks	1,400 of 1,700	Yes	Mandatory (arbitration)	Bargaining
Providence (179,213)	Lodge 3, FOP	All ranks	395 or 420	Yes	Mandatory (arbitration)	Bargaining
Rochester, N.Y. (296,233)	Rochester Police Locust Club, ICPA	P,D,S,L	665 of 665	Yes	Mandatory	Bargaining
San Francisco (715,674)	San Francisco Police Officers Assn., ICPA	P,D,S,L,C	1,700 of 1,920	No	Mandatory	Lobbying

Table 2-1 (cont.)

City (1970 Population)	(1) Organizations and National Affiliations	(2) Ranks Represented by the Organizations	(3) Approximate Numbers of Members and Eligibles	(4) Certified Exclusive Representative Status	(5) State Collective-Bargaining Legislation	(6) Type of Union-Management Relationship
Seattle (530,831)	Seattle Police Guild, ICPA	P,D,S	1,111 of 1,120	Yes	Mandatory	Bargaining
Vallejo, California (71,710)	Vallejo Police Officers Assn., Ind.	All ranks	89 of 89	Yes	Mandatory (arbitration)	Bargaining

Notes:

General: The information in this table is current as of late 1971, and thus some items may have been superseded by subsequent developments.

Column 1: Includes only those organizations which represent a wide range of members' employment interests and excludes social, specific-benefit (Police Pension and Annuity Association, etc.), and racial (Afro-American Patrolmen's League, etc.) organizations. State affiliations are not listed.

Column 2: P = Patrolmen, D = Detectives, S = Sergeants, L = Lieutenants, C = Captains, DI = Deputy Inspectors, I = Inspectors, DCI = Deputy Chief Inspectors. "All ranks" means that the union represents all the civil-service ranks and some of the exempt ranks above captain, but this usually does not include the chief and the assistant chiefs.

The fact that a union represents detectives does not necessarily mean that there is a separate detective rank in that department.

bIn Omaha, Local 1 represents the patrolmen and detectives in one negotiating unit and the sergeants and lieutenants in another unit.

Column 3: These figures come from a variety of sources, but mostly from the parties.

aThe two unions in Boston and the two unions in Detroit have agency shop agreements with their respective cities.

Column 5: Mandatory = The police have a statutorily protected right to form and join unions and the city *must* bargain collectively with such a union.

Silent = No state law exists to regulate police collective bargaining.

(Arbitration) = State law provides compulsory binding arbitration for the settlement of police union-management negotiating impasses, with the exception of Vallejo's arbitration procedure is part of a recently revised city charter.

California law provides that cities must "meet and confer in good faith" but the state has no regulatory agency to enforce the law's requirements. Los Angeles and San Francisco were still in the process of establishing official bargaining systems at the time of the field visits and had not formally certified the respective organizations. The San Francisco union has bargained a noneconomic memorandum of understanding with the city's police commission.

Column 6: See text for explanation.

3. Representatives of the police employee organization initially meet with the police chief or his representative for the express purpose of developing mutually acceptable proposals on salaries and/or working conditions for submission to the city council. The council acts on such proposals, reserving the right to accept or reject. When the police chief and the employee representatives fail to reach agreement on an issue, the parties may have the right to appear and present their positions before the council; review or mediation may or may not be sought through involvement of persons or agencies outside the department. This alternative is called "consulting."

4. Representatives of the police employee organization meet directly from the outset of negotiations with a committee that represents the city council and/or the mayor's office. The purpose of the meetings is to develop a mutually acceptable policy on wages and/or working conditions. Provisions may or may not exist for mediation or review by persons outside the department. This is called the "bargaining" alternative.

Our field-study information indicates that these are not mutually exclusive alternatives. Almost all of the unions studied engaged in a variety of these activities. For example, the Boston patrolmen's union bargains collectively over many employment conditions, lobbies with the city council or the state legislature over others, and meets with police department executives over others. The alternative listed in column 6 is the most formalized (or highest-order) relationship which existed at the time of our study (as noted, bargaining relationships were being established in Los Angeles and San Francisco). There is a high correlation among the bargaining alternative, mandatory state bargaining legislation, and the existence of exclusive-bargaining representative status.

Rival Unionism

In each of four cities—Baltimore, Buffalo, Cleveland, and Cranston—two unions competed for the membership and allegiance of some or all of the ranks at the time of our field visits. In Baltimore, Cleveland, and Cranston the competition appeared to have as its ultimate goal exclusive representation rights for the contested ranks. In Buffalo the Silver Shield Club (patrolmen) did not appear to be attempting to displace the PBA as the department's exclusive representative but rather to pressure the PBA to more actively represent the interests of patrolmen.

Four other cities—Boston, Detroit, Hartford, and Omaha—had resolved union rivalries prior to our visits. In 1967 the Boston Police Patrolmen's Association and the Collective Bargaining Federation (now known as the Superior Officers Federation) competed in a representation election for the right to be the patrolmen's exclusive representative. The two separate units (patrolmen; superior officers) were established following the preferences of the voters. In Detroit the Detectives' Association and the Lieutenants and Sergeants Association agreed to merge (and retain the latter name) after the department eliminated the formal distinction between uniformed and plainclothes lieutenants and sergeants. In Hartford the International Brotherhood of Police Officers (NAGE) successfully challenged former AFSCME Local 234 for the right to be the department's exclusive representative. In Omaha John Cassesse's NUPO successfully challenged former AFSCME Local 531 for the right to be the department's exclusive representative (and, as mentioned earlier, to lose this status within two years as the Omaha union went independent).

While the majority pattern in our study was for the existing organization(s) to have unchallenged representation rights, there has been some kind of recent or continuing interorganizational rivalry in eight of the twenty-two cities. It is difficult to draw conclusions about the effects of these rivalries on the quality of the union-management relationships. It appears that direct interunion competition tends to make some unions more aggressive in their dealings with management than they would otherwise be.

Local Union Governance

Since this is not a comparative study of union locals among several occupational groups, it is difficult to make evaluations about the conduct of internal union affairs. Using the existing literature on private-sector local-union governance, it appears that police unions are not governed in a manner radically different from other unions.[59] In general, rank-and-file members tend to be rather apathetic and show little interest in union affairs unless a "hot" issue is current. Most union decisions are made by a small group of activists who are reelected to office as long as they satisfy a majority of the membership. As in private-sector unions, members and leaders appear to be primarily concerned with "bread and butter" issues, that is, those economic and noneconomic issues which directly affect working conditions such as wages, pensions, seniority provisions, and so forth. The importance of various issues will be discussed in Chapter 3.

The police unions we studied appear to be as internally democratic as other unions with which we are familiar. The longest term of office for elected leaders was three years, with many unions providing for annual elections. In several unions recently there have been spirited election contests for top office (San Francisco, Omaha, Pittsburgh, New York [detectives], Detroit [superior officers], Boston [patrolmen], Philadelphia, and Milwaukee). In some unions, candidates for top office are limited to those currently holding another union position (e.g., stewardship, board of directorship, etc.), thus limiting the access to important decision-making positions. On the other hand, the local nature of police unions means that the members and leaders are geographically close, and this closeness is accentuated by the fact that local-union leaders are almost always full-time policemen who are well aware of the daily concerns of the rank-and-file. In the unions in nineteen cities the elected leaders appeared to be the primary decision-makers, while in three cities (New Haven, Baltimore [AFSCME], and Omaha) the chief union officials were nonelected business agents. In two of these cities (New Haven, Omaha) the business agents were former policemen, so in all unions except one, the leaders were practicing or former policemen. It is our judgment that locally elected policemen leaders, in close and direct touch with the membership, make most of the substantive union decisions.

Summary

In this chapter we have attempted to show that police employee organizations have existed in some form for many decades and that when police militancy erupted in the 1960s, organizational forms already existed to convey its expression. We discussed the causes of this militancy and argued that it was largely a function of the employment relationship and the community environment in which the department functioned. Finally we looked at the nature of the police labor movement and attempted to show that it is essentially local, independent police-only employee organizations that express the militancy and impact on department management. The next three chapters look at how these organizations exert pressure on management in support of their goals.

3

The Nature of Police Labor Relations

This chapter examines the nature of union-management interaction in the private and public sectors in order to establish an analytical base for a more detailed examination of police union power in the next two chapters.

Labor Relations in the Private Sector

Since practices in the private sector have served as the reference point for most of the municipal union-management relationships that have emerged, we use the private-sector model as a point of departure. It is difficult to talk about *the* practice of collective bargaining because of the wide variations among the thousands of union-management relationships which exist;[1] however, it is possible to abstract and focus on the primary factors governing the union-management relationship.

The Economic Context

In the private sector the primary constraints upon the union-management relationship are economic: business firms are assumed to be profit-maximizing organizations; the product markets from which the firm receives its revenues, and the labor, capital, and raw materials markets which determine the firm's costs, pose the primary constraints upon the firm's operations.[2]

The union too is subject to economic constraints. While it is generally acknowledged that unions have raised the relative wages of members 10-15 percent,[3] it is also true that union wage policy over the long run is severely constrained by factors affecting the supply of labor, the production function, and the demand for final product. Wages rise more rapidly in tight labor markets, less rapidly in loose labor markets, and for individual firms in crisis situations union wages may remain constant or even fall. Similarly in a competitive market given consumer choice among substitute products, increases in labor costs which force up the firm's prices can adversely affect the sale of the finished product and lead to a reduction in the firm's relative demand for the union labor.[4]

Bilateralism

The private-sector union-mangement relationship is assumed to be bilateral: a single hierarchy of employees and their spokesmen (union) interacting with a single hierarchy of managers and their spokesmen (management).[5] An important factor contributing to this bilateral focus in the analysis of private sector union-mangement relationships is the relatively monolithic nature of the business firm. Compared to governmental organizations (to be looked at shortly), the business organization is characterized by a tight hierarchical structure in which the lines of decision-making authority are carefully drawn and observed. Operationally, this means that for industrial-relations purposes the firm speaks with a unitary voice, and interactions with union representatives are channeled through the firm's industrial-relations officials.

While bilateralism is the rule, there are exceptions to this two-party paradigm. For instance, it can be argued that the continual availability of governmental dispute resolution machinery (the National Labor Relations Board, the courts, the Federal Mediation and Conciliation Service, Railway Labor Act dispute resolution procedures) and the frequent intervention of the federal government into union-management affairs (whether via unfair labor practice proceedings by the NLRB, suits for breach of contract in federal court, wage guidelines, or FMCS and presidential mediatory efforts during contract negotiation impasses) tends to expand the bilateral relationship into a multilateral one. As we shall see, however, both mangement and the unions are reluctant to exploit governmental intervention on a continuing basis for fear of future, unwanted intervention on the basis of earlier precedent. To date the private-sector experience has essentially favored bilateralism.[6]

The Concept of Power in Private-Sector
Collective Bargaining

There are almost as many definitions of power as there are writers on the subject. A general definition which we favor defines power as the extent to which A can get B to do something that B would not otherwise do.[7]

Bargaining Power. This general definition can be refined for specific application to the union-management relationship. In the unionized private sector, non-supervisory employment conditions are determined via contract and grievance negotiations between union and management representatives. The parties are driven to come to mutually satisfactory terms, particularly during contract negotiations, by the costs which might be incurred if they fail to agree. For example, the workers might strike, forcing a partial or total loss of production, sales, and revenue for the firm and work and paychecks for the employees, or the employer might lock out with similar results. Since for most issues each side is at odds on what constitutes a satisfactory settlement (the firm has a constant incentive to minimize costs and maximize efficiency, and the employees have a constant incentive to maximize income and security,) agreement occurs not voluntarily because of altruism but rather because of the threatened or actual use of power.[8]

Chamberlain and Kuhn offer a general model of bargaining power: the union's bargaining power consists of its ability to increase mangement's costs of disagreement (the usual cost-imposing action is a strike) or to decrease management's costs of agreement (for example, allowing the employer unlimited mechanization rights if he agrees to provide income guarantees to those presently employed). If the costs to management of disagreeing with the union's terms are high/low relative to the cost of agreeing with them, the union's bargaining power is increased/decreased.[9]

Bargaining Power as Economic Costs. It is possible to be more specific about how union power in the private sector operates through economic mechanisms. Rees, citing Marshall, relates the union's bargaining power to the elasticity of demand for labor.[10] The more inelastic the demand for union labor, the smaller the effect of a given wage increase on the employment of the union's members, and the greater the union's influence on members' wages (and, hence, the greater its bargaining power). Marshall cites four conditions that affect the elasticity of the demand for union labor: demand is more inelastic (1) the more essential is union labor in the production process, (2) the more inelastic the demand for the product, (3) the smaller the union labor cost/total cost ratio, and (4) the more inelastic the supply of the other factors of production.

Given that the market is the source of this power, unions usually exploit this power through market intervention: the planned strike, wildcat strikes, slowdowns, consumer boycotts, the use of the union label, secondary boycotts, and control of the labor supply.[11] However, not all applications of union power are negative (i.e., increasing the firms cost of disagreement). Some unions have instead worked with management to lower management's costs of agreement to the union's terms. For example, the United Mine Workers gave the coal operators a free hand in the mechanization of the mining processes in return for very high wages and monetary fringe benefits for the employed miners, and the International Longshoremen's and Warehousemen's Union agreed to let the shipping companies mechanize the longshoring processes in return for employment and retirement guarantees for incumbent longshoremen. Just as with union tactics to increase mangement's costs of disagreement, so do union efforts to decrease management's costs of agreement operate through economic markets.

Summary

The analysis in this section has focused on three factors that govern private-sector union-management relationships. These three factors are summarized as follows:

1. The union-management relationship is shaped by the constraints imposed by economic markets.
2. For each bargaining unit a bilateral relationship exists between a single representative of employee interests and a single, relatively monolithic organization of managers.
3. The union's bargaining power, expressed in terms of the costs of agreement and disagreement, consists primarily of the ability to impose economic costs on management.

The Public Sector: The Case of the Law-Enforcement Industry

Public-sector labor relations can be distinguished from private-sector labor relations on each of the three criteria cited above: the primary context of the union-management relationship is political (rather than economic), the union-management relationship tends to be multilateral (rather than bilateral), and bargaining power involves the imposition of political costs (rather than economic costs).

The Political Context

The most obvious difference between private and public labor relations is the economic context of the former and the political context of the latter.[12] The continued existence of local government organizations does not depend upon satisfactory performance in economic product markets. Rather, these organizations provide a variety of services, many of them monopolistic (there is only one fire department, one park service), financed by revenues which usually have no direct cost-price connection with the services provided (the police department does not send a bill to burglary victims when the burglar is apprehended). A second factor, beyond the absence of competitive markets in characterizing the context of public-sector bargaining as political is the fact that the top executives in these organizations are elected by the voters on the basis of their political appeal rather than their administrative abilities.[13]

Because of these monopoly characteristics and the fact that municipal taxpayers must share in the costs of government whether they use certain services or not, government managers relative to those in the private sector are in a position to pass along increases in costs without much fear of losing customers in the short run (though they may lose customer loyalty, that is, votes).[14]

This is not to say that public managers can ignore market forces in the long run (indeed several cities in the 1970s are experiencing fiscal crises), but rather it is to say that political factors rather than economic factors may be the dominant decision variables in responding to the challenges posed by economic constraints. The specific nature of the implementation of economic constraints (e.g., what services will be cut or new services cancelled, what new taxes will be imposed, etc.) are ultimately decided by elected officials, and these implementations of economic constraints are mediated by the elected officials' interpretation of their actual and potential political implications.

How this works in practice may be seen in the experience of two cities in this sample. In Cleveland policemen and firefighters and in Dayton firefighters were among the last employees laid off when budget stringency necessitated reductions in city employment. Since protective service compensation is higher than the pay of most other city employees, a purely economic decision rule would have meant that at least some of these employees could have been laid off sooner; that they were not reflects management's decision that the protective services are among the most important provided by the city (and personal safety one of the most potent political issues). While the economic context was relevant, political criteria were dominant.[15]

The Concept of Multilateralism

In recent years many cities have established collective-bargaining relationships with unions of their employees. While these relationships have the same conceptual bilateral form as in the private sector, the municipal context provides the union an opportunity for expanding the bilateral relationship into a multilateral one.

"Multilateral bargaining" may have different meanings in different contexts. According to McLennan and Moskow, who coined the phrase, it means that more than two parties are involved in the collective-bargaining process. This involvement may occur directly at the bargaining table or more typically on the fringes of the bargaining relationship (which formally is conducted by the two direct parties to the agreement.) To be able to participate, a third party must be able to impose a direct cost on at least one of the direct parties to the agreement.[16]

Thomas Kochan offers an operational distinction between bilateral and multilateral bargaining based on the channeling of union-management interactions through formally designated negotiators:

It is assumed that a bilateral bargaining process is one in which a formally designated management negotiator or negotiating team represents the city in direct negotiations with a corresponding negotiator or negotiating team representing the employee organization. The purpose of these two individuals or groups is assumed to be to reach a tentative bargaining agreement. When an agreement is reached, the negotiating representatives take the agreed upon package back to respective organizations where it is then ratified and implemented. An extremely important assumption in this operational definition of bilateral bargaining is that all interactions between city officials and the employee organization are channeled through the formally designated negotiators. In addition, these negotiators are assumed to serve as the public spokesman for the management on bargaining issues, that is, no other city officials are expected to publicly comment on the bargaining issues without first clearing their comments with the formal city negotiators. Given this characterization of a bilateral bargaining process, multilateral bargaining will be operationally defined as acts which constitute violations of this pattern of behavior.[17]

The movement from bilateralism to multilateralism is inherent in the structure of the public sector. First, the pricing and monopoly characteristics of municipal government discussed above serve to increase the interest of many citizens and interest groups in the outcome of municipal union-management interactions, especially those concerning monetary items.

Second, the vertical separation of governmental decision-making authority among federal, state, county, and municipal levels; and at each level, the horizontal separation of decision-making authority among the executive, legislative, and judicial branches; and within each branch among various bodies, offices, and office-holders means that many government decisions involve a variety of managerial decision-makers. For our purposes, the best example is the fragmentation of municipal control over personnel issues. In our research we found that authority over monetary items may be shared among the executive branch (which often prepares the budget), the legislative branch (which may modify, reject, amend, and must ultimately approve the budget), and the civil service commission (which sometimes prepares salary recommendations for the city council). Some cities even have charter provisions, approved by the voters, which determine police pay and fringes. Authority over nonmonetary items may be shared among police department management, the police commission (if any), the civil service commission, the personnel director, the city attorney, the city manager or mayor's office, and the city council.[18] This dispersion of managerial authority means that interest groups seeking to influence managerial decisions are provided with multiple access points.[19]

Third, since top management consists of elected and appointed officials responsible to various electoral constituencies, interest groups, and other elected and appointed officials for their presence in office, and since these decision-makers may have ideological convictions and/or electoral or interest group pressures that may cause them to oppose each other on various municipal issues, the potential payoff to interest groups interceding in the municipal decision-making process may be high.

Finally, the city's hired labor-relations representatives take their directions from these elected or appointed politically motivated officials.

In this environment, then, it is not unreasonable for the union to attempt to exploit these elements of multilateralism. For example, union representatives may make an "end run" around the city negotiator to the mayor or city councilmen to improve the deal offered at the bargaining table; the union may go directly to the voters for their approval of police employment issues through referenda; or the union may lobby for improved pensions in the state legislature after having been denied a similar request at the bargaining table. Given the multiple access points to management and given the political currency the police have in "law and order issues" multilateralism may be the only rational behavior for the union to follow.

Since multilateralism is one of the keys to understanding the specific dimensions of police-union power discussed in the next two chapters, we now turn to a more detailed examination of the concept.

Governmental Multilateral Bargaining. It is useful to distinguish between governmental and community multilateral bargaining.[20] Governmental multilateral bargaining refers to the involvement of nonlabor relations mangement officials in the union-management bargaining process:[21] elected or appointed officials with no designated labor relations responsibility. This kind of multilateral bargaining occurs because of union exploitation of the divided managerial authority structure and the "political" nature of holding municipal office.

Governmental multilateral bargaining had occurred in almost every city in the sample. As usually practiced, these multilateral efforts included union interactions with various city officials (usually elected ones) designed to secure agreement with union demands to which the designated city negotiators would not agree. These multilateral efforts, frequently called "end runs" because they attempt to achieve gains on bargainable subjects by circumventing the institutionalized bargaining procedures, paid off for the union when the elected officials involved believed that it was better "politics" to agree to union demands than not to agree, that is, the elected officials perceived that they could gain more political benefits by agreeing to some or all union demands than by refusing. This was especially true as election time approached.

These union-management interactions away from the bargaining table were implemented in a variety of ways. In a midwestern city in 1971 the union negotiated directly with the city council after the council refused to give adequate negotiating authority to the city negotiator. In six cities management negotiators related instances of union leader-city council member interactions during the contract negotiation process. Six other cities yielded examples of union leader-mayoral interaction during the bargaining process. The purpose of these extracurricular interactions with elected officials was to "get more" than could be obtained by limiting union-management interactions to hired negotiators. Some of these union-elected official interactions took place in the context of union demands—electoral support *quid pro quo* (i.e., the union provides political support at election time (or promises of same) in return for benefit increases (or promises of same)).

Community Multilateral Bargaining. Community multilateral bargaining is identified by the direct interest and involvement of citizens and community groups in the process and outcomes of interactions between union and management.[22] This interest and involvement may be expressed directly in the voting booth on police issues, or it may be channeled or expressed via elected officials, but the distinguishing characteristics are either a relatively high level of public interest in particular union-management issues and concomitant attempt to influence the outcome of these issues or else the necessity for the expression of voter preferences on particular issues. It should be noted that there is no hard-and-fast dividing line between governmental and community multilateral bargaining, particularly when citizen interest and involvement is channeled through elected officials.

One type of community multilateral bargaining is channeled through government officials but results from a high level of public interest in police activities.[23] This interest frequently focuses on law enforcement rather than monetary issues. An example is illustrative:

—In early 1970 policemen in Hartford shot three criminal suspects in a one-month period, killing two of them. All three were either black or Puerto Rican. The city's minority communities rose up in angry protest and demanded that something be done to restrict this kind of police action. At a stormy meeting the city council voted to establish a council committee with subpoena powers to see if some restrictive police gun use guidelines should be established. The city's policemen were incensed, and their union vigorously fought against this committee's investigative efforts. After an eleven hour negotiating session between union representatives (primarily the union lawyer) and the committee, the committee's powers were substantially reduced and the police offered their previously withheld cooperation. This agreement also ended what appeared to be a very real police strike threat. There was a great deal of black, brown, and white community interest in the affair, with the minorities and the liberal whites backing the efforts to establish police gun guidelines and the majority of the white citizenry supporting the police union in its opposition efforts. The city council apparently responded to this public support for the union position, for it ultimately voted against adoption of new gun guidelines.[24]

Another example can be seen in the Seattle police union's informal negotiations with the county coroner's office to change the coroner's inquest procedure involving police on-duty homicides. This occurred in the wake of a police rank-and-file uproar at a coroner's jury verdict that an alleged black fire-bomber, shot by the police, was killed "by criminal means." The police perceived that this verdict resulted from the pressure created by the local black community's angry reaction, and in particular by the demonstrative crowd present at the actual coroner's jury inquest proceedings.[25]

This type of interaction is not limited to nonmonetary issues. In San Francisco, which has no institutionalized collective-bargaining procedure for determining economic items, union interactions with city officials over monetary fringe benefits were influenced by the unofficial but influential involvement of representatives of the downtown business community.[26]

A second type of community multilateral bargaining occurs when the police union goes to the voters for direct implementation of some union goal. These union-voter interactions may deal with either economic or law-enforcement issues. The most publicized example of the latter is the New York City PBA's campaign against newly-elected Mayor Lindsay's civilian review board. After failing to block the formation of the board in early 1966, the union gathered enough petition signatures to have the issue placed on the ballot, won a court battle to keep the issue on the ballot, and then went to the city's voters with a well-financed (in excess of $500,000) and hard-fought public relations campaign. This campaign accurately tapped voter sentiment, for the board was buried by a two-to-one vote.[27]

More commonly, this type of community multilateral bargaining deals with direct labor-relations issues. Police unions in San Francisco, Oakland, Los Angeles, Omaha, Cleveland, Pittsburgh, and Philadelphia have gone directly to the voters and "bargained" for either increased benefits or the implementation of procedures designed to obtain increased benefits in the future. In San Francisco and Cleveland the police unions put police-pay charter amendments on the ballot and then convinced the voters to approve them.[28] Police unions in San Francisco, Oakland, Los Angeles, and Omaha put measures on the ballot which would increase their pensions. Police unions in Pennsylvania worked for voter approval of a 1967 ballot measure to amend the state constitution to permit the implementation of compulsory arbitration of police and fire union-management impasses.

Legitimate objections may be made to the inclusion of these kinds of union-voter interactions under the label of "bargaining." Admittedly, the use of that term in this context is much looser and refers to a process much different from the traditional union-management interaction across a negotiation table. However, even a cursory examination of some of the union communications directed at the voters reveals a vague theme of an exchange of equitable treatment of the police in return for better law enforcement for the public. In any case, these kinds of union-voter interactions do come under the rubric of police labor relations, and it seems reasonable to expect that voter agreement with police-union ballot objectives is exchanged for something, even if it is nothing more than a feeling of "having supported our local police."

Applications of the Multilateral Concept. We found multilateralism to be an especially useful concept in observing two kinds of situations—union management interaction in cities where no institutionalized bargaining procedure existed and, in cities with collective bargaining, union management interaction over issues that cannot be decided at the bargaining table.

At the time of the field study, San Francisco, Los Angeles, Cleveland, and Baltimore did not have official collective bargaining.[29] In the absence of such formal procedures, the police unions in these cities have used tactics such as private lobbying with various managerial officials, public lobbying via appearances at city council, civil service commission, or state legislative hearings, involvement in the election campaigns of various candidates, putting police measures on the ballot, and in general using the activities available to political interest groups.

These same kinds of political interactions are also used by police unions in cities which have collective-bargaining systems to deal with a variety of issues which affect police employment conditions but which are not subject to determination via the collective-bargaining process. Several of these kinds of issues will be discussed in Chapter 7. One example that relates to the chief's ability to manage is the 1969 lobbying battle waged in the New York State Legislature between the city of New York and the PBA over the city's efforts to amend a state law in order to allow the police department to establish a fourth shift during high crime hours. Where employment issues cannot be implemented without the approval of the voters or other governmental bodies we found that police unions were quite capable of using the entire arsenal of political processes necessary to influence government decision-making.

Summary

As we discussed earlier, unions in the private sector use the institutionalized collective-bargaining framework for dealing with employers over almost all substantive employment conditions through interactions regularly confined to the formally designated managerial labor-relations representatives. In contrast, because of municipal management's fragmented authority structure and political nature, the necessity for many employment conditions to be changed via the legislative, electoral, or judicial processes, and the lack of institutionalized collective-bargaining procedures in some cities, police unions cannot and do not rely on the institutionalized collective-bargaining procedure to the extent that private-sector unions do. In addition to collective bargaining, police unions include lobbying, electoral politics, and other political activities among their self-interest efforts. Thus, when analyzing police-union activities, it seems more accurate and appropriate to talk about police labor relations than limiting the analysis to police collective bargaining.

This multilateral spectrum of police labor relations is illustrated in Figure 3-1. Our field research yielded examples of union interactions with all of the potential adversaries mentioned in the diagram. While some of these managerial officials play a much more important role in police labor relations than others, the research findings show that the police unions in our twenty-two-city sample

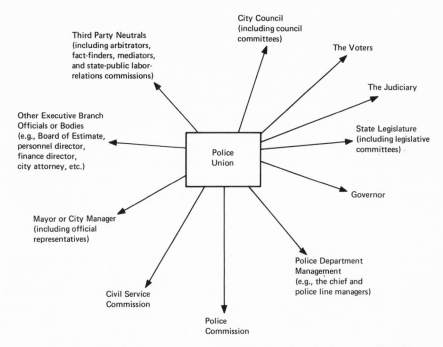

Figure 3-1. The Potential for Multilateral Labor Relations: Possible Union Adversaries

used a variety of different influence methods to interact with all of these managerial targets in their attempts to participate in the determination of a wide variety of employment conditions.

We can now summarize the distinctions between private sector and law enforcement labor relations.

1. The union management relationship in the public sector is shaped immediately by the constraints imposed by political markets rather than economic markets.

2. For each bargaining unit in the public sector, there tends to exist a multilateral relationship between a single representative of the employees and a multifaceted or fragmented organization of managers representing diverse interest groups as opposed to the bilateral relationship that characterizes the private sector.[30]

3. Thus the union's bargaining power in the public sector consists of its ability primarily to manipulate the political costs of agreement and disagreement of the various managers rather than the economic cost manipulation that characterizes union power in the private sector.

In the next two chapters we utilize this multilateral model of public-sector bargaining to analyze the use of power in police labor relations. Chapter 4 looks at the contextual variables which add to or detract from the union's bargaining position vis-à-vis management while Chapter 5 analyzes the activities which the union can manipulate directly in its relations with management.

4

The Contextual Dimensions Affecting Police-Union Power

The context in which bargaining takes place is an important determinant of the relative power of the parties. In this chapter we will look at how the economic, political, and statutory environments of bargaining, the structure of bargaining, and the characteristics of the work place and work community affect the exercise of power by management and the unions.

From a practitioner's point of view, the most important thing about power is that he have more power than his adversaries in order that he may secure agreement on his own terms; the exact sources of this power probably are of secondary importance. For analytical and expository purposes, however, we have found it useful to distinguish between the contextual sources of power discussed in this chapter (those which affect the union's ability to achieve its goals but which in the short run cannot be meaningfully manipulated) and the application of directly manipulatable sources of power (discussed in Chapter 5).[1]

The material in this and following chapters is concerned with giving specific meaning to the conceptual framework developed in the previous chapter. There is no attempt to measure power either absolutely or relatively between parties, for as Murray Edelman has said, "except in static situations hypothesized by academicians, power is not a measurable entity like physical pressure."[2] Further, since power has meaning only in terms of the specific costs of agreement and disagreement associated with each issue or demand,[3] since the number and kind of issues vary from one city to the next, and since power relationships are dynamic and change over time, it makes little or no sense to construct aggregate measures of power relating to some point in history.

The Economic Context

Four economic factors that affect the strength of the union's bargaining position with management are: local labor-market conditions, the ability of comparable groups to raise their wages, the cost of living, and the city's ability to pay. Just as in the private sector, a police union's bargaining position is enhanced if the employer is having difficulty hiring qualified personnel at the going wage, if there are strong inflationary pressures, if other highly visible groups of employees have been winning generous settlements, and if the employer can afford to pay more. Conversely, a police union's bargaining position is weakened if there is a queue of qualified applicants, if there are minimal inflationary pressures, no strong orbits of coercive comparisons, and if the city is facing bankruptcy.

The Local Labor Market

The relationship of supply and demand and wages and bargaining power is well documented throughout the literature.[4] We emphasize the local labor market here because as discussed earlier the delivery of services is local and very few departments recruit far beyond their own boundaries. We did not collect data relating vacancies and wages because of the situations in several cities where additional positions had been created for political reasons with no intention of their actually being filled in the short run.

During the 1960s a tight labor market and a politically volatile environment were factors that kept the level of unfilled positions relatively high. After the 1970-72 recession, however, many agencies found that the high salaries offered patrolmen (e.g., as of January 1, 1973 top patrolmen pay in New York City, Oakland, San Francisco, and Los Angeles exceeded $14,000 exclusive of overtime, longevity, night shift differential pay and other monetary fringe benefits) had resulted in an excess supply of qualified candidates.[5]

Coercive Comparisons

When the union finds local labor-market comparisons with similarly qualified employees no longer useful, it extends the definition of "relevant" comparisons to other highly visible and better paid groups of employees. The San Francisco union attempted to compare themselves with construction craftsmen in 1971;[6] Boston in 1967-68 used the much higher New York City patrolmen's pay as its reference point. Police unions may institutionalize these pay relationships to their advantage, as has been done in the San Francisco, Oakland, and Cleveland charter provisions, which officially peg changes in police pay to changes in the pay of other groups.[7] The institutionalization of these relationships, which are accomplished via the manipulation of power sources examined in the next chapter, gives the union an opportunity to control which wages are used for comparison purposes, but the union has no control over the changes in reference group pay.

One way in which these coercive comparisons may be expressed in a relatively strong manner is via the "catch-up" principle. Police-union leaders may point out that by comparison with particular reference groups they are inequitably underpaid and thus their compensation should "catch-up" with these reference groups in order that equity be established. An example of this phenomenon occurred in Rochester during the 1970 negotiations when the union wasted no opportunities in pointing out that Rochester police pay was significantly lower than police pay in some of the surrounding suburbs where the police jobs allegedly were easier (certainly the suburbs did not have the ethnic and racial tensions that Rochester had).

The Cost of Living

A rapidly rising cost of living, which deflates the real value of salary increases, adds to the union's bargaining power in that it creates an issue which transcends all of the internal interest group boundaries and thereby contributes to the solidarity essential to the use of power sources. The period since 1966 has been such an inflationary period, and the unions in this sample have used increases in the cost of living to bolster their bargaining position.

The City's Ability to Pay

A fourth economic factor affecting the union's relative strength is the city's ability to pay. Whereas the union never really is able to influence local labor-market conditions, changes in the cost of living, or the wages of reference groups, in the long run it can have some influence on the city's ability to pay. Four unions in our sample attempted to strengthen their bargaining position by working to increase city revenues by: campaigning for the passage of a referendum to establish a city payroll tax; lobbying in the state legislature for a bill enabling the city to levy a sales tax; campaigning for the incumbent governor's slate during an election in return for favorable consideration over the amount of state financial aid their city would receive; and lobbying in the state legislature for approval of the mayor's budget (the solvency of which depends upon the level of state financial aid).

However, in spite of the union's long-run ability to influence the city's ability to pay, in the short run a police union faces a relatively fixed economic context, for even if the union can influence the flow of revenue (including state and federal aid) or the ability to generate new revenues (including taxpayer resistance, which is discussed in the next section) it still has little control over competing claims on those revenues.

In summary, the economic context is an important factor in the union's bargaining power and the rate of increase in patrolmen's pay levels. As the economic environment in the cities has deteriorated in recent years, the rate of increase in patrolmen's salaries in cities over 100,000 has declined: from 10.5 percent in 1968-69 to 8.9 percent in 1969-70 and 5.5 percent in 1970-71.[8] However, the economic context is only one of several affecting the union's bargaining power. In this next section we look at the dimensions of the political context.

The Political Context

The economic variables mentioned in the previous pages are generally composed of discrete and easily measurable units, for example, the cost of living has increased 5 percent, the police in an adjacent city received a 10 percent pay increase, and so forth. Unfortunately, it is not as easy to measure the political environment in which a police union operates.

The Balance of Political Power

The most important aspect of the political system is the balance of political power, or more specifically the location of *de jure* and *de facto* governmental decision-making authority relevant to police-connected issues along a concentrated-diffuse continuum. The analysis in Chapter 3 emphasized that official managerial decision-making authority tends to be widely diffused. In contrast, *de facto* political decision-making authority usually tends to be less diffused.[9] For example, political power in Mayor Daley's Chicago is quite centralized in the mayor's office;[10] on the other hand, political power in New York City is much more decentralized and is spread among various offices, office holders, and other people who do not control each other's behavior.[11]

Rather than determining some absolute measure of political power, in this context the important consideration is the extent to which the union has room to maneuver—whether or not there is a "balance of power" political environment which enables the union to increase its bargaining power by forming mutual support alliances with various actual or potential office holders or other political influentials. Differences in room to maneuver can best be examined by citing some examples:

—In one city outside the twenty-two-city sample the union has no political leverage. The mayor, through an all-pervasive patronage system, controls the local majority political party, the city's executive branch, the city council, the local judiciary, and a large number of votes in the state legislature. Although he is the union's primary adversary, the union has endorsed him twice for reelection. When asked why, the union president replied "because he's got the only game in town."

—In another city there is no dominant political machine either in the city or the state. The union gained an advantage in its bargaining position several years ago as two mayoral candidates tried to out-promise each other in wooing police support during a close and hotly contested election campaign. The union was able to secure large increases in economic and noneconomic benefits, due in part to the campaign promises made by the new mayor.

—In a third city the police union aided the leading mayoral candidate by endorsing him, giving him a small campaign contribution, and having the articulate union leader campaign for him. Very soon after he was elected, the new mayor signed a generous two-year police contract.

In the long run the police union in any city can work to cultivate political alliances and influence in city hall, the state capitol, party headquarters, and so on. To do so entails some expertise in the *quid pro quo* nature of political life, whereby the union helps particular interest groups or politicians obtain their goals (election of candidates, passage of referendum issues, passage of legislation) in return for their support for particular union goals (direct benefit increases for the membership, union security measures, etc.). At any point in time, however, the union must accept as given the political power structure in the relevant community.

"Law and Order" Politics

The 1960s saw the emergence of new and radically different lifestyles among some groups and the emergence of demonstrations and confrontation political tactics by racial minorities, students, and others who demanded a larger voice in the determination of their own lives. The 1960s also saw the emergence of large-scale public fear of criminal activity; by 1968 citizen fear of violent street crime had become so widespread that "crime" was a major issue in the presidential election campaign of that year.[12]

This increasing saliency of the crime and law and order issues during the late 1960s-early 1970s has helped make the police a more potent political force than they were during the tranquil 1950s when fewer demands were placed on them.[13] Law-and-order politics can be an important source of union power, since public opinion on this issue may make it costly for an elected official to oppose union demands and thereby appear "anti-police." The Hartford gun guidelines example cited in Chapter 3 and the widely noted overwhelming referendum defeat suffered by New York City Mayor John Lindsay's civilian review board in 1966 are concrete examples of "law and order" political leverage exercised by two unions.[14]

Political Ideology

While police unions desire management officials to be economically liberal (at least regarding police salaries and fringes), the police unions in this sample generally espoused a "hard line" on law enforcement-related issues. Various unions have vigorously resisted restrictions on the police use of weapons, have energetically worked to defeat civilian review boards, have condemned managerial actions which facilitate citizen identification of police officers, have espoused "get-tough" civil disturbance control policies, and have roundly condemned Supreme Court decisions, "liberals, do-gooders, and bleeding-hearts," and any person or organization who espouses any changes which would impinge on the discretion of police officers in the performance of their duties. This hard line on law enforcement issues has resulted in frequent police-union endorsement of, or informal membership support for, political candidates who exhibit "conservative" stances on many social and political issues. The most widely noted example of this support of conservative candidates was the significant police interest in the presidential candidacy of George Wallace in 1968.[15]

It is in the context of this expressed police political conservatism that Don Berney has advanced the thesis that politically liberal mayors have much more difficulty in dealing with police unions than do politically conservative mayors.[16] He cites as evidence the relationships in New York City (Mayor John Lindsay), Boston (Mayor Kevin White), Cleveland (former Mayor Carl Stokes), and Detroit (former Mayor Jerome Cavanaugh) between liberal mayors and their respective police unions.

While we would agree with him that politically liberal mayors do have a harder time dealing with their police unions than mayors with a conservative image, our research suggests that these difficulties stem less from broad ideological differences than from specific mayoral intervention in the operation of the department—some of which actions may relate to ideology and some of which may not. Proposals to require name tags, hire civilian traffic directors and desk clerks, and institute a Model Cities program with some community control of police (Boston); the establishment of a civilian review board, and the attempt to implement a fourth shift (New York City); the withdrawal of all white officers from the area of a 1968 shoot-out with black militants (Cleveland); and one city's perceived bad faith at the bargaining table (Detroit) are issues that the police and their unions perceived as inimical to their interests. The ideological differences may add some fuel to the fire and serve to reinforce antagonisms, but police union-liberal mayor conflict seems to be primarily a result of the formulation or implementation of specific mayoral proposals.

Another factor emerging from the clash in ideologies is the visibility and appearance of being powerful, which the union gains from interacting with liberal mayors on these issues. This image of power is further enhanced if a police union is able to successfully block the implementation of mayoral proposals (via the tactics discussed in the next chapter) as happened repeatedly in Boston, for example. Having liberal mayors against whom to tilt contributed significantly to the powerful images enjoyed by the patrolmen's unions in Boston, Detroit, New York, and Cleveland.

The City's Priorities

The political analogy to the city's economic ability to pay is the degree of the city's *willingness* to pay for police services. Since most city services (police protection, fire protection, welfare, parks and recreation, street maintenance, etc.) have no direct cost-price connection with revenues, and since there are usually more competing claims for city funds than funds available, the amount of money (both absolute and relative) allocated to each particular service depends in large part upon city officials' funding priorities. In turn, these priorities are shaped by city officials' own preferences and their perceptions of voter preferences for allocating the city's revenues (herein lies a major application of the power discussed above under the law and order heading). If city officials accord high priority to funding police services, this willingness acts as a source of union power by making it easier for the union to obtain economic benefits.

A variety of examples illustrate the power of the police in this regard. Chicago's Mayor Daley, who controls the allocation of the city's revenues, has made his policemen among the highest paid in the country. In Cleveland, which had budget difficulties sufficiently severe to require the lay off of hundreds of employees, fire and police officers were the last to be laid off and the first rehired. Detroit, under similar circumstances, laid off several hundred temporary civilian employees but retained all its policemen and firefighters even though the layoffs were necessitated by the cost of implementing police and fire arbitration awards. In Dayton layoffs occurred in every department except police. To cite a contrary example, in Berkeley, California, after the 1971 election of a "radical" slate of four (of nine) city councilmen, the police department budget came under sharp attack.[17]

The Statutory Context

Police union-management relations are regulated by a variety of state laws and local ordinances. The most important of these are the state collective-bargaining laws, which mandate that cities bargain collectively with city employee unions if a majority of the relevant employees desire to do so, and the other statutes, which regulate the many kinds of political activities in which police unions are active. This section will examine the statutory "rules framework" as it impinges on police-union activities, with the focus on the collective-bargaining statues, which regulate much of the police union-management interaction.

Bargaining Statutes

Students of industrial relations have commented extensively on the decisive effect the legal protection afforded by the 1935 passage of the National Labor Relations Act had on the growth of collective bargaining in the private sector.[18] This same effect has also been observed in the public sector:

The importance of a statute authorizing and protecting collective bargaining for public employees cannot be overemphasized. In the absence of such a statute, collective bargaining exists largely at the sufferance of management. A public agency may enter into good-faith bargaining on its own volition; however, considerations of self-interest inevitably assert themselves so that it is virtually impossible for management to divorce its role as an adversary from that of the arbiter of the bargaining process.[19]

As reported in Table 2-1, eighteen of the twenty-two cities in this sample are in states that have legislation mandating police collective bargaining with a recognized employee representative; in addition Dayton and Cincinnati have city ordinances that provide similar mandates. Of the eighteen cities, only Los Angeles and San Francisco have yet to establish such a relationship. Only Baltimore and Cleveland have neither state legislation nor local ordinances providing for recognition and bargaining.

The existence of a mandatory bargaining statute, since it tends to guarantee the implementation and use of collective bargaining, strengthens the union's position. Exclusive representation gives the union a status it previously had not enjoyed. Similarly, the accompanying institutionalization of the collective-bargaining process (with its negotiating teams, lists of demands, timetables and deadlines, and attendant publicity) provides a great deal more visibility than did the lower keyed processes of union-management relations which preceded it—lobbying at city council and civil service commission hearings, in the mayor's office, and so forth. Further, in most cases the end result of the collective-bargaining process is a written agreement that visibly confirms the union's role as an equal with management in the determination of a wide variety of employment conditions. Several union spokesmen commented on these benefits: as they explained, the existence of a mandatory bargaining law means that management can no longer treat employee representatives as suppliants who are deserving of only a few minutes' time at a city council hearing or in the mayor's office; rather management is required to negotiate as equals with union representatives in good-faith attempts to reach a mutually satisfactory agreement.

In addition to enhancing the union's status, the existence of a bargaining statute may also increase the incentive for the union's use of direct action. Job actions as a source of pressure on management are usually more effective in a bargaining context than they are in a lobbying relationship, if only because the public is more aware of the legitimacy of the organization and the legitimacy of the interaction. Thus Detroit patrolmen conducted a ticket slowdown and "blue flu" in May-June 1967 during the second year of collective bargaining in order to create pressure on management after the union became convinced the city was not bargaining in good faith; the Vallejo policemen went on strike in July 1969 during their first year of bargaining after the city council rejected a tentative agreement negotiated with the city manager's office; and in their first year of bargaining under New York's Taylor Law, Rochester police waged a combination speedup-slowdown in July 1968 because of the city's refusal to agree to a one-year wage reopener in their two-year contract, which was signed before the city received an unexpected several million dollars in state aid.

Another important contextual change that may be occasioned by the introduction of a bargaining statute is the provision for third-party intervention in the event of impasse. However, since unions and managements usually exercise a large measure of control over the introduction of third parties into disputes, impasse resolution procedures are treated as a manipulatable source of power and discussed in the next chapter.

Other Relevant Statutes

Because a significant portion of the labor-relations interaction occurs away from the bargaining table, other legislation is important in establishing the statutory context. For example, police unions are regulated by the statutes establishing referenda ballot requirements and statutes regulating the campaigns of candidates for public office.

The most important aspect of the nonbargaining statutory context is the division of authority in municipal employment matters between cities and the state legislatures. Cities usually are creatures of the state and have no legal authority other than that which is expressly delegated to them by the states. In many states the legislatures have retained a substantial degree of authority over some of the employment conditions of municipal employees. The fact that state legislatures exercise this control means that police unions sometimes must interact with the state government to influence these employment conditions. Further, the fact that state legislation supersedes city ordinances on some issues creates an incentive for police unions to try and obtain from the legislature what they cannot obtain from the city. For example, in several states the legislature must approve changes in police pensions (e.g., Washington, Illinois, Ohio, New York); thus unions in those states must lobby in the legislature to implement pension changes; the FOP in Pittsburgh was able to lobby a significant change in their city's discipline procedure through the legislature, over the objection of local officials; New York City and Boston patrolmen have lobbied numerous bills affecting employment conditions through their state legislatures. Police (and fire) unions in Pennsylvania, Michigan, and Rhode Island have secured the passage of compulsory arbitration statutes sometimes over the opposition of municipal management. What is significant about the division of home-rule authority between cities and legislatures is that it extends the multilateral nature of police labor relations by providing the unions with additional managerial officials with whom the union may seek its objectives. In the next chapter we take up the fruits of this lobbying in greater detail.

Another aspect of the nonbargaining statutory context is the legislation regulating political activity by police officers. Several states have "little Hatch Acts," modeled after the federal Hatch Act, which contain broad restrictions on political activities by state and local government employees, and many cities have similar kinds of ordinances. In fact, in this sample it was common for police departments to have rules that restricted the political activities of police officers. For example, forty-five of forty-eight police departments responding to our questionnaire indicated that they had official policies regarding political activity. In general, these policies, ordinances and statutes allowed an officer to vote and privately express his political opinions but tended to prohibit campaigning for or making contributions to a political party or club, or holding office.

Our research indicates that these restrictions are rarely honored or enforced. Unions in our sample endorsed, campaigned for, and made contributions to candidates for office, financed and campaigned for ballot measures, lobbied in mayors' offices, city councils, and state legislatures, and in general engaged in a wide variety of political activities. The field interviews did not uncover any instances where police unions were punished for such activities—though in at least two cases individual policemen were punished.[20] On the basis of both union and management interview responses, it appears that city management's *de facto* policy regarding political activity by police unions appears to be one of "benign neglect."[21]

In summary, while the police have changed the statutory context to their advantage through passing laws that mandate bargaining or require binding arbitration as the last step in the bargaining process, it is also true that in the short run a police union must accept the statutory environment as given, and thus we have treated it as a contextual dimension of power.

The Structure of Bargaining

In this section we examine the effect of the form of municipal government, the role of police management in labor relations, unit boundaries, and bargaining timetables on police-union power.

The Form of Government and Bargaining Responsibility

For the purposes of this discussion we have categorized the cities in our sample as either mayor-council or council-manager. Within this dichotomy we have also distinguished between weak mayor and strong mayor cities, not so much on the basis of *de jure* mayoral decision-making authority relative to the council, but rather on the basis of the relative degree of mayoral participation in, and control of, labor relations.[22] Examples of strong mayor cities would include Boston,

New York, New Haven, Buffalo, and Seattle: the executive branch prepares the city budget, the city negotiators receive their instructions from the mayor, and at times the mayor himself may negotiate directly with the union (frequently in an attempt to reach a last minute bargaining settlement). In other strong mayor cities, state arbitration laws (Providence, Cranston, Philadelphia, Pittsburgh, and Detroit) or the city charter (San Francisco) may have circumscribed the role of the mayor's office in labor relations—though the executive branch still has labor-relations responsibility and still plays an important role in the determination of nonbargainable issues.[23]

In weak mayor cities the council plays the dominant role in labor relations (Milwaukee, Omaha, Los Angeles). In council-manager cities the appointed labor-relations representatives are formally attached to the city manager's office. In some cities (Oakland, Rochester, Vallejo) the city council provides negotiating directions to these representatives; in other council-manager cities (Cincinnati, Hartford, Dayton) the city manager directs the bargaining process (though the city council may provide financial and policy guidelines for the city manager). Cleveland and Baltimore are not included in this classification since neither has a police collective-bargaining system.

Beyond making the obvious point that the type of governmental structure influences union-management interaction patterns and suggesting that the presence of an appointed city manager instead of an elected mayor may reduce the union's political leverage, it has not been possible to discern any distinct union advantages or disadvantages that unambiguously are a function of the form of city government.

In strong mayor cities the union frequently is able to exert considerable political leverage in the executive branch (a point to be discussed under the heading "Electoral Politics" in the next chapter). In weak mayor cities and council-manager cities, union contact with the mayor tended to be minimal. In one council-manager city the union president explained that the union interacts with the mayor only because he has a vote at city council meetings, and that the union pays no more attention to him than to other councilmen. In two weak mayor cities union interviewees mentioned that their unions had minimal dealings with the respective mayors and concentrated their efforts on city councilmen.

In one council-manager city in our sample the manager was able to remove the council from active participation in the collective-bargaining process by convincing the council (which was elected at large) that it was less costly politically to let him handle labor relations than to become involved themselves. Prior to this time the union leadership had lobbied continuously, packed the council chambers during meetings, played Republicans against Democrats, and been involved in election campaigns. Subsequently, the union changed leadership, moving to a leader more inclined toward collective bargaining.

The Role of Police Management in Labor
Relations

In the early days of police collective bargaining, police managers in several cities were excluded from the bargaining process by the mayor or manager's office. Experience with exclusion, however, has shown in several cities that it can often work to the union's advantage: police management interviewees in Cranston, Dayton, and Omaha objected to seniority clauses negotiated by the city prior to the time police agency management was actively involved in bargaining; in New York City, city negotiators agreed to a portal-to-portal pay plan, which the department claims cost much more than anticipated and severely restricted their flexibility in assigning men to temporary duty away from their regular duty stations. The absence of department management from the bargaining table or the lack of consultation with police management meant that city negotiators did not have sufficient information to properly evaluate union proposals. As police officials and city officials acquire more collective-bargaining sophistication, it is likely that they will arrange for a fuller role in bargaining for police officials.

Police officials' prime concern in the bargaining process generally is to protect managerial prerogatives from union encroachment. However, on some monetary items, especially wages, police executives may be quite supportive of union demands. Police officials generally are in favor of more rather than less pay for their men. First, they believe that higher pay contributes to increased morale and more effective job performance, and, second, the greater the pay increases at the bottom of the police pay hierarchy the greater the pay increases at the top. In field interviews several chiefs or assistant chiefs were quite explicit in their support of union monetary demands—though they had not publicly supported the union's position. While it is difficult to assess how this top executive support for rank-and-file demands affects the union's power, the union's bargaining table leverage certainly is not reduced when police executives support the union's demands.

Another structure to emerge in three cities because of inexperience was the grant of total authority over nonwage items to the chief. In the private sector, of course, this could not happen since all interactions occur through the industrial relations representative; in the public sector, however, it is another legacy of the divided managerial authority structure in municipal government. For example, Detroit originally had a policy that formally divided labor relations authority between the police department and the city's executive-branch labor-relations bureau. The city office bargained for all cost items (which had to be approved by the city council), while police department representatives bargained with the union over noncost items. This separation was part of a city-wide policy to give department heads noneconomic labor-relations authority in an attempt to ease the negotiating burden on the labor-relations bureau (and, according to one source, to enable the city to stall the unions by buck-passing). The system has since been abandoned because it proved dysfunctional; the Detroit Police Officers Association was able to play one bargaining table against the other. Because of the separate bargaining there were never *quid pro quo* exchanges between economic and noneconomic demands; and the union was able to exploit police managements' lack of labor relations expertise.

A similar division existed in Los Angeles, though much less formal because Los Angeles did not have any institutionalized collective bargaining. The city administrative officer and the city council maintain close control over cost items, and the Los Angeles Fire and Police Protection League informally negotiated with police management over many noneconomic items. This arrangement may change as Los Angeles implements a collective-bargaining system.

Rochester briefly had a similar division, but it appeared to be by default rather than the result of an official labor relations policy. In 1970 the Police Locust Club negotiated with the city manager's office over economic items and because of a great deal of administrative and political confusion, the city allowed the union to meet directly with the police commissioner over noneconomic items. The new city negotiator hired at the end of 1970, who was formerly president of the city's firefighter local, said that in the future *all* negotiating would be done through him.

The strongest reason for having only one negotiating forum, of course, is that collective bargaining is essentially a trade-off process: economic items may be traded for noneconomic items, and the relegation of these two categories to separate negotiating forums reduces the trade-off potential in the bargaining process. Given that the union usually takes the initiative in bargaining, this reduced trade-off potential tends to work to management's disadvantage.

Unit Boundaries

As in the private sector, the size and shape of the bargaining unit may have an effect on union strength. The most obvious relationship is between the size of the unit and the union's ability to deprive a city of police services. As mentioned in Chapter 2, police bargaining units are limited to one or more ranks in a single department in a single city, generally excluding any civilian employees of the department.

In the event of a job action, this narrow construction of the appropriate bargaining unit raises management's power relative to the union's because of the city's ability to secure temporary replacements from neighboring municipal police departments, county deputy sheriffs, the state police, and the National Guard. For example, although approximately 90 percent of the Vallejo police went on strike in July 1969, the city was able to maintain a police presence through the use of county sheriffs and the state police.

Equally important, if the bargaining unit is limited to patrolmen, the union's ability to create disruptive pressure is reduced by the availability of superior officers for street duty. For example, New York City management used sergeants and detectives on patrol duty and was able to maintain a police presence during the January 1971 strike. In Milwaukee patrolmen were the only real participants in the January 1971 strike (although sergeants and detectives are in the union), and management had enough superior officers and county sheriffs to adequately patrol the streets. The experience in this sample of cities suggests that with these narrowly drawn units, police management can obtain enough law-enforcement personnel to maintain public order. This is not to suggest that a police strike poses no threat to the public health and safety, rather that, in this sample at least, the threat has been more potential than real.

Unit Boundaries and Organizational Militancy. Cohesion and solidarity within the union may be partly a function of unit boundaries. In this sample three patrolman-only organizations (Boston, New York, and Detroit) are probably the most visibly militant and aggressive organizations: all three have energetically opposed specific actions of the mayors in their cities; all three repeatedly challenge managerial actions through their contractual grievance procedures; and all three have engaged in a wide range of legislative, judicial, and electoral activities in pursuit of their members' interests.

While no conclusions can be drawn from such a limited sample, we would suggest that the absence of superior officers from these organizations increases the cohesiveness of the membership, which in turn contributes to the development of an organizational aggressiveness that might otherwise be diffused among the several ranks. Patrolmen naturally have less managerial consciousness and less organizational responsibility than the superior officers. In addition, patrolmen generally are younger and less socialized into the police paramilitary mentality of obedience than are the superior officers.[24] They are more inclined to challenge orders that appear unjustified, and when an employment dispute develops, they appear more willing to take some kind of organized overt action. In short, a patrolmen-only based organization is not exposed to the "leavening" influence that might be supplied by superior officers.

Bargaining Timetable and Deadlines

In the private sector the collective-bargaining process proceeds inexorably toward the all-important contract expiration deadline. While the initial expiration date may be postponed voluntarily, at some point a firm expiration date will establish a "deadline at which all the bluffs are called, all the speeches must end, and either the parties agree on contract terms or both will incur the costs of a strike."[25] In other words, eventually there will be a contract or there will be no work.

Policemen, however, have no right to strike and there is no tradition of "no contract, no work." Instead, in many cities police bargaining is characterized by a noticeable absence of pressure to reach agreement: the New York City patrolmen's contract expired at the end of 1970 but the PBA and the city did not agree to a new contract until July 1972; the Milwaukee contract also expired at the end of 1970—the two sides finally agreed to a new contract in December 1971; the city of Hartford and the local police union reached agreement in October 1971 on a contract to replace the one which had expired the previous March; in New Haven the contract beginning January 1, 1969 was not signed until late May 1969; and in Rochester the agreement reached in mid-October 1970 was retroactive three-and-one-half months until July 1. Other examples could be listed.

Perhaps the most important factor in understanding the lack of time pressure in police bargaining is the easy granting of retroactivity by most jurisdictions: the union loses nothing by not reaching agreement when the previous contract expires. Retroactivity also allows the union to take full advantage of municipal election campaigns.

—In one city the police contract expired on June 30, 1971. By that date the only thing to which the two sides had agreed was that any settlement would be retroactive to July 1. During our field visit in July, the union president appeared to be in no hurry to consummate a new agreement. A close mayoral election race was heating up for culmination in early November, and it appeared that he wanted to play off the incumbent against his challenger in order to get the best possible agreement.

—Similarly, at the time of the field visit in August 1971 the Boston patrolmen's union appeared to be in no hurry to affect a new agreement even though the previous one had expired a few months earlier. One explanation is that the union hoped to take advantage of the existing mayoral election contest between incumbent Kevin White and challenger Louise Day Hicks.

Although collectively bargained changes in police economic conditions must be paid out of the city budget, we found no particular rigidities in the relationship between budget deadlines and retroactivity. A majority of the police contracts negotiated in the eighteen cities with bargaining procedures were approved prior to the implementation of a new budget. However, retroactive agreements have been negotiated in at least nine of these cities (Seattle, Milwaukee, Dayton, Buffalo, Rochester, New York City, New Haven, Hartford, and Boston), and many of these agreements were reached after the start of a new budget year. Interviewees in several cities said that retroactivity and budget implementation posed no serious problems for bargaining. For example, the city negotiator in one large city explained that at times bargaining may be largely a contest between the ingenuity of city accountants in hiding contingency funds in the budget to cover expected and retroactive wage increases and ingenuity of union accountants in estimating how much is hidden. (Police bargaining in this city is noted for its retroactive settlements.) These results suggest that when the budgetary and bargaining processes conflict, the bargaining process will not necessarily be subordinated to the time constraints of the annual budgetary process.[26]

It is difficult to say which side benefits most from this bargaining and budgetary flexibility: during inflationary periods the city benefits from the maintenance of the *status quo* in monetary police employment conditions; money that would have been paid out during a retroactive period can be used elsewhere. On the other hand, retroactivity removes or makes much looser any time constraints operating on the union and thus provides union leaders with enough flexibility to use the local electoral and other political processes to maximum advantage. Flexible time constraints also may work to both sides' advantage simultaneously. For example, in one city the union negotiator regularly allowed negotiations to run far beyond the contract expiration date as a way of reducing rank and file expectations. As the men yearned more and more for their lump sum retroactivity check and the increase in their weekly paychecks, they became more "realistic" in their expectations and ultimately the city and the union reached agreement.

Characteristics of the Work Group and the Work Environment

Finally we consider the nature of work group and the nature of the work environment as important components of the context of collective bargaining. Particularly we will look at group cohesion and the police function as they affect relative bargaining power.

Group Cohesion

Group cohesion usually emanates from a shared community of interest or outlook among members of a separately identifiable group. This common outlook is most often the result of frequent interaction with other group members, shared values among group members and shared experiences, especially stressful or dangerous experiences.[27] Because policemen share experiences, especially dangerous and stressful ones unknown to other members of the society, they tend to form cohesive groups.[28] Two well-known manaifestations of this group cohesiveness are the extreme urgency with which policemen respond to "officer needs assistance" calls and the "blue curtain" of secrecy with which policemen protect one another from punishment for proscribed behavior.[29]

Group cohesion has long been recognized as one of the primary determinants of the effectiveness of interest group activity.[30] In general members of more cohesive groups show a greater willingness to support a unified course of action in the pursuit of group goals than do members of less cohesive groups. Thus a highly cohesive group would be characterized by a general psychological willingness among group members to agree to, support, and participate in courses of action in pursuit of group goals. In our sample, despite the fact that strikes are illegal and in violation of the tradition of the police service and the oath to which all patrolmen swear, approximately 95 percent of Milwaukee patrolmen and 90 percent of Vallejo police officers participated in strikes in those cities, and approximately 85 percent of New York City patrolmen participated in the January 1971 wildcat strike. Several city management interviewees mentioned that the police and the firefighters formed the most cohesive municipal unions in their respective cities and they believed that this cohesiveness resulted in a propensity to be more aggressive in pressing for attainment of their goals.[31]

This occupational cohesion is reinforced in most of the sample cities by the *de jure* and *de facto* existence of exclusive organizational representation. By contrast, Baltimore and Cleveland were the two cities with dual unionism and competition for police officer allegiance, and this lack of organizational cohesion has undermined the natural occupational cohesion that exists and has made it more difficult for any of these four unions to establish a solid record of obtaining benefits for their members.[32] One Baltimore incident illustrates how this lack of organizational cohesiveness can be detrimental to union goal-attainment:

In 1968 representatives of the two Baltimore police organizations went to the state capitol to a meeting of the House of Delegates members from the city of Baltimore for the purpose of lobbying for a bill which would have reor-ganized the police department's personnel services board (the city police department is technically a state agency). At the meeting, the representatives of the two organizations spent much of the time bad-mouthing one another. This internal factionalism so infuriated the chairman of the city legislators' delegation that he literally ripped the bill into little pieces. That particular police union bill died a dramatic death.[33]

The degree of group willingness to support any particular course of action depends in large part upon the issues under consideration. A particularly salient issue will engender an increased willingness to agree to and support a course of action than will an issue which arouses little membership interest. Our research suggests that the most salient issues are those which the police see as external ·threats to their existing rights, interests, or benefits or incidents which the police regard as unfair treatment. Examples of such issues and the police response include New York Mayor Lindsay's 1966 attempt to establish a civilian review board and the patrolmen's union fight against it; the Hartford gun guideline controversy described in Chapter 3; a threatened strike by policemen in Seattle over a coroner's jury verdict (described in Chapter 3); the 1971 wildcat strike in New York City, which started when the state's high court issued an unfavorable ruling in a patrolmen's union pay suit after the members had been assured that victory was certain; the 1969 strike in Vallejo prompted by the city council's rejection of a tentative agreement reached with the city manager's office; and the 1970 "blue flu" in Pittsburgh to protest some racially-motivated transfers.

While it is true that police union leaders can manipulate their members' group cohesiveness by utilizing information flows to the rank and file and perhaps exaggerating the importance of certain issues, it is also true that they cannot create issues where none exist. In the six instances cited above, for example, the police unions were responding to management initiated issues which were perceived as genuine crises. For these reasons we treat the degree of internal cohesion as a contextual rather than a directly manipulatable source of power.

The Police Function

The police are charged by society with enforcing the law and maintaining order.[34] To be able to perform these broadly-defined duties, the police have been given unique coercive authority. They are the only group in society that can legitimately apply coercive force against everybody else. Their coercive authority is seen in their ability to issue traffic citations and to arrest and incarcerate offenders. Further, they are permitted to use force in the performance of their duties, including the right to "shoot to kill" under certain circumstances. Consequently in the performance of their duties the police have a constant potential for imposing negative sanctions on citizens with whom they come in contact.

For the purpose of this analysis, this police monopoly on legitimate coercion has three major effects: to the extent people are apprehensive of police officers, their apprehension contributes to police isolation from the rest of society,[35] which in turn contributes to police solidarity or cohesiveness vis-à-vis the external society.

Second, the fact that many citizens view the police officer as the ultimate societal authority (especially the uniformed patrolman with his many symbols of authority—the military style uniform, the military style automobile and his nightstick, sidearm, and handcuffs) may create an image of power not available to other groups of employees. How this image works in practice to augment police union power is illustrated by a union spokesman in one city who said, "The city council is scared of us—they seem to think we're going to come into the council chambers and start shooting holes in the ceiling." While it is extremely difficult to measure this very subjective and intangible effect, it is possible that police unions may appear powerful in part because they are composed of policemen.

Finally, because the police are seen as the last bulwark between society and lawlessness, the police unions have been able to capitalize on "law and order" politics. We discussed this point earlier in the chapter but it bears repeating here. Gifford provides a vivid description of how politicians in the New York State Legislature are responsive to requests from the men in blue:

Most legislators, from their roles as politicians and lawmakers and from their frequent contacts with policemen, have a certain affinity for the men in blue and therefore are receptive to requests by organizations that represent them. . . . No matter how fiscally conservative a legislator may be, he generally finds the arguments in behalf of shorter hours or better pensions for policemen more appealing than similar arguments in behalf of faceless bureaucrats sitting at desks in some vast city or state agency. Asked about such proclivities toward the uniformed force, legislators commonly respond, "They deserve it; they have rough jobs."[36]

Related to this point of the perceived essentiality of police services for the maintenance of public safety is a fear of the withdrawal of these services: the Boston (1919) and Montreal (1969) strikes are often cited as evidence of what happens when these services are withdrawn. The strike, however, is a manipulatable source of union power and is discussed in the next chapter.

Summary

The complete list of determinants of police-union power is quite lengthy, and certainly we cannot ascertain all of these dimensions in looking at how twenty-two police unions achieve their goals. However, our research has suggested that the economic, political, and statutory contexts, the structure of bargaining, and the work environment are important determinants of the relative power of the parties. In the next chapter we look at how the unions manipulate the power available to them.

5

The Manipulatable Dimensions of Union Power

This chapter examines those sources of power which union leaders may manipulate directly, that is, those over which the union leader exerts some discretion as to their use: to adopt a win-lose or cooperative approach at the bargaining table; to take the city to court; to lobby an ordinance through the city council or a bill through the state legislature; to call a strike or other job action; to invoke arbitration, or just to threaten any of these actions. We consider each of these in order.

Negotiating Expertise

At the Bargaining Table

The union's reservoir of negotiating expertise relative to management's constitutes a direct source of union power: who is better prepared factually; who is the more persistent; who is the better bluffer; who has a better understanding of the negotiating process; and so forth. How these skills may pay off can be seen from the following two examples (the first illustrates the value of persistence, the second the value of relative experience):

—In contract negotiations, the city agreed to provide the men's uniforms, and the two sides were negotiating the exact quantity to be provided. At one point the city offered one pair of trousers, and the union demanded two. Both sides clung to their positions. However, the union representative was very tenacious and would not discuss any other subject until the trouser issue was settled. Finally, in exasperation the city agreed to provide two pair of trousers in order to proceed to other subjects.

—In one city the union lawyers had considerable experience representing private-sector trade unions. During negotiations for the first two contracts, their official adversary was a young and relatively inexperienced city negotiator. The union lawyers, who were the union's chief negotiators, used their experience and their opponent's lack of it to influence the tactical course of negotiations, including the intervention of third parties. In both sets of negotiations the union obtained very substantial economic and noneconomic gains, including some contractual language that gave the union a very substantial voice in the making of police employment decisions. While city and police representatives told us that they agreed to many union proposals in a spirit of cooperation, the union lawyer said that at one point he was afraid the mayor was going to fire the city negotiator because of the numerous tactical mistakes he made.

73

While the persistence demonstrated in the first example probably would not be sufficient to obtain agreement on items of major importance, and while many unions are not represented by such highly skilled negotiators, these two examples illustrate how relative negotiating expertise can be a source of union advantage in the bargaining process. An incident from a third city shows how the union's lack of negotiating expertise (this was the first police contract negotiation) cost it benefits it otherwise would have obtained (the story was told by the city negotiator):

—In these first contract negotiations the local leaders were assisted by an international union representative. The city negotiator claimed that he and the international representative spent much of the negotiating session time explaining to the local leaders how the collective bargaining process worked. Eventually the city and the union agreed on a contract which included a 15 percent wage increase and a $2 per week dependents' insurance contribution from the city. However,the local leaders boycotted the scheduled joint press conference to announce the tentative settlement and successfully urged the membership to reject it. The international representative was so angered by this breach of good faith that he withdrew and left the local leaders on their own. Apparently the local leaders felt they had to match the 17 percent increase the city's firefighters had recently obtained. The city offered an additional 2 percent wage increase (which, when added to the previous 15 percent, totalled 17 percent), but simultaneously withdrew the $2 per week dependents' insurance contribution. The city reportedly had no intention of pushing this point and would have retained the contribution had the union objected. But the local union leaders agreed to its deletion, and thus on this issue they snatched defeat from the jaws of victory. Similarly, they were either unaware or did not care that the 17 percent increase was actually an approximate 13.5 percent increase over the year: 10 percent at the beginning of the year and 7 percent seven months later.

Attitudinal Patterns

The union's reservoir of negotiating skills is an important direct source of power as we have seen in the examples cited above. A more subtle exercise of power may be the recognition of the importance of moving from conflict to cooperation as management begins to accept the union's legitimacy. Three examples illustrate:

—During negotiations one year, the union went on strike. One of the important features of the dispute was the city council's strong displeasure at seeing the union represented by two lawyers from another city. These men were looked upon as "outside agitators." In subsequent years the union has used as its chief negotiating representative a local attorney who also handles the legal business of several of the city councilmen. While the union does not officially negotiate with the council, the council keeps firm control over the negotiation process and individual council members may meet informally with union representatives. The council has approved all tentative agreements since the strike, and the union has been satisfied with the benefits it has obtained. The union president is convinced that much of the reason for these successes lies with having this lawyer represent the policemen. As the union president said, "It's amazing how easy it is to reach agreement among friends."

—In another city the union's founder and first president was a very determined individual who kept the organization together during the early days of adversity. After the union had become the certified exclusive representative, had bargained a solid first contract, and had more than a 90 percent membership ratio, this man was pushed out of his presidency by a coalition of other leaders of the union. We were told this was done largely because the former president was a very abrasive individual who almost automatically antagonized managerial representatives no matter what the issue was. The man who replaced him was much less abrasive, and union-management interactions became much smoother.

—In a third city, one with more than one police employee organization, police management interviewees were critical of the approach adopted by the top leaders of one union in grievance negotiations. These union leaders reportedly relied more on a belligerent attitude than on factually-supported cooperative efforts to seek favorable resolution of grievances. Managerial officials apparently responded in kind and appeared to the authors as being more reluctant to enter into compromise settlements of grievances than they might otherwise be. In contrast, these same management interviewees had substantial praise for the grievance negotiation approach of the leader of another union. While this union leader was staunchly protective of his members' rights and interests, he reportedly was factually well-prepared, maintained a cooperative demeanor, and did not act in an antagonistic or belligerent manner. Managerial officials appeared to be more willing to try and reach grievance settlements with this union leader than they were with the leaders of the other union.

Informal Negotiations

The analysis in Chapter 4 showed that much police union goal-directed activity occurs outside the collective-bargaining process. Many of these other activities, including discussions with the chief and lobbying with various officeholders, can be thought of as informal negotiations. The role of lobbying as a source of union power will be examined later in the chapter, but the interpersonal aspect of it is examined here because it deals with the same kind of attitudinal and negotiating variables involved in collective negotiations.

Negotiating, whether it be labeled lobbying, horse-trading, an exchange of favors, or anything else, is an integral part of political life. As one eminent political scientist notes, "One of the most important skills in politics—one of the reasons why the practice of politics is an art—is the ability to detect a bargaining position and to guess correctly how much it diverges from the adversary's 'real' position."[1] As outside researchers, the authors could not witness the actual use of negotiating skills, but some indirect evidence is available that shows how the union's ability to obtain its goals is enhanced by having representatives who are skilled in the interpersonal arts of political negotiations. Gifford's analysis of New York City PBA representatives and their lobbying portrays these men as being highly skilled in the nuances of the lobbying process, and the PBA's record of lobbying successes in Albany suggests that these skills are valuable.[2]

> In another city in the field sample the police union had acquired an impressive record of obtaining desired legislation in the state legislature and the city council, much of it over the mayor's opposition. When union-mayoral relations were at their most antagonistic, a meeting was arranged between the elected union leaders and the mayor, which ultimately resulted in an exchange of electoral support for job benefits (as well as a cooling of tempers). When asked how all this was accomplished, the union president gave substantial credit to one of the union's lawyers (whom he constantly referred to as "the magician") and his personal friendships, acquaintances, and general access to many local and state politicians.

Thus, if a police union has leaders or representatives who are skilled in the interpersonal arts of political negotiations, the union's ability to obtain its goals is enhanced.

Lobbying

Lobbying is usually defined as soliciting members of a legislative body with the intent of influencing legislation. As at least two other authors have observed, this definition is too restrictive and ignores the two other branches of government.[3] Consequently, for our purposes, lobbying will be defined as direct contacts by interest group representatives with public officials for the purpose of improving the probability of attaining group objectives, provided that such contacts occur outside such institutionalized forums as collective-bargaining procedures and litigation. This definition, then, includes legislative lobbying (directed toward members of a legislative body); executive lobbying (directed toward members of the executive branch); public, or on-the-record, lobbying (an appearance at a city council meeting or state legislative committee hearing); and private or off-the-record lobbying (a meeting behind closed doors with the mayor or the governor).[4] The content of these lobbying interactions can range from a simple request for equitable treatment to a mutual benefit exchange (e.g., certain union demands in return for electoral endorsement) to a union threat that a strike will occur if the union's terms are not met.[5]

Legislative Lobbying

At the local level legislative lobbying consists of union contacts with city council members and at the state level with state legislators. The following examples illustrate the variety of situations in which police unions lobby:

—In one city during collective negotiations it became apparent to the union that the city council had given the city negotiator almost no authority to negotiate over money items. Police-union representatives went to the council-members and the two sides agreed to negotiate directly over money items.

—During contract negotiations in another city a $1,000 pay raise became a sticking point in the minds of the rank-and-file. Union representatives and city negotiators could not reach agreement, so the union met directly with the city council finance committee. They agreed on a settlement, including the $1,000 raise, but the union president realized he did not have the five votes necessary to secure full council approval. Accordingly, the union president packed the council chamber with police wives and children on the crucial day. Then, in side chambers, he played the Republican majority caucus against the minority Democrats, including threatening a strike if the raise was not approved. At the public meeting the council approved the raise.

—In Boston the mayor proposed to have the police wear name tags on their uniforms. The union immediately filed a formal grievance and carried it to arbitration. In the meantime union representatives introduced a local option bill in the state legislature which would ban the wearing of name tags. By working with key legislators who were eyeing higher political office and police-union political support, the union was able to get the bill passed. Using the same methods of operation, the union was able to get the city council to adopt the bill (and override the mayor's veto). The arbitrator subsequently ruled that the city had the right to require the wearing of name tags, but his decision was moot because of the council's adoption of the legislation prohibiting name tags.

—Another city experienced a protracted and bitter contract negotiation dispute. After months of no agreement the union decided that fact-finding might be a vehicle to obtain more benefits, and proposed that the dispute be submitted to a fact-finder. Union representatives then lobbied various city councilmen to obtain council approval for fact-finding. The union lobbyists were opposed by the city negotiator, who tried to persuade the councilmen to unilaterally implement the city's last offer. The council voted to submit the dispute to fact-finding.

—The Pittsburgh police union went to the state legislature several years ago and obtained legislation that drastically modified the police department's internal disciplinary process (this legislation applied only to the city of Pittsburgh). A few years later they successfully lobbied, along with other Pennsylvania police and fire unions, for the passage of legislation that provided for compulsory arbitration as a means of resolving police and fire negotiating impasses. More recently the union went to the legislature and lobbied for legislation that would have required all departmental transfers and assignments be made on the basis of seniority. The bill died in committee, largely because of the strenuous resistance to it from the mayor.

—Police unions in Michigan, Rhode Island, Pennsylvania, Wisconsin, and California have conducted serious lobbying campaigns in their respective state legislatures for the passage of legislation providing for compulsory arbitration as a means of settling police and fire-union negotiating disputes (most of these campaigns were conducted jointly with fire unions). Only in California (of the states in this sample) were these efforts unsuccessful.

In addition to the goals mentioned in the examples above, police unions have lobbied in state legislatures for the passage of collective-bargaining legislation, pension benefits, changes in the penal code, elimination of city residency requirements, state financial aid to cities, approval of the city budget, vacation and holiday benefits, changes in moonlighting restrictions, and a wide variety of other employment conditions.

Executive Lobbying

In the above examples the union representatives contacted elected legislators. The following examples illustrate these same kinds of union solicitations to elected and appointed executive officials:

—In one city the union attempted to put a charter amendment on the ballot providing for increased retirement benefits. The union leaders took their proposed amendment to the city council and lobbied with various council members to approve it for the ballot. At one point it appeared that the council would kill the amendment, so the union went to the mayor and asked for his assistance. The mayor intervened with several councilmen on the union's behalf, and the council approved the amendment for the ballot.

—In another city the union sought an agency shop provision from police department management (which had noneconomic labor relations authority). Management representatives staunchly refused. The union, which had actively supported the mayor in the previous year's election campaign, then went to the mayor's office and obtained the agency shop clause.

—Changes in San Francisco police pay are made according to a city charter provision that pegs police pay to the highest pay for police officers in any other California city over 100,000 population.[6] In August 1969 the city council voted a 12 percent police pay raise, ostensibly on the basis of an opinion by the city attorney, an elected official up for reelection the following November, that San Francisco patrolmen were entitled to parity with the senior patrolman rank in Berkeley. While the Berkeley rank is reserved for those patrolmen with a specified combination of college education, training, and experience, the city attorney said that the duties of Berkeley senior patrolmen and San Francisco patrolmen were essentially the same and thus the latter group was entitled to the higher rate.[7] According to interview data from a former union leader, the city attorney issued this opinion after the local police union, going through the chief's office, had brought it to his attention.

It would be extremely difficult to determine what factors influence the selection of lobbying targets. The most obvious factors to be considered are the decision-making authority of an official over the issues involved and the chances of success that a union leader estimates in lobbying that official. In some situations the union may lobby both legislative and executive officials over a single issue.

Some data from our questionnaire suggests that police unions make more lobbying contacts with legislators than with top executive officials. Table 5-1 contains data provided by forty-nine police department respondents about various types of activities used to achieve union goals. If council and committee appearances are counted as public lobbying, then police unions have much more lobbying contacts with legislators than with top executives at both the city and state levels.

Table 5-1
Frequency of Selected Union Activities

Number of times selected union acties were reported by police department questionnaire respondents (N = 49)[a]

MUNICIPAL LEVEL

Activity	Number of Times Reported
Legal action	16
Informational picketing of public buildings or public officials' homes	11
Newpaper advertisements	22
Getting public endorsements from civic or political groups	29
Appearing before city council or council committees	44
Lobbying with city-council members	29
Lobbying with mayor and/or city manager	24
Other	7

STATE LEVEL

Activity	Number of Times Reported
Legal action	6
Informational picketing of public buildings or public officials' homes	1
Newspaper advertisements	7
Getting public endorsements from civic or political groups	8
Appearing before legislative committees	30
Lobbying with state legislators	28
Lobbying with the governor's office	6
Other	1

[a]This was an open-ended question which asked the respondent to list each specific issue over which the union was active and to associate the issue with the above lists of activities.

The Relationship between Lobbying
and Bargaining

Lobbying is the time-honored method by which interest groups secure benefits from the government. Before the advent of institutionalized collective bargaining, police unions regularly appeared before city councils and state legislatures seeking benefits. While this study did not collect any definitive "before" and "after" data, comments from several interviewees suggest that the introduction of a formal bargaining process has tended to reduce these *public* lobbying efforts over items subject to determination by contractual negotiations; such efforts do continue over items not included in the scope of bargaining (e.g., pensions, residency requirements, changes in other ordinances or statutes, etc.).

Our research suggests that private lobbying continues to thrive even after bargaining is institutionalized. This off-the-record lobbying can be used to work for benefits not included in the scope of bargaining. Also, as several of the above examples indicate, private lobbying is used to supplement union-management interactions at the bargaining table. As mentioned in Chapter 3, interviewees in at least thirteen cities related instances of union-leader contacts with city elected officials during the course of the bargaining process. In addition, unions may lobby the city council to approve the agreements negotiated with the executive branch since such agreements usually are not self-implementing. Consequently, it appears that lobbying and bargaining are complementary activities rather than substitutes for each other, and that bargaining does not eliminate union lobbying efforts but instead tends to make them less overt.

Private lobbying fulfills a function similar to the collective-bargaining process in that it enables union and management representatives to meet off-the-record to discuss police union objectives. In some circumstances private lobbying may be even more attractive to the union than bargaining because it enables the union leaders to meet directly with elected officials to discuss an unlimited variety of subjects rather than with hired negotiators to discuss matters within the scope of bargaining.

Electoral Politics

The union's ability to contact and influence the relevant electorate to support union objectives is another broadly defined source of power. Electoral political activity includes molding public opinion, especially during bargaining; going directly to the voters on particular ballot measures; and participation in the election campaigns of candidates for office.

Publicity and Public Opinion

An important aspect of any political interest group's efforts to secure benefits from the government is the state of public opinion regarding that group and its efforts.[8] Public opinion is a much more important variable in public-sector labor relations, where it may emerge as votes and where elected officials are extremely cognizant of its perceived changes, than in private-sector labor relations, where direct economic considerations are paramount.[9] Like other political interest groups, police unions generally try to develop and maintain support for themselves and their objectives among a majority of the electorate. While almost all union electoral political activity seeks to influence public opinion, the focus in this subsection is on union publicity efforts during the collective-bargaining process.

In a few cities, the two sides actually honored publicity moratoriums during formalized contract negotiations. However, field research in newspaper archives revealed that it was quite common for the union and management to use regular news coverage to explain their positions to the public and to seek public support for their goals (though these publicity efforts usually did not include the divulging of the actual interactions across the negotiating table). Comments from a few union leaders indicated that they placed significant value on getting adequate news coverage, and thus union activities were planned with one eye toward the local news media.[10]

Our research indicated that police unions generally did not spend much money to influence public opinion during the bargaining process. Since important police union-city disputes, impasses, or other interactions have high news value, police unions usually can count on adequate news coverage to explain their position to the public. Probably the most notable exception to this reliance on free news coverage during collective bargaining occurred in Rochester in 1970:

—The union and the city had been negotiating over a new contract. Negotiations had reached an impasse, and the dispute had been submitted to fact-finding. Mindful that the fact-finders had great freedom to make recommendations, and that the city council could accept or reject the fact-finders' recommendations, the union set out to show that the police had a lot of public support. It conducted an extensive public relations campaign that included newspaper, radio, and TV ads, voter mailings, and a house-to-house poll. The union president claimed that the campaign resulted in an "overwhelming" demonstration of public support for the police and their bargaining demands. Although the fact-finders subsequently recommended huge wage and fringe increases, and the council voted unanimously to adopt their recommendations, it is difficult to pinpoint the role played by the union's public relations efforts.

Another method the police may use to seek public support for their demands is informational picketing. Cranston police officers picketed city buildings for several months during a lengthy bargaining impasse in 1967-68.[11] Police in Oakland and New Haven picketed their respective city halls in 1969 during contract negotiations disputes. Omaha police also picketed city hall in 1969 during a pay dispute (other issues also contributed to the Omaha picketing). While this form of publicity seeks to visibly inform the public of the dispute (police picketing usually has high news value), it also seeks to create some political embarrassment or liability for city officials thereby increasing management's costs of disagreement.

Sometimes the union will seek to mobilize public opinion over issues unrelated to bargaining. Detroit patrolmen in 1969 picketed the local courts building in an effort to mobilize community sentiment against Recorder's Court Judge George Crockett, who had released the suspects arrested after a shoot-out with police in which one officer was killed.[12] The Detroit's patrolmen's union also circulated petitions seeking public expressions of support for the union's efforts to have the judge removed from office.[13] During the Hartford gun guideline controversy examined in Chapter 3 the police union asked for and received expressions of public support for its position of adamant opposition to the city council's creation of restrictions on the police use of firearms.[14] This example also indicates how a union may be able to substitute news coverage for purchased advertising. However, this is not always the case. Police unions frequently buy newspaper advertising to influence public opinion. This is especially true of "hot" issues that have aroused much interest and emotion among the police and parts of the community, as in the case of the alleged black fire-bomber in Seattle in 1970,[15] and the Detroit patrolmen's efforts to remove Judge Crockett from office discussed above.[16]

This field study was not designed to measure the impact of union publicity efforts, but presumably the efforts described in this section do have some impact upon the citzenry, even if only the mobilization of latent citizen support into overt support. Of course, the strongly-worded advertising of the type purchased in the New York City 1966 civilian review board campaign and in the Seattle and Detroit examples cited above may alienate as many citizens as it attracts.

Issue Electoral Efforts

Another reason for police-union contact with the voters is to seek their approval or rejection of particular referenda dealing with issues (as opposed to candidates) affecting the police. These measures may deal with economic or noneconomic police working conditions, procedures which the union may use in future interactions with management, or other issues which affect union goals. The most widely noted instance of the exercise of this kind of union power was the New York City PBA's successful 1966 campaign to defeat the civilian review board. Several other examples indicate the variety of issues for which police unions in this sample have campaigned:

    —In San Francisco the city charter regulates most employment conditions, so the union regularly goes to the voters with many issues: in the June 1968 election for retirement benefits (the union won); the June 1970 election for eliminating firefighter pay parity and for fringe benefits (the union lost); the

November 1970 election with a measure that would allow the city council to grant fringe benefits by ordinance rather than by charter amendment (the union lost); and the November 1971 election that sought permission to reorganize the department (the union won; this measure also was supported by the chief, the mayor, the city council, and the police commission).

—The union in another city reportedly spent $340,000 on a narrowly successful charter amendment that increased pension benefits for policemen and firemen. The money was spent on media advertising, doorbell ringing, telephoning, distributing literature, and purchasing voter lists.

—Many years ago the Omaha union successfully went to the voters with a charter amendment to provide a five-day, forty-hour workweek. More recently (1968), the union obtained voter approval of a charter amendment providing time-and-one-half pay for overtime, but the voters simultaneously rejected increases in retirement benefits and disability pay.

—FOP lodges in Pennsylvania joined with the firefighters to secure voter approval of a state constitutional amendment on the November 1967 ballot, which allowed the legislature to pass an act providing for compulsory arbitration to settle police and fire negotiation disputes. The voters approved the measure by a 3½ to 1 margin, and with this overwhelming popular mandate the legislature passed an arbitration act at its next session.

—In 1968 the police and fire unions in Detroit engaged in an unsuccessful effort to convince the voters to reject a city-sponsored measure that reduced police and fire pension benefits. In Oakland in 1972 the police and fire unions successfully appealed to the voters to reject a city-sponsored measure that might have reduced pension benefits.

—In Cincinnati the police union (and the other city unions) recently campaigned for the passage of a city payroll tax measure. It passed and increased the city's ability to pay. A few years earlier, the police had unsuccessfully opposed a firefighters' union ballot measure incorporating police-fire pay parity in the city charter.

—In Cleveland in 1967 the police and fire unions successfully went to the voters with a two-pronged charter amendment that provides police with pay 3 percent higher than the highest police pay in other Ohio cities over 50,000 population and provides for police-fire pay parity.

Candidate Electoral Efforts

The third major type of union electoral politicking involves participation in the election of candidates for office. As mentioned in the section on lobbying and in the Chapter 3 section on governmental multilateral bargaining, we encountered situations in several cities where officeholders had traded benefit increases or support of union objectives for perceived union support, particularly at election time. Some of these efforts amounted to nothing more than informing the union and the members that the elected official whole-heartedly supported their demands. In other cities, however, the police unions and the potential or actual officeholders have engaged in more direct exchanges:

—In a western city the police union actively supported the leading mayoral candidate during the 1969 municipal election campaign. Very soon after the election the new mayor signed the city's first full-fledged collective-bargaining agreement with the union. This two-year agreement contained substantial wage and fringe benefit increases (including wage increases of 10 and 7 percent on top of 12 and 6 percent in the previous two years). Interview comments portrayed this first contract as the new mayor's exchange to the union in return for its support.

—In April 1971 the San Francisco Police Officers Association began negotiations with the city's police commission over a noneconomic "memorandum of understanding." On September 22, 1971 the POA endorsed incumbent Mayor Joseph Alioto in his bid to be reelected on the November 1971 ballot (in what was regarded before the election as a close race). On October 28, 1971 the POA and the police commission, which is composed of three mayoral appointees, reached agreement and signed the noneconomic contract.

—In 1970 Boston Mayor Kevin White tried to become Massachusetts governor. He failed to get the Democratic regular organization's nomination, so in the party primary he ran as an independent and was endorsed by his long-time political foe, the Boston Police Patrolmen's Association. In return for the endorsement he changed the regular police weekly schedule from five days on and two off to four days on and two off (which increased annual days off by 17), guaranteed the patrolmen two men in all patrol cars, and agreed to a minimum-manning guarantee (that at least 50 percent plus one of the patrol cars in each police district would be on the street during night hours). The mayor won the primary election nomination (but lost in the general election).[17]

These three examples are indicative of the benefits that unions perceive as theirs in exchange for involvement in partisan politics. While the first two cases cited might be considered merely coincidental, consider the following coincidence involving the New York City patrolmen's union dispute over the pay ratio between patrolmen and police sergeants:

—Mayor Lindsay, eyeing the November 1969 election and anxious to avoid disruptions of municipal services, in late 1968 or early 1969 agreed to a reestablishment of the old 3.5 to 3.0 pay ratio between sergeants and patrolmen even though the city was already in the process of moving to a new 3.9 to 3.0 ratio in order to establish parity between the police sergeants and fire lieutenants (pay parity between patrolmen and firefighters had existed since 1898). This pay-ratio agreement contributed to the PBA's acceptance of a new contract in early 1969, but it did not prevent police opposition to Lindsay's reelection; the city's later efforts to avoid implementation of the ratio eventually led to the five day wildcat strike in January 1971.[18]

In the three examples cited earlier the emphasis was on the positive, that is, the union provides political support in return for benefit increases. In the New York City example benefit increases were given in the hope of reducing or eliminating police and police union hostility at the polls. Other examples of more negatively-oriented union electoral involvement include the following:

—In Buffalo a mayoral-proposed community-peace-officer plan designed to increase black and Puerto Rican membership on the police force came under sharp police attack. After the city council approved the plan in 1971, the uncertified patrolmen's association put out a special issue of its newspaper devoted to condemning the CPO plan, and singled out for special condemnation was a councilman who at the last minute switched his vote in favor of the plan. One of the patrolmen's group leaders said that the group flooded this councilman's district with this edition and did whatever else they could to mobilize community sentiment against the councilman. Soon after, according to our interviewees, the councilman announced he would not seek reelection.

—In another city the union president mentioned that the thrust of the union's involvement in the previous municipal election was to work for the defeat of a strong challenger to the incumbent mayor. Even though the challenger was a former policeman, the union feared that he would establish some kind of civilian review procedure if elected.

—In Boston the mayor was able to secure, over strong union opposition, a 5 to 4 city-council approval of his plan to hire fifty civilian clerks for the police department with the intention of freeing fifty policemen for street duty. One of the councilmen who voted for the plan was a former policeman who in the past had counted on the police vote. In the municipal election a few months later, the patrolmen's union opposed his reelection bid. He lost.[19]

The Politics of Disruption

The politics of disruption refers to a police union's ability to disrupt the delivery of normal services to the citizenry. The public press has labeled these disruptions "job actions," and they range from full-fledged strikes (by whatever name known, including the "blue flu," "continuous professional meeting," "job action," etc.) to such other tactics as work slowdown (refusal to perform certain parts of the job, most commonly a refusal to write traffic tickets), or work speed-up (enforcing all laws, most commonly writing many times the normal amount of traffic tickets). In general, the purpose of these disruptions of normal services is to create political pressure on management to accede to union demands. The following examples of police-union disruptions in this research sample give some indication of the pressures these disruptions are intended to create:[20]

—In January 1971, after nearly a year of negotiations, the Milwaukee patrolmen went on strike to create pressure on the city to accede to union demands. Interview comments revealed that the union expected that disorderly and lawless behavior would increase, that normal economic and social interaction would be slowed because of citizen fear of such disorderly behavior (e.g., that banks would not open, that people would stay home from work, etc.), and that these behavioral and attitudinal changes would create sufficient pressure on the city to improve its offer. Instead, public apathy appeared to be the prevailing mood, business went on as usual, the city did not improve its previous offer, and the patrolmen returned to work under a court injunction. A large part of the reason for the strike's failure to create the hoped-for pressures on management was police management's ability to maintain a "police presence" on the streets. By canceling days off, instituting twelve-hour shifts for nonstriking detectives and superior officers, and using county deputy sheriffs, police management was able to create the impression of adequate police services being provided to the city.

—In January 1971 85 percent of the New York City patrolmen participated in a five-day wildcat strike in response to an unfavorable state court of appeals ruling in their union's pay-ratio suit.[21] The city was apprehensive, but police management was able to maintain a "police presence" on the streets by canceling days off, instituting twelve-hour shifts, and using almost all available nonstrikers, superior officers, and detectives on patrol duty, with the result that no increases in lawless or disorderly behavior were reported. The walkout ended when, among other things, a state court judge promised to "expedite" the pay-ratio implementation trial.

—In July 1969 Vallejo policemen and firemen jointly struck the city after the city council rejected tentative agreements reached with the city manager's office. While there was the expected public concern over the absence of public-safety services, the city streets were patrolled by the state highway patrol and county deputy sheriffs, and no major fires occurred. The four-day strike did cause enough pressure that the city agreed to the terms of the original tentative agreements and amnesty for the strikers.

—In May 1970 Rochester police engaged in an eight-hour strike prompted by an evening mass standby order for the day shift (resulting from rumors of racial disturbances). Aggravating the situation was the fact that this took place in the context of ongoing contractual negotiations with the city in which one of the union's demands was time-and-one-half pay for such overtime duty rather than the straight compensatory time off currently being paid. Sheriff's deputies were called in to patrol the streets, and the brevity of the strike contributed to any absence of abnormal disorderly or lawless behavior. The strike ended when the city agreed to resume negotiations (the city had refused to negotiate after the first strike vote was taken), pay time and one half for overtime, and grant amnesty to the strikers.

—In May and June 1967 Detroit patrolmen conducted a traffic ticket slowdown and "blue flu" to put pressure on the city in contract negotiations and as a response to what the patrolmen perceived as undue pressure to increase city revenues by writing large numbers of traffic tickets. The job action started as a ticket slowdown and escalated into a "blue flu" when management suspended several officers for not writing enough tickets. The "blue flu" afflicted one-third of the patrolmen, but the city was able to maintain substantial police services by canceling days off and instituting twelve-hour shifts for nonstrikers and superior officers. The "blue flu" apparently was aimed at the mayor because of union perceptions of bad faith bargaining by city negotiators (who reported to the mayor) and union perceptions of mayoral pressure to levy punishments for not writing enough traffic tickets. The disruptions ended when the city agreed to submit the contract dispute to fact-finding. The subsequent fact-finder's report led to some very large pay and fringe benefit increases for Detroit patrolmen.

—In April 1970 several hundred Pittsburgh policemen caught the "blue flu," protesting some racial transfers in some of the city's district stations (white officers were transferred out of a ghetto district and black officers were transferred in). The "blue flu," which lasted for three days, did not involve the entire force and thus the city was still able to provide substantial police services. The influenza virus vanished when the city, at a city council hearing attended by 600 policemen, agreed to arbitrate the transfers (the arbitrator upheld management's right to make the transfers).

This first category of disruptions of normal police services essentially deals with job actions which withhold a substantial proportion of a city's police services—and thus deserve to be labeled as strikes. A second category of disruptions involves the disruption of normal police services, but on a much smaller scale than in the above examples. This second category includes such job actions as slowdowns, speedups, and the controlled illness of a small fraction of the force, where the police are still performing the majority of their law-enforcement and order-maintenance duties. Job actions in this category seem to be intended primarily to dramatically inform the public of a union-management dispute, to politically embarrass management officials, and/or to warn management that larger-scale disruptions are possible. While it is difficult to accurately draw the line between the two categories, the following four examples are illustrative of this second kind of disruption of normal police services:

—In October 1968 the New York City PBA launched a two-pronged job action to put pressure on the city to offer better terms during contract negotiations. Patrolmen issued no traffic or parking tickets, and approximately 20 percent of those scheduled for duty each day called in sick. These disruptions ceased after the city obtained an injunction, and the dispute was resolved two months later when the members voted to accept a substantially improved city offer (including city agreement to restore the 3.5 to 3.0 patrolman pay ratio with the sergeants).

—In the summer of 1968 the Boston Police Department changed the existing practice of assigning men to ride buses on certain high-crime routes from an off-duty paid detail basis to an on-duty regular assignment.[22] In addition, the department assigned one man per bus instead of the former two. In protest twenty of the twenty-two men assigned to the bus details called in sick for two days, but to no avail. The department retaliated by suspending the men for four days.

—During late 1969 and early 1970 the Boston patrolmen's union and the city were negotiating a new contract. To put pressure on the city to agree to the union's terms, the union organized a paid-detail strike. For several days the patrolmen refused to accept any paid details, thus depriving many private parties of the protective services normally provided by off-duty police officers. Soon afterward, the city and the union reached agreement on a new contract.[23]

—During early August 1969 many of the black officers in the Hartford department (members of the Connecticut Guardians) engaged in a week long "sick-out" to protest what they called departmental "segregation." They complained that black officers were assigned almost solely to patrol duty in the black ghetto rather than being integrated throughout the geographical and functional range of departmental assignments. Their work stoppage was successful in that they received a lot of publicity and management agreed to an expanded range of assignments for black officers. However, since blacks comprised less than 15 percent of the department's personnel, and since not all the black officers struck, the strike did not significantly reduce the police services available to the Hartford citizenry. Instead it created "civil rights" political pressure upon the city to accede to the black officers' demands.[24]

The Essentiality of Police Services

The key to understanding the political pressure created by police job actions is in the perceived essentiality of a police presence on the street. That police services are perceived as essential is demonstrated by the nearly universal exclusion of the police from any proposal that public employees have the right to strike (including the two states which currently allow certain public employees the right to strike but explicitly exclude the police and fire services—Hawaii and Pennsylvania).[25] A job action is intended to deprive the citizenry of a portion of these essential services, with the extent and the seriousness of the deprivation directly correlated with the percentage of police participants and with the specific services not being performed. This can range from a total cessation of work (by 95 percent of the Milwaukee patrolmen) to a refusal to write the usual number of traffic tickets (by Detroit car and motorcycle patrolmen). This deprivation of essential services is intended to increase public concern and create pressure upon the city's elected officials to take steps to restore the deprived services—that is, to accede to some or all of the police union's demands.

Public officials feel that their concern with lawlessness in the absence of a police presence is well founded, citing the violence which erupted during the 1919 Boston police strike and the 1969 Montreal police strike to support their case. Our research suggests, on the other hand, that in the large majority of cases there were few if any reported increases in disorderly behavior during the job actions cited above.[26] To elected public officials who have the responsibility for public safety, however, the threat of a police strike, regardless of the probability of violence constitutes a great deal of potential power even when discounted for past experience elsewhere. Moreover, previous experience suggests that this potential power is greater in larger, high-density, multiracial cities than in homogeneous small cities and towns because the potential consequences of disorderly and lawless behavior are much higher in the former.

It could be argued that the impact of a police strike on the community is economic: no traffic citations mean a reduction in revenue; providing temporary replacements during job actions incurs a cost whether it is overtime for nonstrikers or payments to neighboring jurisdictions for use of their manpower; and litigation necessitated by disruptive action costs money. Our research suggests, however, that while economics cannot be ignored, it is not useful to view the strike as an economic weapon. First, and most important, reductions in revenues or increases in costs affect an extremely small portion of the city budget.[27] Second, municipal governments do not operate in purely economic markets. If city income is reduced or costs increased, decisions about which city services will be affected will ultimately be made on the basis of political criteria.

Disruptive Picketing

A final form of disruption is disruptive picketing. Unlike informational picketing, discussed earlier, disruptive picketing is intended to disrupt the services performed by others. Three examples illustrate:

—During the 1969 name tag dispute in Boston, the patrolmen ringed downtown headquarters with pickets, thereby preventing union tailors (from the ILGWU) from entering the building to sew the name tags on uniforms.

—In a 1971 contract negotiation dispute, Trenton, New Jersey, policemen placed pickets at numerous intersections around the city in an attempt to disrupt truck deliveries. This "blockade" was accompanied by a ticket-writing speedup, and while the blockade generally was unsuccessful, the city did increase its monetary offer.[28]

—In the informational picketing case in Cranston discussed earlier, some picketing was carried on at the site of the new police station, which was fully completed and ready for occupancy except for the fact that the parking areas had not yet been paved. Construction unions for a long time were unwilling to cross the lines thus delaying the utilization of the new facility.

Dispute Resolution Procedures: Binding

Another important source of union power is the ability to obtain third-party intervention in employment disputes. It is argued that this is a source of union power because much of the intervention occurring in the cities in this sample appears to have enabled police unions to "get more" than they otherwise would have obtained. These third-party mechanisms can be either compulsory or voluntary, with binding or nonbinding resolution of dispute. This analysis will focus on litigation, compulsory binding arbitration of contract disputes, and grievance arbitration.

Litigation

Litigation is an important direct source of union power: the New York City PBA went to court to force the city to implement the 3.5 to 3.0 pay ratio with police sergeants (which finally resulted in a $2,700 retroactive payment to each patrolman); the Baltimore AFSCME local went to court and won the right for its president to publicly criticize the police commissioner and not be disciplined for doing so; the Omaha union went to court and successfully blocked the lateral entry of a policeman from an annexed suburb. The Oakland union won a ruling that a city-charter wage increase formula set a floor for annual wage increases and not a ceiling as the city contended. The Los Angeles union won a favorable ruling in a prevailing wage case that resulted in a substantial pay increase. The Seattle union challenged the county coroner's inquest procedures regarding police-involved homicides (and obtained an out-of-court settlement) and in another action won a ruling prohibiting the chief from using polygraphs (lie detectors) in an internal corruption investigation.

Obviously police unions do not win all of the cases they file but sometimes the act of filing *per se* may achieve desired goals. Some examples illustrate:

—In Buffalo in April 1970 several policemen responded to a radio call that shots had been fired at a police car. The officers allegedly assaulted the black occupants at the location where the shots were assumed to have been fired. The victims claimed they could identify the culprits, so the police commissioner ordered all men on duty during that particular shift to stand in identification lineups. The men refused, saying that their constitutional rights were being violated, and the union took the case to federal court. The federal circuit court eventually ruled against the union and the lineup was held, but by this time more than a year had elapsed and the chances of making an accurate identification were reduced. The lineups had not been completed at the time of this research.

—In another city the chief changed the shifts from eight hours with paid lunchtime to eight-and-one-half hours with unpaid lunchtime. The union claimed he violated a contractual provision calling for an eight-hour workday, but the chief responded that the men only "worked" eight hours during the eight-and-one-half hour shift. The union took the case to court. The chief, fearful of a huge retroactive overtime bill if the union won, reinstituted the eight-hour shifts. The union lost at the trial court, but the department continued the eight-hour shifts because the union said it would appeal. At the time of the field visit the issue had not been resolved, but the union's lawsuit had the desired effect of shortening the workday during at least an eight-month period.

—In 1959 the city of Philadelphia established a civilian review board (later known as the Police Advisory Board), and in 1963 Rochester established its own Police Advisory Board. While neither of these boards had the authority to directly punish police officers, they were empowered to receive complaints of police misconduct, investigate, and make nonbinding disciplinary recommendations. In 1965 the police union in each city challenged the respective PAB in court. In both cases the trial courts upheld the union's challenges, but both of these verdicts were overturned on appeal. However, these final appeal verdicts were not issued until 1969. In the interim both boards became *de facto* dead letters because of their inability to operate. In both cases the boards eventually ceased to exist entirely because of elected official hostility (manifested via a lack of funds for board operations), but both boards became inoperable much earlier during the union-initiated court battles.[29]

The importance of litigation as a union weapon is demonstrated by the fact that all of the union representatives interviewed said that their unions have regular access to legal services and that the unions are frequent parties in court cases. Some of the unions in the larger cities may have many cases in court simultaneously with a battery of lawyers hired to argue them.

Litigation plays a much larger role in police labor relations (and in public sector labor relations generally) than in the private sector. As mentioned in Chapter 3, private-sector unions seek their substantive goals primarily through the collective-bargaining process; when they do go to court (or to the NLRB) it is usually over procedural matters.[30]

This description does not apply to police labor relations largely because the courts traditionally have been, and continue to be, the forum in which disputes involving government decisions have been resolved. In addition, many police conditions of work are not determined via the collective-bargaining process. Moreover, there is no well-developed body of municipal labor law that works to keep the courts out of the labor-relations process. Finally, grievance arbitration provisions are less common in the police service, and thus employment rights disputes are less likely to be resolved by an arbitrator and more likely to go to court than in the private sector.

A direct parallel to litigation can be found in union decisions to bring cases before state administrative agencies established to regulate public labor relations (similar to the NLRB in the private sector). In a few cities these rulings have had an important impact upon the structure or process of police labor relations: for example in Boston and Omaha the state agencies made unit determinations over the objections of one of the parties. We do not intend to examine the role of administrative agencies *per se*, first because ten of our twenty-two cities are in states with no agencies or no agency with jurisdiction, and second, because in states where such agencies do exist it appears that their primary involvement, aside from unit determination, is in impasse resolution—a subject to be discussed shortly.

Compulsory Interest Arbitration

Unions in six of the cities in the sample—Providence, Cranston, Philadelphia, Pittsburgh, Detroit, and Vallejo—have available to them compulsory arbitration procedures for the resolution of police union-management bargaining impasses.[31] If the union and the city cannot reach agreement, the dispute *must* be submitted to an arbitrator for final and binding determination. The discussion in this section focuses on the first five cities since the Vallejo police have not used their arbitration procedure.

The ostensible reason for the existence of these arbitration procedures is the perceived essentiality of police and fire services for the continued maintenance of public health and safety. Recognizing that policemen and firemen might withhold their services even though they have no right to do so, the state legislatures in Rhode Island, Pennsylvania, and Michigan enacted statutes forbidding public safety work stoppages and providing for compulsory and binding arbitration to settle union-management impasses over new contract terms.

In the five cities in our sample where compulsory arbitration was used, the unions won highly favorable settlements. To say that compulsory arbitration is a source of union power we would have to show that the arbitration award was more than management would have given otherwise. While we were not able to develop such a sophisticated measuring instrument, we do have some heuristic evidence: In all five cities management interviewees universally condemned arbitration (usually on the grounds of the amount of the award and the fact that the arbitrator does not have to fund the award and is not electorally responsible to the taxpayers who do provide the funds) while in all five cities union representatives unanimously supported arbitration (usually on the grounds that arbitration provides a means of securing fair and equitable employment conditions without having to use the strike weapon) with union spokesmen in two cities saying, "it's the only power we've got." Additional support for the assertion that the union *perceives* arbitration as a source of power (relative to the way management views it) comes from the fact that in the Michigan, Rhode Island, Pennsylvania, California, and Wisconsin legislatures it was the unions who sought arbitration and certain management groups who were opposed.

While we can't measure whether arbitration increases the union's power, we can argue that arbitration may be a less expensive source of power (both financially and politically) than the direct action necessary to achieve the same result. The primary cost to the union of arbitration proceedings is financial (hiring expert witnesses, gathering supporting data, preparation of exhibits, and sharing in the cost of the arbitration proceeding), whereas if the union were to pursue a bargaining-political action approach they might incur the costs of lobbying, publicity, job actions, and so forth, and while they might gain a great deal, they might lose a great deal (public suport in a strike, political capital spent to no avail, etc.). One of the advantages of conventional compulsory arbitration as it was practiced prior to the final offer experiments now being waged was that while the union might get less than it had requested, it would surely get more than management had offered—downside risk was minimized.

Politically, compulsory arbitration allowed the union leader to duck the question of whether to engage in a job action. For the union leader with a militant, young membership anxious to press any advantage including the strike, compulsory arbitration offers a safe haven in a stormy sea. To date few union leaders have been disappointed in their expectations.

Compulsory Grievance Arbitration

The grievance procedure provides a vehicle through which the union can seek redress if management violates these contractual terms of employment. While the unions do not win all their grievances, numerous union and management interviewees commented that the presence of a union contract with accompanying union enforcement of the contractual conditions has improved police department personnel practices and "kept management on its toes" when making personnel decisions (e.g., assignments, transfers, disciplinary actions, etc.), especially in Boston and Detroit where the patrolmen's unions were most aggressive in policing their contracts.

Police unions in ten of the twenty-two cities in the sample—Boston, Buffalo, Cranston, Dayton, Detroit, Hartford, New Haven, Omaha, Providence, and Rochester—have multistep grievance procedures culminating in final and binding arbitration. According to union and management interview responses, these arbitration provisions have given these unions a much stronger voice in the determination of actual working conditions by referring disputed items to a third party who may be more willing to agree to union interpretations than the managerial representatives with whom the union must deal at the pre-arbitration steps. The unions believe that this has resulted in benefits which were previously unobtainable.

—A group of Boston patrolmen won an arbitration award that provided a total of $13,000 in retroactive overtime payments for out-of-turn work (the contract calls for all work outside of regularly scheduled shift hours to be compensated at time-and-one-half) in the department's communications control room.

—Many Boston patrolmen benefited when another arbitrator agreed with the union's position that night-shift men on sick or injured leave should have their shift differential pay included in their paychecks because it was part of their regular compensation (the department was paying them only their base salaries while they were on sick leave).

—The Buffalo union won arbitration awards which granted higher pay to several men who had worked temporarily in a higher classification and which provided for an hour's pay to each man required to stand inspection outside of regularly scheduled duty hours.

The arbitration procedure also can be used to temporarily protect the *status quo* from perceived undesirable changes even though the arbitration award ultimately may be unfavorable:

—The Boston union was able to buy enough time via the grievance and arbitration proceedings on the name tag issue to get the state legislature to pass a local option bill banning the wearing of name tags (if an identifying number is worn) and persuade the city council to adopt it so that, when the arbitrator finally issued a decision upholding the city's right to require the tags, the issue was moot.

—Similarly, the Detroit patrolmen's union was able to stall the introduction of name tags and flap holsters via the the grievance procedure. While the arbitrators eventually ruled that management has the right to require name tags and flap holsters, the union was able to prevent their introduction for considerable periods of time (more than two years for name tags).

Dispute Resolution Mechanisms: Nonbinding

The two most common forms of nonbinding dispute resolution mechanisms are mediation and fact-finding. Mediation is a noncoercive process in which a third-party neutral works behind the scenes to achieve some kind of agreement (by maintaing the flow of communication, suggesting alternative resolutions, persuasion, etc.). If the mediator fails to achieve an agreement, he will withdraw from the dispute. Fact-finding is a procedure by which a third party gathers evidence from the parties and then issues a recommended settlement to the dispute. Typically, these recommendations will be released privately to the parties and then to the public if the dispute persists. The apparent rationale behind public recommendations is that the publicity creates pressure on the parties to settle the dispute.

Fact-finding

If a fact-finder makes recommendations that strike a "reasonable" middle ground somewhere between management's best offer and the union's final demands, and are consistent with the relative power of the parties, there is a strong presumption in favor of both parties accepting these recommendations. In this sample fact-finding recommendations, especially public ones have tended to become the basis for settlement.[32]

Experience in five cities illustrates: in Buffalo and Detroit in 1968, in Boston and Rochester in 1970, and in New York City in 1971-72 large wage increases were implemented after the issuance of fact-finding recommendations; in three of the five cases the amounts recommended by the various fact-finders were the amounts of the final wage increases. Fact-finding has been an important factor in Milwaukee police bargaining since the first negotiations in 1961; fact-finding also followed the 1971 strike. Currently there is an experimental compulsory arbitration statute in effect lobbied through the state legislature by the Milwaukee police union.

As we mentioned earlier in discussing compulsory arbitration, we cannot show that fact-finding leads to greater settlements then an all-out struggle in the bargaining arena, but we can suggest that it is likely to lead to results favorable to the union at a lower cost both financially and politically than would a full program of lobbying, publicity, and job actions. Because fact-finding is not binding, however, the union leader is still open to pressure from the rank and file to pursue these options *after* fact-finding, and the city is free to reject any fact-finder's recommendations it perceives as favoring the union. It may be for these reasons that police unions have sought binding arbitration even where fact-finding was previously available.

Mediation

Mediators may act as go-betweens to reduce feelings of animosity and to save face; at times they may be able to clarify issues to both sides in such a manner as to reduce the areas of disagreement, and at times they can help where one or both of the parties is unsophisticated. This tends to work to the union's advantage in the typical dispute over economic items since it is the union that is attempting to get management to shift from the *status quo.*

—Union interviewees in one city gave decisive credit to a state-supplied mediator in getting the city to make an "acceptable" offer (i.e., more generous economic terms than the city had previously offered).

—In another city the two sides had agreed on a first-year wage increase and were haggling over the second-year increase. The city told the mediator that it would give a cost-of-living plus one percent increase for the second year, and the mediator relayed this offer to the union. However, the mediator added his own little twist: he told the union cost-of-living plus one percent with a seven percent minimum. The union accepted, and the city reluctantly agreed for fear that a refusal would be seen as bad-faith bargaining.

Mediation and fact-finding, at least as practiced with police unions in this sample, work to the union's advantage in the same manner that arbitration does. Again, while no claim is advanced that these dispute resolution mechanisms will always result in a solution favoring the union more than the city, the examples cited in this section indicate these methods can and do yield benefits for the union that *might* not otherwise be obtained. These dispute resolution mechanisms are treated as manipulatable sources of power because the union often has some discretion in deciding when they will be used.

The Power of Anticipated Reactions

As mentioned earlier, the view adopted throughout this study is that union-management relationships ultimately are based on the power each party can use in its quest for desirable terms. Since union-management relationships are basically power relationships, frequently the representatives of each side may resort to the use of threats to increase the other party's perceptions of the costs of disagreement. A threat to strike at the expiration of the current contract is probably the most commonly used threat in private-sector collective bargaining, and it is becoming increasingly common in the public sector as well.

It can be argued that this type of union activity should be considered under the heading "the politics of disruption," especially since most actual disruptions, with the exception of wildcat actions, are preceded by threats. For example, union interviewees in two cities told of incidents where the explicit use of threats—one a strike threat, the other a threat to "empty the union's treasury" to publicly castigate elected officials for not properly supporting public safety—produced pay increases that might not otherwise have been obtained. It can be argued that management's response to these and similar threats is done in anticipation of the union's exercise of power.

However, the power of anticipated reactions as used here refers to certain union efforts to prevent management from taking action rather than the typical use of threats to "get more": the power of anticipated reactions refers to management's expectations of union reactions to a potential action by management.[33] More specifically, the concern here is with union efforts to maintain the desired *status quo* (on nonmonetary issues).

Bachrach and Baratz have argued that there are two "faces of power" relevant to the study of political processes—the power which is exercised in the decision-making process, and the power which bears on the nondecision-making process, with nondecision-making defined as "a means by which demands for change in the existing allocation of benefits and privileges in the community can be suffocated before they are even voiced; or kept covert; or killed before they gain access to the relevant decision-making arena; or, failing all these things, maimed or destroyed in the decision-implementing stage of the policy process."[34] The following two examples indicate how the power of anticipated reactions may prevent managerial actions and thus contribute to the attainment of desired aspects of the *status quo:*

—In one city with a large black population and a history of poor police-black. ghetto relations (including one major riot), police department management has been plagued with the "long gun" problem. For some time after the riot many patrolmen carried their own rifles and shotguns on duty (many of which were purchased through a discount arrangement the union established with the National Rifle Association). In addition, the long guns were frequently brandished in a conspicuous manner (e.g., carried in plain sight when out of the patrol car; carried to the door of a house when responding to a call; carried in plain sight when in the patrol car; etc.). The researcher heard conflicting reports about whether the department had been able to eliminate the use of personal weapons and have them replaced with departmental-issued weapons. The department had an unwritten policy that long guns should be carried inconspicuously (e.g., not to be carried outside the cars, kept in the trunk, etc.), but interview responses agreed that many patrolmen, particularly in the ghetto precincts, regularly violated this policy. When asked why management never codified this policy in a written order that could be enforced with official disciplinary sanctions, one candid managerial inter- viewee replied that if the long-gun issue were ever put to the test, "the department would eat it." Perhaps much of the reason for keeping the long-gun issue in the nondecision arena can be found in previous events or circumstances: when one precinct commander, in an attempt to defuse an extremely tense racial situation, ordered his men not to take long guns on patrol, the men refused to leave the station house until he relented; and in the past the union has let it be known via the grapevine that if the use of long guns was proscribed, all of the department's patrol cars might simultaneously develop "mechanical difficulties" and be delivered to the police garage as unsafe to operate.

—In another large city police productivity has been a prime concern of department and city management, yet all patrol cars are manned by two men. In its efforts to make better use of available police manpower, the city has not attempted to institute the use of one-man cars even though it has an arbitrator's decision giving it the explicit right to do so. Perhaps the reason can be seen in the union president's emphatic comment to the researchers: "One man cars are a guaranteed strike issue in this city."

It is extremely difficult for the outside observer to accurately assess the role of anticipated reactions in police union-management relationships, since by definition a successful outcome prevents potential issues from becoming overt issues decided in observable decision-making processes.[35] However, the antici- pated reactions illustrated in the above examples are a very definite source of union power.

Other Direct Sources of Power

The Nature of the Issue

The use of power in any context is tied to the issue involved. Power-based interactions are conducted over specific issues rather than abstract concepts.

Thus the nature or content of any particular issue will strongly influence the union's selection of an appropriate management adversary and will be influential in the determination of each side's costs of agreeing and disagreeing.

Managerial Decision-making Authority. The nature of the issue often determines where in the multifaceted governmental hierarchy the union will have to, or want to, apply pressure. As we discuss later in Chapter 8, one broad cut is between wages, hours, and conditions of work, which are usually attacked through the bargaining process, and issues of law enforcement policy, which are usually attacked through political processes. A second distinction can be made between terms and conditions of employment which can be handled within the bargaining process and those for which it is necessary to seek revisions in the city charter through referendum. A third distinction can be made between issues within the jurisdiction of the municipality and those reserved exclusively to the state legislature—such as pensions in several cities in our sample where the pension system is statewide and can be amended only by action of the legislature.

Costs of Agreement and Disagreement. "Either side's capacity to get agreement on its own terms depends upon its specific demands. The more one side asks for, the higher the other's cost of agreeing relative to disagreeing, and the smaller the likelihood of the latter conceding."[36] In other words, management may offer more resistance to a demand for a 25 percent wage increase than a 10 percent increase or to a demand for retirement at half pay after twenty years than half pay after thirty years.

Union-management bargaining over noneconomic issues is similarly affected by such estimates.

—In 1969-70 the Pittsburgh union went to the state legislature to secure a bill providing that assignments and transfers would be made on a straight seniority basis. City management perceived a very high cost if the legislature legislated city compliance with that union demand, and according to field interviews the mayor's vigorous lobbying against the bill was largely responsible for its demise. The city has also placed a high cost on the union-lobbied, state-legislated police department's trial board system in which imposition of discipline is controlled by the rank-and-file rather than by top management. The city has tried unsuccessfully to get the legislature to rescind the plan, tried unsuccessfully to have an arbitrator rule on it, and at the time of our field visit was fighting the trial board system in court.

Relations with the Firefighters

An analysis of police-union power would be incomplete without some examination of police-union relations with firefighters' organizations. Policemen and firemen have had close ties for many decades. Together they constitute a city's protective services, frequently they are structurally united in a municipal department of public safety, and historically there has been significant movement between the two services (with many more policemen becoming firemen rather than vice versa). In many cities and states the two groups have their own public safety retirement systems separate from those of other public employees. Most important, in many U.S. cities (and in most of the larger cities) there has been a long tradition of police-fire pay parity.[37] In this section we will look briefly at police-fire relations to see how they affect police union strength.

Joint Political Activities. Police and fire unions have made a number of alliances (mostly temporary) for the purpose of engaging in a variety of joint political activities: the Cleveland police and fire unions combined in 1967 to secure voter approval of a dual ballot measure that made the police the highest paid in Ohio and provided for police-fire parity; the police and fire unions in Detroit and in Oakland combined to urge voter rejection of city ballot proposals to alter their respective public safety retirement systems; in state legislatures in Michigan, Pennsylvania, and California police and fire unions have joined forces to lobby for compulsory arbitration of public safety negotiation disputes; and in Omaha the police and fire unions combined in 1968 to seek voter approval of various public safety fringe benefits. Los Angeles had a unique organizational arrangement until 1972 with policemen and firefighters belonging to the same organization.[38]

Joint Bargaining. In this field sample at least, formal joint collective bargaining does not appear to be as widespread as joint political activity. Police and fire unions in New York, Seattle, Buffalo, and Cincinnati have bargained jointly on occasion, and in 1969 the Vallejo police and fire unions conducted coordinated bargaining and a joint strike. None of these have been permanent alliances.

Parity. Protective-service pay parity may affect police unions' ability to secure wage increases since any increase in their salaries is automatically passed on to the firefighters. This larger impact unit makes it more costly for the city to agree to police wage demands than if the police bargained only for themselves. New York City provides the ultimate example of how broad an area of direct impact may become:

> —Because of various contractual ratios and political customs, the city is obligated to give various multiples of any wage increase negotiated by the patrolmen to the police sergeants, lieutenants, and captains; firefighters and fire lieutenants; sanitation men; transit authority police; housing authority police; and correctional system officers (even though each one of these groups constitutes a separate bargaining unit).[39]

This police union resentment to police-fire pay parity is a relatively new phenomenon. In the precollective bargaining era the firefighters generally took the initiative in using traditional political interest group tactics to push up public safety wages, while the police reaped the benefits. In the late 1960s the wage initiative shifted to the police, largely as a result of their emergence onto the center stage of "law and order" politics and the fact that it was easier to recruit qualified candidates for firefighter positions than for police work.

Police unions in New Haven, Hartford, Vallejo, San Francisco, Cincinnati, Oakland, Buffalo, and Rochester have all attempted to break parity or willingly agreed to management's attempt to do so. Tactics included filing unfair labor practice charges, referenda to break parity clauses in city charters, and straight bargaining at the table.

That feelings run deep is indicated by the fact that in five cities union interviewees roundly condemned parity as a "parasite" clause which gave the firefighters the same pay as police for performing allegedly easier jobs and which limited the police unions' ability to bargain freely for whatever they can get. These were obviously not the same cities in which policemen still lag behind firefighters. Arbitration awards in Detroit and Pittsburgh gave the firemen larger wage increases than the police (though in both cities parity was reestablished), and in another city with no collective bargaining the police union leader told one of the authors that he had informed city officials "in no uncertain terms that the police had better get everything fire gets." A police union leader in Chicago said that in that city there is pay parity but the firemen have superior fringe benefits.

As with so many other dimensions of police-union power, it is difficult to determine to what extent these joint police-fire ties help or hinder police unions. On the one hand, pay parity enlarges the unit of direct impact and increases the city's costs of agreement with police wage demands (in 1969 in Boston, city management went even further and reached agreement with the firemen in an alleged attempt to use parity to "box-in" the patrolmen with a relatively cheap pattern settlement—the patrolmen's union leaders successfully resisted). On the other hand police-union leaders in at least five cities commented that joint activities with the firemen enhance the political influence of each group beyond what would exist if the two groups went their separate ways. Further, some management spokesmen said that the firemen deserve the lion's share of the credit for such joint lobbying and electoral victories as the Michigan and Pennsylvania arbitration statutes, and another author has commented on the firefighters' superior political abilities.[40] Thus it seems that while police-fire parity constrains a police union's wage demands at the bargaining table, police-fire political alliances give the police more influence than they would have if they acted alone.

Summary

*The Political Context and
Collective Bargaining*

Police unions have a wide range of directly manipulatable sources of power available to them—strikes and other job actions, dispute resolution procedures, lobbying, and issue and candidate electoral politics. While these sound like the same tactics available to unions in the private sector, they differ in two important respects. First, the environment in which strikes and job actions are effective is political rather than economic in nature, for example, a police job action is undertaken to create political pressure on particular political officials rather than to shut off city revenue (though the nonissuance of traffic citations marginally reduces city revenue). Second, in the police service the unions are able to bring their whole arsenal of weapons to bear on the determination of the substantive terms and conditions of work, whereas in the private sector political activities are limited to gaining procedural advantages that may later be exploited at the bargaining table. Thus police unions may bargain collectively, lobby with elected officials, go to the courts, or make electoral *quids pro quos* in order to obtain improvements in substantive employment conditions (e.g., higher wages, more fringe benefits, improved working conditions, etc.) and to obtain their procedural objectives (e.g., a mandatory bargaining law, a compulsory arbitration ordinance, a more advantageous position in the local political influence system, etc.). Nonetheless, while police unions may have many cost-manipulating activities they may use, the collective-bargaining process—with its written contract, visibility, and attendant dispute resolution mechanisms—is the most important vehicle through which the average police union in this study sought to improve the employment conditions of its members.

This is not an unreasonable finding when one considers that the political avenues had always been available to the unions who had learned long ago that while political power is quite potent, it requires political capital which is difficult to accumulate but which is expended quite rapidly.

*The Nature of Quid Pro
Quo Exchanges*

Presumably one of the advantages of the collective-bargaining process is that it facilitates the potential for *quid pro quo* exchanges in which both sides may come out ahead. In the private sector these exchanges are usually spoken of as productivity bargaining and examples often cited include the Kaiser Steel settlement of 1959, the bituminous coal agreements and the East and West Coast longshoring agreements. In the public sector all of these economic *quid pro quo* are equally attainable under the prerequisite economic conditions; the dimension which distinguishes police and public-sector bargaining from the private sector is the addition of the potential for political *quid pro quo*—that is, the union can lower management's cost of agreement (instead of concentrating on increasing the costs of disagreement) by trading political support for desired changes in employment conditions. We have cited examples of this type of behavior throughout this chapter. Whether these exchanges will work in or against the public interest remains to be seen.

In the last three chapters we have developed a model of the sources and uses of power in police labor relations. In the next three chapters we look at the impact of the exercise of that power.

6 Police-Union Impact on the Potential for Professionalization

Police executives anxious to professionalize the police service are concerned that professionalization and unionization are incompatible. In this chapter we look at two aspects of this proposition: the potential for professionalization of the police service and the impact of the unions on this potential. We found more agreement and less consensus on the subject of police professionalization than any other we encountered: agreement that professionalization is essential; no consensus as to what constitutes professionalization, professionalism or indeed, the profession of police officer. Our first task, then, will be to seek to distinguish among the concepts of profession, professionalization, and professionalism and to compare these with two concepts that seem more applicable to what is happening in the police service: the struggle for professional status and the development of a professionally led department.

Vollmer and Mills adopt a quite useful distinction between profession and professionalization:

In our discussion . . . we avoid the use of the term "profession" except as an "ideal type" of occupational organization which does not exist in reality, but which provides the model of the form of occupational organization that would result if any occupational group became completely professionalized. In this way, we want to avoid discussions of whether or not any particular group is "really a profession" or not. In accord with Hughes' experience we feel that it is much more fruitful to ask "how professionalized" or more specifically "how professionalized in certain identifiable respects" a given occupation may be at a given point in time.

We suggest therefore, that the concept of "profession" be applied only to an abstract model of occupational organization, and that the concept of "professionalization" be used to refer to the dynamic *process* whereby many occupations can be observed to change certain crucial characteristics in the direction of a "profession" even though some of these may not move very far in this direction. . . .[1]

Professionalism, then, is defined as the ideology found in many occupational groups in the process of professionalization. "Although professionalism may not lead an occupation very far down the road toward professionalization in every instance, it is an integral part of the process."[2]

Rarely, however, are these definitions used in the police service. Rather, the police tend to use these terms somewhat more loosely than they are used here. When the police speak of a "professional" department they usually are referring to a department in which efficiency and managerial rationality are emphasized to the exclusion (or attempted exclusion) of political criteria as a basis for decision-making. It is in this sense that O.W. Wilson refers to professionalism in his work on police administration, and it is in this sense that the Los Angeles Police Department is held up as a model of the professional police agency.[3] For example, at the time of one field visit the leaders of a police union in a midwestern city had recently returned from a visit to Los Angeles, and they spoke to the researcher in glowing terms of the "professional" character of the LAPD. When pressed to define "professional," they referred to the absence of interference from city hall, the modern police building, the shiny new equipment (especially the computers) inside the building, the neat and clean appearance of uniformed officers, and the specialist rather than generalist nature of many LAPD jobs. Consequently, it seems that a professionally led department is one of the essential components of the ideology of professionalism in the police service.

Another concept confused with professionalism *is the struggle for professional status*—the quest for the trappings of professionalism, for example, autonomy, professional authority, and the power to determine the appropriate character and curriculum of the training process. Failure to distinguish among professionalization, a professionally led department, and the struggle for professional status has clouded all previous discussion of the impact of police unions on the potential for professionalization. Therefore, before we get to the actual discussion of the impact of unions we will attempt to develop these concepts a bit further.

Professions and Professionalization

Sociologists and other academicians who are concerned with occupations have themselves failed to agree unanimously on what constitutes a profession, but they do generally agree on the set of characteristics from among which they may select criteria for determining the extent to which professionalization has occurred in a given occupation. Kleingartner summarizes the work of seven scholars in the field and finds that four or more support the following characteristics: intellectual training, specialized knowledge, altruism, practicality, self-organization, and ethical codes.[4]

Possession of several of these characteristics usually means that the occupation had achieved professional status. This has two important consequences. The first is "professional authority"—the concept that the professional is supposed to know more about what is good for his client than either the client or the public. The second is the power of the profession to determine the appropriate character and curriculum of the training process. This is, in effect, an extension of professional authority—since the profession knows more about its area than the laity, it should be the sole arbiter of criteria for professional training and by extension, certification.[5]

It is important to remember that professional authority and control over certification, curriculum, and training are proferred to an occupation by the public because that occupation has met the criteria (listed above) for becoming a profession. In contrast, much of the discussion relating to unions and professionalization in the police field is, in fact, a discussion of the impact of unions on the struggle for the trappings of professionalism. We question this as the appropriate level for analysis. First, however, we must ask what is the legitimacy of the police claim for the fruits of professional status, that is, have they professionalized?[6]

The Process of Professionalization

The process of professionalization assumes that certain prerequisite criteria have been met. First, it is assumed that the specialization on which a profession is built is at the occupational level as opposed to the individual or organizational level. Second, it is assumed that the occupation stresses process rather than product and that the reward structure of the occupation reinforces this orientation. Third, it is assumed that there exists a body of knowledge peculiar to the occupation which is codified, which can be transmitted on an abstract plane, and which is subject to investigation and verification and is continuously under review.[7]

Occupational Specialization. The first assumption, occupational specialization, is an essential prerequisite because only at this level of specialization do we generate a sufficiently broad base of common problems to begin to derive the general intellectual premises or lore on which a profession is founded. If specialization ceases at the level of the individual, his horizon is limited to his own experience. Organizational specialization broadens this horizon to include interaction with and observation of others and the development of an organizational or geographic base from which principles of behavior may be derived. Occupational specialization encompasses the experience across many organizations and geographic areas and allows for the development of broad principles of behavior that are a prerequisite to professionalization.

In the police service, the emphasis is on organizational specialization. The police officer specializes at the department rather than the occupational level. For example, it is widely felt that the officer must understand and be responsive to the political criteria for his particular city or even his division or beat, a fact often cited when arguments are made against lateral entry.[8] An example of occupational specialization, on the other hand, would be an emphasis on police intervention in marital disputes or interpersonal dispute intervention generally. Similarly, acknowledgement of the importance of the political style of the city to the type of police training process would indicate a shift from organizational to occupational specialization in the sense that it would help remove one of the often cited roadblocks to lateral entry.

Process Orientation. Professions police themselves and improve themselves by an emphasis on the process by which ends are accomplished. A reward structure is established which reinforces good practices and punishes bad practices through exclusion if caught. This combination of positive rewards and sanctions for deviant behavior is also considered an efficient way to reinforce the learning process.

In the police service the current reward structure emphasizes product rather than process. Within police agencies where the emphasis is on fighting crime, attention is focused on the uniform crime reports and index crimes, arrests by patrolmen, and clearances by detectives. The reward structure associated with these output measures is the opposite of a reward structure emphasizing due process and the rights of individuals. A change in the reward structure emphasizing process would be consistent with professionalization. This is not to say that doctors do not emphasize curing the patient or lawyers do not emphasize winning the case. Rather it is to say that while professional persons are as much concerned with product as are police officers, they emphasize the processes by which these products are sought, and those who engage in unethical or bad processes are punished when caught.

Conceptualization. The third prerequisite to professionalization is the existence of a body of knowledge or lore at an occupational level of generalization (applicable over a large variety of circumstances and times) subject to conceptualization and abstraction so that it can be transmitted symbolically and subjected to thought, discussion, and revision on the basis of experience. Prerequisite too, however, is the need to agree on some focus for the occupation. For example, in the medical field "health" is the broad focus; in the legal field "justice" is the broad focus. In the police field no broad definition of function, such as fighting crime or providing service, has yet been agreed to by academicians, practitioners, and politicians.[9]

Given the organizational level of specialization and the fact that the police occupation field has yet to settle on an agreed primary focus, it is not unexpected that we find training for the police function an essentially organizational responsibility.[10] Furthermore, the nature of this training tends to be anecdotal, oral, and by observation as opposed to formal and conceptual, with postacademy socialization playing a major role in the structuring of police officer behavior on the street.[11]

Our first concern, then, in evaluating the impact of unions on the potential for professionalization is that we have a definition of professionalization against which we can measure the union's accelerating or retarding effect. In this section, we have suggested that the union's impact may have to be measured on the extent to which it is one of the factors preventing the police service from reaching the take-off stage for professionalization. In the next section, we will question the extent to which it would be possible for the police to achieve professional status even if these prerequisites were met.

Professional Employees in a Highly
Structured Organization

There is a literature suggesting that the form of an organization from which occupational (or professional) services are delivered is an important factor in determining the extent to which professionalization can occur (or be maintained) in that occupation or profession. This is of particular interest here because the organizational form identified as least conducive to professionalization—bureaucracy or highly structured organizations—is the form most commonly associated with police agencies.

Professional occupations are commonly practiced in one of three major settings: the individual practice, the professional organization, and the nonprofessional organization. The doctor or lawyer in an office by himself is said to be in individual practice. The lawyer, engineer, or scientist working for a large business corporation is an example of a professional working in a nonprofessional organization. The law firm, medical clinic, public school or social work agency are examples of the professional working in a professional organization, and this is where we would classify the police agency if the police occupation had professional status.

Professional organizations such as these, however, can (and must) be further distinguished by certain features of their organizational structure. For example, in medical clinics and law firms everyone continues to practice his profession whether he is a manager or an employee; however, in the public school or social work agency when an individual is promoted to supervisory status, he ceases to teach or to see clients in his capacity as a social worker—he gives up his "professional" duties to assume those of a manager.[12]

Professional organizations can also be distinguished by the degree of autonomy employees enjoy in the practice of their profession. In the law firm or the medical clinic, professional practice is governed by the rules of the profession as determined by the professional association or by the laws of the state as drafted, in large part, by the professional association. In the public school or the social work agency, however, employees are at least partially subordinated to an externally imposed administrative framework.[13] Most important, says Scott, this administrative framework significantly reduces the amount of professional autonomy exercised by the individuals in these organizations.

An elaborate set of rules and a system of routine supervision control many if not most aspects of the tasks performed by professional employees so that it is often difficult if not impossible to locate or define an area of activity for which the professional group is responsible individually or collectively.[14]

Hall cites two reasons for the existence of external controls, both of which reflect the fact that the public has not accorded the occupation professional authority. First, the service performed is a public service and second, the public, feeling that it knows as much about the subject as those in the occupation, has retained control through a lay board.[15] The formal distinction accorded these two types of professional organizations is the "autonomous" organization (such as law firms and medical clinics) and the "heteronomous" organizations (such as public schools or social-work agencies).

The reason we have presented this discussion here is because it seems that the police agency is clearly a heteronomous organization in which lay boards, city councils, and legislatures have established the administrative framework and defined the function of the police without consulting the police in the same way that nonprofessionals control the state boards which set standards for teaching certificates, and lay members of the board of education set education policy in the community.[16] The identification of the police agency as a heteronomous professional organization is important to the discussion of police professionalization because Hall presents an interesting paradox and policy question.[17]

If the occupation is a true profession, then practicing the profession in a heteronomous organization would be dysfunctional in the sense that domination by a lay board will undermine the morale and professional status of the professionals in the organization. On the other hand, if the occupation has not achieved professional status, then the heteronomous organizational form allows for community control.[18]

Many police agencies would like to establish their own standards, methods, criteria for admission, qualifications for officer training, and, indeed, inputs to law-making. The justification cited is usually the professional experience of the police and their professional prerogatives. However, in light of the discussion above, the granting of professional authority and relinquishing of lay control is only valid if the professionalization process is well along. In the case of the police, we have argued that these conditions do not hold; the police are seeking the fruits of professional status before they have become a true profession. In this next section, we will look at the impact of the union as it relates to both of these areas.

The Impact of Unions

Earlier, we indicated that police *professionalization* cannot occur in the absence of certain prerequisites—occupational specialization, a process orientation, and a learning model more formal than the oral tradition now prevalent. It is our contention that the impact of police unions on professionalization can be discussed only in the context of their impact on achieving these prerequisite conditions. Anything else is a discussion of the impact of unions on the "shadow" rather than the "substance" of professionalization. In this section we will discuss both aspects.

Union Impact on Achieving the Prerequisites
for Professionalization

For our purposes, some discussion of the police function and some agreement as to what constitutes the proper role of the police in a democratic society would eliminate several roadblocks to achieving an occupational locus of specialization, a process orientation, and the basis for a formal-learning model. For example, if the police function were to be considered broadly as encompassing both social service and crime fighting, then there would be an incentive to acknowledge the relevance of social science training to a potential police officer and to at least examine the extent to which specialization must be limited to a particular department.

Kelling and Kleismet in an excellent article identify three myths concerning police work that serve to delude the public about the true nature of the police function: the myth of the police officer as a crime fighter; the myth of the command structure as an effective control on police behavior; and the myth of the omnipotence of the police as crime fighters, which carries over and influences their behavior in other areas.[19] So long as these myths are accepted, say the authors, it will not be possible to effect the changes necessary to achieve professionalization.

Specifically, if the public were to be educated to the fact that most crime will not be solved because of technological and other constraints and, therefore, that the police are not omnipotent, it would ease the pressure on the police to attempt to foster this image even when they themselves know it is an impossible situation and a hypocritical one. If the public were to inquire more fully into what it is that the police actually do, and found that only 20 to 30 percent of the patrolman's job deals with crime,[20] they might be more open to a discussion of what is involved in the police function, what training is necessary, what reward structure appropriate, and so forth. If the myth about command staff control were explored, the public would become aware of the great deal of discretion actually afforded the officer on the street. At this point, there could be more intelligent discussion of whether bureaucratic or professional control were the more appropriate model in the police situation.

In short, a critical evaluation of the police function is prerequisite to the process of professionalization. As we shall see in the next section, it is not clear that full-blown professionalization is the ideal state for all police agencies or for all jobs within a police agency. It may be that an organizational level of specialization is the appropriate one for many if not most police agencies or that there are types of police agencies among which lateral entry may occur or particular police jobs within which lateral entry may profitably occur. The limiting factor is the speed with which these examinations of function will be disseminated and the extent to which the findings will be accepted and acted upon.

The impact of unions on the prerequisites to achieving professionalization will depend in large measure on the position they take with respect to the dissemination, study, and utilization of the findings from the various studies of the police function. It is our feeling that the unions will be active in this process of dissemination, study, and utilization but most likely in a reactionary way. Like all employee organizations (and professional societies) they have a stake in the *status quo* and must be shown some reason why change is necessary and offered some incentive to participate in change. In the following section we examine the extent to which the unions in this study sample became involved in issues broadly characterized as involving professionalization.

The Impact of the Union on
Specific Issues

The efforts we will discuss in this section deal almost completely with the trappings of the professionalism issue rather than the complete model of professionalization offered in the previous sections. For example, we will discuss the attitude of unions toward increased formal education—an issue always cited in discussions of professionalization. Yet in none of these situations is there a discussion of "education for what" or how do we use the educated officer differently in order to increase professionalization. The conventional wisdom assumes that increased education is synonomous with professionalization—a position we have rejected. On the other hand, exposure to education does allow for abstraction of knowledge, distinction between process and product, and the development of an occupational outlook.

Education. There is a wide range of alternatives to be considered under education: education as an entry requirement; education as a requirement for promotion; education just to receive additional compensation. Also to be considered are the amount of education; the grade necessary to qualify; the type of courses allowed; the dollars to be received for increased education; who pays the cost; the scheduling difficulties; and what to do with those men who do not want to get advanced education.

We have seen examples where the city initiated an advanced education requirement and examples where the union initiated the requirement. We have seen cities opposed to advanced education and unions opposed to advanced education. The union objections usually centered on the point that not all the men were interested in an advanced education and that since everyone was required to do the same job, they should receive the same pay. In both cases where the city was opposed, a bill had been put through the state legislature making education incentives possible (on a local-option basis). The cities were objecting in the one case because of the excessive cost (30 percent minimum for a master's degree) and in the other because of the wide latitude in the bill as to what constituted an acceptable topic for a course which qualified for incentive. In Detroit and New York, the issue of college credit for promotion at a future date has come up but in neither city has it been resolved. In one midwestern city, the union proposed a two-year college requirement for entry; the chief is opposed. In a second midwestern city, the city proposed a two-year college requirement for entry; the union is opposed.

In summary, it is difficult to discern a pattern regarding unions and education. Unions are accepting of educational incentive programs where they have a substantial input into the design of the program (usually via collective bargaining) and if a longevity pay arrangement is established concurrently to take care of the older officers who have no inclination to return to the classroom. However, the variance in the union's position on the issue of educational standards, the fact that educational credits accumulated in one department are not transferable to another department, and the fact that many of the unions in this sample saw increased education as a means to secure more dollars and break parity with the firefighters serves to emphasize the organizational locus of the occupation. A resolution of the relationship between educational standards and professionalization would require a broadening of horizons.

Minority Recruitment. We briefly discuss recruitment here because it does relate to the question of professional standards. Admission requirements for police work, especially as they relate to education, age, weight, height, eyesight, and personal background are quite stringent. Minorities have complained that these standards are artificial and that they systematically discriminate against blacks, especially in the sense that it is difficult for any youngster to grow up in the ghetto and have no adverse contact of record with the police. Again we are in a position where a policy decision very much related to function is being argued abstractly or on the basis of misinformation. For example, in the major metropolitan areas, it may well be that a significant number of black and Spanish-surnamed officers will be required to provide a *full* range of social and crime-fighting services to the minority communities. While a college-educated white officer might be an asset to a metropolitan department such as New York City, his value in Harlem might be somewhat less than that of an officer who was raised in that environment. Therefore, instead of referring to "lowering" the standards of the agency in order to recruit minorities, we might speak of flexible standards or changes in standards necessary to achieve the goals of the organization. Many departments have made an effort to increase minority representation in their departments. This section deals with the attitudes of white majority unions and black police associations on this point.

—In 1970 the mayor of Buffalo proposed a new police classification that would be an extension of the existing almost all-white cadet program. Those appointed as Community Peace Officers (CPO's) would get one year cadet training and take a civil-service promotion exam to become a patrolman. The program, paid for with federal funds, was designed to increase minority representation. The usual entrance hurdles were to be lowered in an attempt to get increased black and Puerto Rican representation in the department. Preference for the CPO program was to be given to blacks and Puerto Ricans. The union vigorously opposed the plan and tried to stop the city council from adopting it. Failing that, the union has gone to court claiming the plan is unconstitutional, discriminatory, violates city charter, state law, and so forth. The union has also stressed the impact on current eligibles on the civil-service list and the current cadets who have yet to be appointed patrolmen.

—Similarly, a 1969 trainee program in a western city was opposed and eventually defeated by the union and the department jointly who argued primarily that the control of the program was first in civil-service hands and then city personnel department hands, but not in police department hands. The trainee program was the impetus for a clause in the union's contract specifying that the department shall notify the union in the event of a reduction in entrance standards below the base established by the civil-service test of 1965. A new program has started in this same city under Model Cities: black community service officers (CSO) will handle social service calls in the field; participants will be able to become regular patrolmen, but if they do not, the CSO program will have its own hierarchy so that a man who does not make patrolman may remain a CSO. The program is under department rather than city-hall control. The union is apprehensive, seeing it as a trainee program with a new name, but it has gone along with department assurances that the police control the program and that undesirables will be excised.

—In a California city, the union opposed lowering height and weight requirements but the civil service commission adopted the new requirements anyhow. In a western city, where the height requirement was dropped, the union is attempting to get it raised by means of a referendum, which would give entrance requirements control to department heads rather than civil service. In three major metropolitan areas, the unions are opposing plans to allow minor criminal records for recruits. Opposition in all of these cases was based on lowering professional standards.

—In New York City, a consortium of police employee organizations were opposing a plan that would set up a "Model Cities police force" in which officers would have to pass only an "equivalent" examination to be composed by the civil service commission. In Boston, the mayor submitted a Model Cities plan that would have set up a civilian review board, elected a citizen advisory panel to provide guidance for the police in the Model Cities neighborhoods, provided for formal cooperation between police and private black security patrols, and relaxed civil-service standards regarding past criminal records. The city council, in consultation with the union, scrapped the mayor's recommendations and substituted language guaranteeing all rights and benefits enjoyed by employee organizations, especially those won through collective bargaining. On the other hand, in one midwestern city, the department has set a goal of making five out of each eight new hires blacks, and they are conducting a billboard advertising campaign openly slanted to young blacks. While the white-dominated union is not happy, it has been unable to do anything about the campaign.

Black police officers' associations have become increasingly involved in the question of standards and recruitment. While this is discussed more broadly in Chapter 8, we cite several examples here.

—In one eastern city, the black officers' association has sent a proposal to Washington to fund their efforts to help blacks get on the force. Through the medium of the cadet program, the group prepares blacks to take the regular civil-service examination to become a patrolman. For those blacks who pass and must fill time until they are appointed, jobs are found. Four years ago (1969), the association challenged the high rejection rate of black and Puerto Rican applicants as a result of screening by a unit of mostly white patrolman investigators. The result of this protest is the establishment of the candidates review board, which the association claims has led to the reinstatement of 85 percent of the rejected blacks into the entry process.

—In a midwestern city, the black police association in conjunction with the chief, the public safety director, and the civil service commission has become totally involved in the recruitment process for all candidates. Black/white teams conduct background investigations; a black and a white psychologist do group evaluation jointly; and a black/white team also is involved in polygraph testing of applicants. In addition, the black police association helps find black applicants for the examinations and helps prepare them for taking the written test.

—In an eastern city, the black officers opposed the formation of a cadet program on the grounds that it did not guarantee a patrolman's job to a cadet once he became twenty-one. They saw the program as a temporary solution to the pressure blacks were generating for more black officers and would not lend their sanction to it.

In all of these programs, it should be noted the 1970-72 recession has interfered with what may have been the best intentions. Many cities have not hired anyone recently. Moreover, the security of a police career and the relatively high salaries now paid have attracted quite highly qualified candidates to the queues. The result of this labor-market phenomenon is to make more complex and difficult an already difficult and emotional problem. Once again, however, we caution the reader that this discussion of "professional standards" should not be confused with the process of professionalization. Emotion aside, the two are quite separate issues.

Lateral Transfer. The one issue where the unions could have direct impact on increased professionalization would be lateral transfer. As we discussed earlier, it is hard to say whether the absence of lateral transfer provisions is a function of organizational specialization or an excuse for organizational specialization. Regardless, we found no union in our sample that had actively worked for lateral entry. In two cities, we found active opposition. In general, police unions saw all the shortcomings (mostly competition for limited promotional opportunities) and none of the advantages (new promotional opportunities in other cities). This reaction is, of course, quite consistent with American trade unionism generally and its emphasis on job scarcity, job security, and promotional opportunities for the indigenous work force. The discussion never got to the level of the mechanical difficulties of instituting such a plan because it was assumed that the need for active opposition would most likely not arise. In fairness, it should be noted that police management also was opposed to lateral entry, although one chief expressed the opinion that it would be nice if a patrolman with a physical problem such as asthma might be able to transfer to a department in Arizona.

Labor-Management Committees. The participation of employees in organizational policy-making could be viewed as an example of professional status. While we chose to view it as an example of participative management (Chapter 7), we report on it here briefly. We found examples of this kind of arrangement in seven cities in our sample.

In two cities, regular meetings are held to discuss matters of general concern, but limited to working conditions—changes in shift time, court-duty time, seatbelts in the back seat of wagons, and so forth. In a midwestern city, the union is represented through its president on various committees considering policy. In another midwestern city, at the time of our site visit, the command staff, representatives of the two competing unions, and the president of the black police officers' association were meeting regularly once a week to consider policy on a range of issues including use of fatal force, political activities by members, crime statistics, firearms policies, and so forth. San Francisco's newest contract provides for a formal commitment to joint policy-making with the union, while the Hartford contract says "material will not be added to the Police Manual without prior discussion between the Chief and the Union; provided, however, that this shall not be construed to require the Union's approval. . . ."[21] In one eastern city at the time of our visit, the union president was trying to get formal union representation at all command-staff policy meetings in the department. The commissioner has been meeting with him informally, but he wants the union to have an institutional right to attend all policy meetings so the union can have a voice in the planning and implementation of change.

Labor-management committees can be viewed two ways. On the one hand they are requests on the part of the union for the privilege of professional status without the benefit of professionalization. On the other hand they may represent a step in the right direction—an acknowledgement that the man on the street may have a useful input to make to the policy-making process—a recognition of internal or organizational "professional authority." On balance, the effect is probably salutary as a prerequisite to the implementation of change.

Master Patrolman. The concept of the master patrolman, or a position higher than patrolman reserved on a merit basis for those of proven superior ability, is often posited as an example of professionalization.[22] In our study, however, we found that as the master patrolman concept has been practiced, it is more a reach for professional status (in this case, dollars) than an effort at professionalization.

The worst example of which we are aware occurred in a city of 175,000 outside of our sample. Two outside consultants recommended to a fact-finder that a new classification be established to be filled on a merit basis for a combination of advanced education and excellence on the job. The fact-finder, however, recommended a new classification, patrolman II and then grandfathered the entire existing patrol force into this higher classification.

Contrast to this, however, the Vallejo, California contract, which at the initiative of the union provides for a rank of senior patrolman and master patrolman, each to be achieved by a combination of experience and advanced education. In two cities where IACP surveys recommended the establishment of master patrolman status, the unions in each city opposed the concept and neither was implemented. In one eastern city where IACP also proposed the concept, the union bases its opposition on the claim that the police-agent positions with their bonus of $500 per year were nothing but a reward for a college degree.

Los Angeles has come the closest of any city in our sample to developing an approach that meets a long recognized need—the opportunity to create a career ladder in the patrol division. Normally, a man enters the occupation at the patrolman level and achieves maximum career salary in three to five years. To get further pay increases, he must seek promotion to a supervisory position (sergeant) or an investigatory position (detective). This creates an incentive system whereby the best patrolmen are induced to leave patrol for a position with a different set of skill requirements which they may, in fact, not be ideally qualified to fill. A more rational system would be one in which a man could develop a career in patrol without being forced to move into management or investigation if patrol were his strongest field.[23] An outside consultant in conjunction with the city of Los Angeles, the department, and the union did devise a plan setting up four classifications within the context of the patrol division: patrolman I, patrolman II, patrolman III, and patrolman III + 1—a lead worker but not a supervisor. The latter steps are on the basis of education, ability, and seniority. While this does not fit our definition of professionalization, it is a step forward in dealing with a personnel problem that has forced people into supervision or investigation who would have been more effective in patrol work.

In a midwestern city, a special patrol rank was created to provide organizational flexibility. In Chapter 7 we discuss this concept of a specialist classification, which provides a rank attainable through examination that is a staging base for more flexible personnel use among the various specialties within the department. While this is not professionalization, it is an important managerial step forward.

Other Areas. Promotions, promotion examinations and efficiency ratings, the joint test-validation board in New York City, discussions of additional positions, civilianization, manning, civilian review boards, internal investigation, and other topics might be interpreted as professional issues if one were to use as the decision rule the participation of the union in decision-making in areas of professional concern. Given our distinction, however, between professionalization and the quest for professional status, we discuss these issues under other headings.

The Impact on the Potential for a
Professionally Led Department

As discussed earlier, the supervisory, administrative, and management ranks have traditionally been considered natural steps in a police career to which all entrants at the patrol level had to aspire if they desired any significant salary increases after the first three to five years of service. Little attention was paid to training new sergeants, lieutenants, or captains for their increased responsibilities at least in part because the management aspects of their responsibilities were either not recognized or not acknowledged.

The advent of police unions can be expected to have two affects on this situation. First, in many jurisdictions unit determinations specifying patrolmen-only units will heighten the sense of difference between the management and those they supervise. Second, as was true in the private sector, we can anticipate that the existence of unions will cause a shift from *ad hoc* decision-making to some form of management by policy. The net effect of both of these factors should be to force a realization on the police and on police administrators that there is a difference in their functions and that on many levels the relationship between managers and employees is an adversary relationship. Once this realization has occurred, there exists the possibility that supervision and management may come to be recognized as a career independent of patrol. From this point, it is conceivable that professionalization might develop.

As one can see from Table 2-1, there are very few of the cities in this sample where patrolman-only organizations are the exclusive representative for bargaining purposes. If the development of police unionism were to follow the private-sector model, one would expect that as more states passed bargaining statutes covering the police and as there was a development of greater sophistication about the relationship between employee organizations and supervisory employees in the police service, that there would be more emphasis on patrolman-only units. The major question is whether police unionism will follow the private sector in this regard. Our sample evidence suggests that the pattern for the immediate future will tend toward inclusive units. In part, this can be attributed to the lobbying power of the unions who have managed to keep mandatory separation language out of the legislation pertaining to the police. Where the language is permissive, the unions have managed to push through inclusive units as, for example, in San Diego, Los Angeles, Oakland, San Francisco, Richmond, and Vallejo, California. A third factor is that there is no lateral entry at the supervisory levels thus eliminating a natural distinguishing factor present in most other occupations. Finally, unlike many other occupations, both rank and file and management in the police service are recruited from precisely the same socioeconomic group (by definition since there is no lateral entry). For all these reasons we expect an extensive time lag before the police service follows the private-sector practice of rank-and-file only units. However, in the long run we believe that the natural differences between employees and supervisors will assert themselves and the union's role in prosecuting grievances and administering the contract will cause the police employee organizations to reconsider the desirability of all inclusive units..

In Chapter 7 we discuss the impact of unions on the chief's ability to manage. One of our major findings in this chapter is that, in fact, *ad hoc* decision-making has begun to be replaced by policies. This was true in the areas of discipline, transfers, court scheduling, manning, and so forth. This shifting emphasis to process and the awareness of process are hopeful signs for future managerial professionalization.

One significant factor that must be considered in the development of a professional management is the phenomenon of superior officers unions in the police service. In every instance in our sample where there was a patrolman-only unit, there was also a union (or unions) representing the superior officers. What effect this phenomenon will have on professionalization of management we are not prepared to say. To a great extent the superior-officer organizations exist to protect the superior officers' interests relative to the patrolmen in the traditional areas of wages, hours, and conditions of work.

Summary

It is fair to say, as many critics of police unions have said, that police unions do systematically interfere with management's quest for professional status. The actions of most of the unions in our sample regarding lateral transfer, education, master-patrolman status, and recruitment and standards have been essentially negative and, from management's point of view, clearly counterproductive. Moreover, as we point out subsequently in Chapters 7 and 8, these are often examples of unions being able to thwart official policy—a serious question in and of itself.

However, as we have attempted to point out throughout this chapter, we should distinguish between those proposals which will bring about professionalization by establishing the prerequisites from moves made in the interest of attaining professional status and professional authority. As we stated in the beginning, the clearest example of this, to our mind, is the emphasis on increased education without first considering (a) what is the function of the police, (b) what is the appropriate educational preparation, if any, and (c) what is the best place to receive this education—college, in service, police academy, all of the above (and if so, in what sequence). In fact, there is reason to suspect that recruiting potential officers with college degrees may prove dysfunctional unless the nature of the work and the internal reward structure are reconsidered in light of the interests of these new recruits.

The bright spot in the professionalization picture is the potential impact of the police-union movement on the potential professionalization of police supervisory and managerial personnel. To the extent that unionization will drive a wedge between patrolmen and the sergeants, lieutenants, and captains and force a recognition of their differential responsibilities within the organization, we can hope that this realization will open the door to the professionalization of management in police agencies.

In Chapter 7 we consider the impact of the union on the chief's ability to manage and in Chapter 8 we look at the impact of the union on law enforcement policy formulation.

7

Police-Union Impact on the Chief's Ability to Manage

A major concern of any manager faced with unionization for the first time is "what will be the impact of the union on my ability to manage, that is, my freedom to allocate the resources of the organization." In this chapter we consider the impact of the union on resource allocation.

Earlier chapters have emphasized the question "who is management." Our purpose there was to emphasize the fact that a multiplicity of "managers" become involved in the *determination* of the terms and conditions of work in the police agency. In this chapter we are concerned with the *impact* of these predetermined terms and conditions on the department head responsible for the delivery of law enforcement services in the community—the chief of police.

The examples presented here are necessarily reported in summary form. In some cases the reader may detect errors of fact or feel that some conclusion is erroneous. We refer the reader to our discussion of this problem in Chapter 1. We believe some errors are unavoidable; however, the amount of data is sufficiently large so that what patterns do emerge transcend individual error terms when the whole body of data is considered. As the authors of the encyclopedic *Impact of Collective Bargaining on Management* took great pains to point out, collective bargaining is diverse in character and results: each relationship is unique; generalizations that unions usually or always have this or that *particular* effect are hazardous; results of particular techniques of problem-solving vary with the economic, technological, and labor-relations environment; contract clauses do not necessarily reflect labor-relations practice; and leadership changes lead to dramatic changes in the character of labor-management relations.[1] In the following material we have emphasized the kinds of issues and problems constantly being discussed and the range of alternative resolutions achieved by the parties. Most of all, we attempt to stress the commonality of issues.[2]

The Scope of Bargaining: Wages

In this section we will deal with cash wages, the concept of police/fire parity, pay steps and differentials, and pensions.

Wages

The majority of the unions in our sample bargain over wages. However, in Cleveland, Oakland, and San Francisco wages are determined by the conditions of the city charter. In Baltimore and Los Angeles, wages are determined through lobbying with the mayor and/or the city council.

In 1967 the Cleveland police and firefighters supported a charter amendment which automatically set police salaries at 3 percent above police salaries in any city in the state over 50,000 in population; the firefighters got parity in a companion amendment. The city, which had opposed the amendment in the referendum, ceased bargaining with the police on the grounds that their wages and benefits were now mandated by charter. Thus the fringe benefits won by other city employees were not given to the police. This has put a certain amount of pressure on the police-union leaders. Furthermore, while sometimes the 3 percent amendment has paid off when other city employees have not gotten similar raises, at other times the city employees have outstripped the police. However, a complicating factor has been the fact that Cleveland's poor financial position led in 1971 to a freeze on negotiated increases for everyone but police and fire. This was because the police and fire were protected by the charter. This bolstered the union's belief in the charter route. However, economic realities could not be ignored and the city responded by laying off 193 police officers, many of whom were later rehired with funds under the Emergency Employment Act.[3]

In Oakland, the city charter provides that the police shall receive an annual percentage increase based on the annual percentage increase in hourly earnings of production and related workers in the San Francisco/Oakland area. In 1970 the union won a court test in which the court was asked to choose between the city's position that the charter treated the comparison figures as a ceiling and the union's position that the comparison figures were to be considered a floor. Across the Bay in San Francisco, the city charter specifies that police may be paid up to the highest pay for police in any California city over 100,000 in population. This led to a situation in which the San Francisco police sought parity with the master patrolmen in Berkeley. In Berkeley, the master patrolman rank is reserved for those with a college education who have met certain other requirements as well; a patrolman in San Francisco needs only a high school diploma or its equivalent. The city attorney ruled that the duties performed by a Berkeley master patrolman were essentially the same as San Francisco patrolmen and thus the city was bound to pay the same rate. The situation in San Francisco is in flux: the law in California allows for local meet-and-confer ordinances and, as explained earlier the new leadership of the SFPOA is committed to collective bargaining.

In Baltimore, police wages are established by the Board of Estimate which makes recommendations to the city council. The council may delete but it may not add. The mayor controls the board through his appointive power and the two police unions have very little power. In Los Angeles, the union cooperated in implementing a pay plan (the Jacobs Plan), which includes a provision projecting suggested wage increases to the council on the basis of certain benchmark jobs. Thus the plan calls for pay raises each July based on a trend line from the previous July to the current April. In 1971, the July '70-April '71 trend line called for a 7.8 percent increase. However, between April and July the benchmark wages fell off so that 5.5 percent would be a more accurate reflection of labor-market conditions. The result of this imperfection was an impasse between the mayor, the council, and the Police and Fire League. No wage increase had been agreed upon by July.

Three other wage situations are worthy of note: each involves a relationship between wages and new positions. In Buffalo in 1968, the police commissioner requested a 25 percent increase for his men who felt their salaries were too low and who were talking job action. A fact-finder recommended 15 percent for all city employees. The police demanded 20 percent. A later fact-finder recommended paying the extra 5 percent. The city refused. Meanwhile a proposal for fifty extra police officers arose in the city council. The union strongly opposed it, demanding that the money be spent on higher wages. The city ultimately did pay 20 percent after a city labor-relations agency so recommended in the face of a strike threat. The request for fifty new positions was withdrawn,[4] and the firefighters received an additional 5 percent to maintain parity.[5] In a smaller city, the union's high wage policy has contributed to a management policy of reduction by attrition. Even though the town has grown, the department has shrunk by five or six men. The union is unconcerned. They say that if the time ever comes when there are not enough men to answer a citizen request for assistance, there will be sufficient political pressure for new men and those new men will get top dollar because of the union's efforts. In Seattle, one of the local papers criticized the mayor for signing a very generous two-year contract with the union, claiming that the city's plan to create 100 new police positions would have to be revised downward because of the large pay raises.[6]

To summarize, most of the unions in our sample bargained over wages traditionally. Three cities had charter amendments which set wages; two cities still went through the mayor and council for benefits. In only the three cities mentioned above (and possibly Cleveland, although there the problem was more generalized) was there an obvious inverse relationship between wages and employment.

Parity

Police/fire wage parity is one of the principle issues in police bargaining. Of course, the parity is in monthly wage only since there is nearly always a great difference between fire and police hours (usually of the magnitude of 56-48 fire to 42-37 police). Parity has already been discussed in Chapter 5; we briefly review some relationships here. Vallejo, California is the only city in our sample to have broken parity. New Haven, Hartford, and Buffalo tried. In San Francisco, Cincinnati, and Cleveland the city charter requires parity. Seattle and New York are cities where the police used to hang on the firefighters coattails but now this situation is reversed. In Baltimore, the firefighters still lead the way. In Pittsburgh and Detroit, arbitrators have actually given firefighters larger increases than police officers.

Of course, the premier pay-ratio dispute of interest in discussing the impact on management is the one involving police patrolmen, police sergeants, firefighters, and fire lieutenants in the city of New York.[7] Originally, the city had agreed to patrolman/firefighter parity and a ratio of sergeant to patrolmen of 3.5:3. They had also agreed to a ratio of 3.9:3 between fire lieutenants and firefighters. When the Sergeants Benevolent Association successfully established parity between police sergeants and fire lieutenants, this caused the police patrolmen to seek a raise to restore the 3.5:3 ratio in the department and then the firefighters wanted to be brought back in to a parity relationship with the patrolmen, leaving the lieutenants out of line. The city was able to resolve the conflict but in the process incurred a retroactive liability to the patrolmen of approximately $2,700 per man and to officers of approximately $3,300 per man. As was discussed in Chapters 4 and 5, a combination of internal union politics and foot-dragging by the city with respect to its retroactivity obligations led to the one-week strike of January, 1971.[8]

In summary, the impact of police unions on the parity issue, at least in our sample, has been slight. In some cases, the unions have chosen to work along with the firefighters. In other situations, they have been stopped by the firefighters political power. Thus in New Haven, a fire slowdown and picketing led to a contract which will restore parity in 1974. In Hartford, the firefighters signed first with a most-favored nation clause; a similar agreement was under consideration in New York City at the time of our visit. In San Francisco in 1970, the police tried a multi-issue charter amendment to, among other things, eliminate the original 1963 firefighter-sponsored amendment on parity. It lost 3 to 1, partly because of the firefighter campaign against it.

Pay Steps and Salary Differentials
among Ranks

In the police service a patrolman will reach maximum career salary (minus cost of living and longevity) in three to five years. Most proposals for change in the delivery of police services have suggested that this range be increased so that a man might develop a career in patrol without having to seek promotion to supervisor or investigator only to get a pay raise. The unions in our sample have been relatively quiet on this issue. In one California city, the union proposed that five equal salary steps be created in *each* rank and that a man advance one step *within* his rank on the anniversary date of his employment, until he had reached the maximum. This was rejected by the city. In Buffalo, the union was able to successfully negotiate a reduction in the number of steps to maximum patrolman pay from five to two. In part, this was a response by the bargaining representative to the threat of a new patrolman-only organization within the department. The city further eliminated increment steps for all superior officer ranks.

The Jacobs Plan in Los Angeles appears to conform to good personnel practice. With the participation of the Police and Fire League, the Jacobs organization developed a plan creating steps within each rank that were to be filled on the basis of merit. In the patrol division there would be patrolmen I, II, III, and III + 1 (a leadman but not a supervisor). As indicated, the union was quite supportive of the plan, but it did exact some tolls in the implementation process. The plan was originally supposed to eliminate longevity payments but the union insisted they stay in. Similarly it was expected that if a man was reduced in rank, his pay would also be reduced. The union has attempted, especially in the superior officer ranks, to let pay stay at the highest level achieved even if a man is reduced. While the union did inflict some costs on the plan's implementation, this is the one example we can offer from our sample where the union did cooperate in such a project.

Several unions have been involved in raising the percentage differentials between ranks. The experience in Seattle is instructive. Police lieutenants used to make $30 per month more than sergeants but sergeants collected premium pay for overtime while lieutenants did not, thus giving the sergeants higher take home pay. The new 15 percent flat differential will help alleviate this problem. In New Haven, twenty-five years of across-the-board increases had narrowed the differential between patrolmen and sergeants. The three-year contract negotiated in 1968 increased wages on a percentage basis (15, 10, and 10) and the 1971 demand was for a fixed 10 percent between the ranks. The men believed that their struggle to get promoted to sergeant and have more responsibility was not properly rewarded with only an additional $70 per month or so more. Perhaps the best example of union policy toward pay differentials comes from Boston, where in 1968-69 bargaining the Superior Officers Federation secured a contractual set of fixed percentage differentials (22.5 percent for sergeants over patrolmen, 15 percent for lieutenants over sergeants, and 15 percent for captains over lieutenants) in response to negative membership reaction to sharply increased pay for patrolmen.

In summary, like their counterparts in the private sector and elsewhere in the public sector, police unions are interested in the differentials between ranks and steps within ranks. In our sample, however, the level of activity was not exceptional. This may just be a function of not having gotten around to it yet, given the short duration of the bargaining relationship.

Pensions and Retirement Issues

Many of the unions in our sample lobbied in the state legislature for pension benefits—a process discussed in Chapter 5. In this section we will discuss several incidents which are representative of other behavior in the pension and retirement areas. Particularly, we will look at two cities where referenda were taken to the voters and three cities where pensions are a matter between the union and the council.

In one city the union went to the voters in three successive years with three pension charter amendments—each was successful. The first amendment restructured the pension system, increased benefits, provided for widow and orphan benefits and added a 2 percent cost-of-living clause. Contributions by employees were raised by 1 percent—this contribution to be placed in common stocks to finance the cost-of-living increases. The second amendment raised to 65 percent the amount of the pension trust which could be invested in common stocks and increased the number of retirees eligible for the cost of living kicker. The third amendment raised everyone to a $350 maximum pension—retired as well as active. (See Chapter 5 for a description of the effort expended on this third amendment.)

In Detroit, an amendment proposed by the city would have raised the requirements for qualifying for a pension. Under the old system a man was eligible for one-half pay after twenty-five years with no age minimum, and with pay raises every time the actives received a raise. The 1968 city proposal called for one-half pay after thirty years, an age fifty-five minimum eligibility and raises based on the cost of living. The new proposals were to apply only to men hired after the plan went into effect. Police and fire teamed up to fight the plan but they failed to persuade the council not to put it on the ballot and despite a several hundred-thousand-dollar campaign, the plan was adopted by the voters.

In a New England city, bargaining resulted in a study commission being appointed to look at the pension issue. The union, however, decided to go to the city council with two proposals—a twenty-five-year mandatory retirement bill (said to be aimed at "getting" the current chief) and a twenty-year pension. The mandatory retirement was defeated but the pension bill went through. The mayor vetoed the bill claiming that this was not only a bargainable issue but was in fact on the table at that time. The council overrode the veto but the mayor refused to implement the act. At the time of our field visit three firefighters who sought twenty-year retirement were testing the issue in court.

In 1968 the Omaha union in conjunction with the firefighters pushed for an omnibus referendum which included early retirement and vesting of pension rights. The referendum failed but in 1970 the union got both through the city council: a policeman can retire after twenty years with 40 percent pension but must wait to age fifty-five to collect. In Buffalo the union went to mediation and fact-finding before they got the pension requirements reduced from half-pay after twenty-five years to half-pay after twenty years.

In New York City where detective is an assignment rather than a rank, the Detectives Endowment Association has actively sought tenure provisions to keep men from summarily being returned to uniform duty. Failing this they were able (with PBA support) to get a state bill passed which allows a detective's pension to be determined by the highest detective rating he attains even if he is "flopped back into the bag" (returned to uniformed duty).

In summary one can see that there is a diversity to the way in which unions approach the pension issue. Our purpose in this section was to present samples of union behavior which are perhaps better understood in the context of the impact of the failure to rationalize bargaining structure but which deserved mention here.

The Scope of Bargaining:
Hours of Work

In this section we consider the questions of instituting a fourth shift, shift changes, the shorter workweek, paid lunch, overtime, night-shift differential pay, court time, call-in, call-back, standby, out-of-turn work, and roll-call pay. The first three topics are covered under the heading "Direct Impact on Scheduling" and the remainder under the subhead "Indirect Impact."

Direct Impact on Scheduling

The Fourth Shift. One of the recommendations made most often by writers in the police management field and by consultants who evaluate police departments is that the patrol force be deployed on some rational basis related to crime patterns and other needs. Communities traditionally have deployed men in three shifts of approximately eight hours each. Most research has shown that the greatest number of calls for service probably come between the hours of 6 P.M. to 2 A.M. In most cities this period lies within two shifts—the 4-12/12-8 or 3-11/11-7, both of which are equally staffed, meaning an excess of men before 6 P.M. and after 2 A.M. and too few from 6 P.M. to 2 A.M. Thus the recommendation of consultants has been to establish a fourth shift to begin around 6 P.M. and run until the end of the peak crime period.

The question of establishing a fourth shift in the face of union pressure was explicit in only four cities in our sample. In Cleveland, the proposal came from the CPPA in response to a management proposal for a four-day week with ten hour days. In New Haven, management wanted a volunteer tactical squad to work the fourth shift with $500 per year extra pay. The union refused, saying it would agree to doubling up on the 4-12. The city refused the counterproposal and the police used their off-duty time to picket in civilian clothes.[9] When both sides returned to the bargaining table they agreed to a compromise in which the idea for a fixed fourth shift was dropped in return for which the chief got the right to use new men during their first two years of service anywhere he wanted.[10] In Boston, the union wanted an eight-hour day rather than the ten hours then in effect on day shifts.[11] The union went to the state legislature where they were able to obtain a permissive local option bill allowing the eight-hour day if adopted by the city council. The union then lobbied in the city council where they lined up sufficient support to go to the city and through bargaining work out an agreement providing eight-hour shifts, a night-shift differential and, for the city, the right to establish a fourth shift from 6 P.M. to 2 A.M.

In the New York State Legislature during the 1960s, New York City tried many times to change a 1911 state law mandating three eight-hour shifts of equal strength. The PBA took the position that there were not enough men to man three shifts let alone four and that it should be a bargainable issue. The city took the position that this was a management prerogative. In 1969 a bill was passed which gave New York City the right to establish a fourth shift. A fourth shift then was established but it was manned with volunteers as a compromise to avoid a full-scale confrontation. In the most recent contract the parties have agreed to the assignment of a significantly larger number of men to the 4-12 shift, meeting management's manpower needs while still meeting the union's objections to a mandatory fourth shift.

In a third city, the establishment of a fourth shift was not an issue but the assignment of men to the shift became an issue. The union insisted that the assignment of relief men to the 6 P.M. to 2 A.M. shift be solely on the basis of seniority in order to avoid the practice of punitive assignment to that shift. The city accepted this suggestion and made all shift assignments on the basis of seniority with the low seniority men alternating between 10 A.M. to 6 P.M. and 6 P.M. to 2 A.M. Those others who wish to work 6 P.M. to 2 A.M. may do so on a voluntary basis by seniority.

Shift Changes. Changing the hours of shifts was an issue in four cities (although in New York City the issue was still on the table and there was no indication of what might happen). In one of the three cities the chief already had a 6 P.M. to 2 A.M./2 A.M. to 8 A.M./8 A.M. to 6 P.M. arrangement. The 2 A.M. to 8 A.M. shift was a skeletal force. What he sought was the ability to move men freely from one shift to another so that he could beef up the 6 P.M. to 2 A.M. shift. While he had not yet made any changes, he did indicate that he would neither consult the union nor warn them ahead of time even though a bargaining relationship exists in the city.

In a second city the IACP had recommended that a new shift structure be instituted ostensibly to break up a graft operation which had existed in the 8 P.M. to 4 A.M. shift. The rank and file threatened a strike if the shifts were changed but the union leaders were able to talk them out of it. A few months later the new shifts were implemented without trouble. The union then sent two men on a fact-finding trip in 1969 to gather information with which to discredit the IACP. A publicity campaign was launched charging the IACP was unqualified; that it had caused havoc elsewhere; that the shift changes were upsetting the personal lives of the men, and that there was a lack of adequate coverage from midnight to 2 A.M. However, the department held tight until early 1971 when in a unilateral decision they went to a schedule only one hour different from the original schedule.

In a third city, the chief proposed, then put into effect, a plan to change the shift starting time by moving it ahead one hour and to rotate squad-car crews every three months. The union threatened to go to court but never did. They did, however, put a lot of pressure on the chief by way of the council and the mayor. A year later the chief finally restored the *status quo* on rotation but said he had accomplished his goal of breaking up departmental cliques.

Shorter Workweek. In one eastern city, the police had been working a forty-hour week. They wanted shorter hours and the city agreed to a 5-2, 4-2 plan which made weekly hours average out 38.7. In return the city won the right to fill many jobs with civilians, thus freeing sworn men for street duty to make up for the man hours of sworn service lost in the change. In a New England city, management negotiated a 4-2 plan which left the department six men short. The city, however, refused to provide the extra men so the chief is forced to call back people at time and one-half whenever someone is sick. In another New England city, the police were asking for a thirty-two-hour week in the 1971 negotiations as part of their continuing parity drama with the city and the firefighters.

Indirect Impact on Scheduling

Paid Lunch and Roll-Call Pay. These two union demands are difficult to separate. The work day for a police officer involves a roll call prior to the shift which may run as long as one-half hour; this is not part of the shift. To compensate, many departments allow lunch to be taken on company time during the eight-hour shift. The catch is that the lunch time is not really the officer's: he is on call and cannot get a haircut, go shopping, or run some other errand.

In Los Angeles, the work day was eight hours to be worked in eight hours and forty-five minutes. Officers report forty-five minutes before the shift and then take a forty-five-minute break during their eight-hour tour. However, in some sectors the men were unable to get away for lunch. The union suggested overtime pay for those men who could not get lunch. The chief refused and the union filed suit. The judge awarded the suit to the union subject to appeal and ordered the city to set up an escrow account for back pay. The chief responded by cutting the roll call to 23 minutes and lunch to 23 minutes. The Oakland union also won paid lunch time by court action.

In a third West Coast city, the chief changed the work day from eight hours (with an implicit paid lunch on company time) to eight and one-half hours (with a one-half hour unpaid lunch). The union claimed he was violating the contract clause calling for an eight-hour work day. The chief said the men still "worked" eight hours. The union said they were still on duty while eating. The chief didn't budge and the union filed suit asking for a return to the eight-hour shift. The department went back to eight hours afraid of the retroactive overtime bill if the union won. However, the union lost. The judge ruled that an eight-and-one-half hour shift was legal. The department did not reschedule eight-and-one-half hour shifts because the union said it would appeal the decision. The union did not appeal and the eight-and one-half-hour shift was expected to be a big issue in the upcoming negotiations.

In an eastern city the police get one hour for lunch but they are on call throughout the hour. One district commander was receiving grievances from men who were missing the whole lunch period every day of the week. Faced with a shortage of manpower he finally agreed with the union that he would overlook a relaxed atmosphere in low crime periods if the men would continue to respond during lunch hours. This settlement was possible because shifts rotate weekly in their department giving each man only one week in three when he is on a high pressure tour that requires missing the midshift meal.

Cincinnati, Dayton, Buffalo, and New York City have all sought some form of roll-call pay. Cincinnati dropped the demand during bargaining; the Dayton FOP has filed suit seeking this benefit; in New York the issue was on the table. In Buffalo the union has been successful in getting fifteen minutes pay on both ends of the shift for turnout and end of shift time.

Roll call and paid lunch are important issues because many departments use this time for in-service training, announcements, or even closed circuit TV communication with the chief or commissioner. By putting a straight time or overtime price on these minutes, the union may cut them to a fraction of their previous importance. On the other hand, few other occupations require people to report early and stay late with little or no added compensation.

Overtime. Overtime is, of course, an accepted feature in the private sector. The Fair Labor Standards Act has guaranteed most workers time and one-half after forty hours in a week for more than thirty years. In the police service, however, paid overtime has been only of recent origin. Officers traditionally have been compensated for overtime with straight time compensatory time off or more recently with compensatory time off at a time and one-half rate. We present here some few interesting overtime situations. In three cities it was the department itself which brought on the pressure for premium pay for overtime. In Rochester, officers as late as 1970 were getting straight time compensatory (comp) time off for overtime work. In May of that year 150 day men were called in one evening because of rumors of possible civil strife in the minority community. The men rebelled at being called in for straight-time comp time and refused to go out on the street. They took a strike vote but the city refused to negotiate under a strike threat so the next day the men went out for six to eight hours. An amnesty agreement brought them back and ultimately a fact-finding panel awarded them the time and one-half among other benefits.

In 1966 the city council in Boston passed a time-and-one-half overtime ordinance which was vetoed by the mayor. While the council overrode the veto, the mayor refused to appropriate the funds. In 1967 just before the election to determine a bargaining agent for the city's police, the patrolmen's union filed a $300,000 suit against the city for thousands of hours of overtime worked during 1967 summer civil disturbances (and no doubt also for votes in the election). The first contract did give the union time and one-half for overtime.

In one western city the department had a practice of reassigning days off in order to avoid paying overtime to men. The union and the city were able to work out a procedure where reassignment of days off would be for emergency reasons only. In Los Angeles before the Jacobs Plan, the chief had the option of compensatory time off (comp time) or money for overtime. The Jacobs Plan called for money only but the men complained so now once again it is comp time or money but at the police officer's discretion (rather than the chief's) until the money runs out.

In Omaha, in 1968, the police and fire both got overtime at time and one-half by going the referendum route. Cleveland had a plan which awarded straight time comp time for overtime. What an officer didn't take during his career could be converted to *cash* at retirement. The austerity program forced the city to reconsider this policy and now while all previous rights are grandfathered, any new comp time must be taken every thirty days or lost.

The following situation in an eastern city is indicative of the complications which can arise over the overtime issue. Detective is an assignment in this particular city and detectives work a forty-five hour week relative to the patrolmen's forty hours. The union claimed that the 8 percent detective premium it had negotiated was in lieu of overtime for those five hours per week; the city said no—it was a recognition of promotion. Now, however, the union and the city have switched sides. The union agrees with the city's earlier position that the 8 percent is a premium and wants the city to reduce the detective work week to forty hours or pay five hours per week at time and one-half. The city now says that the 8 percent was all along an overtime allowance in recognition of the extra hours worked by detectives.

In summary, the overtime issue is one where the unions are moving toward the standard time and one-half after eight hours in a day and forty hours in one week. This aspect of overtime, however, will probably not have as great an effect on scheduling and deployment as will penalties imposed on call-back, call-in, and standby, which we consider next.

Call-in, Call-back, and Standby. Call-back is the situation in which a man has left the station house and is called back for duty before eight hours has elapsed. Call-in is a call to work on an off day. Standby is a requirement that a man be available on his off day or off time. His physical presence may or may not be required but at least he may not be far away from a telephone, imbibe alcoholic drinks or in general make independent use of his off time. This last category became a real issue during the civil disturbances of the late 1960s.

In 1968 Boston negotiated a four-hour minimum for call-in. Cincinnati has time and one-half comp time or straight time cash (officer's choice until the money runs out) but no minimum for call-back and call-in. Seattle, however, in its 1970 contract provided for time and one-half for call-ins with a four-hour minimum and 50 percent straight-time pay for standby. Rochester provides a four-hour minimum for call-backs and a two-hour minimum for holdovers on a shift, both at time and one-half with the officer's choice of pay or comp time. Dayton has a two-hour recall guarantee. In one city the call-in clause got into the contract because the men used to work parades and other events on their off days for no extra compensation.

In Boston men were often moved from one shift to another with little or no advance warning. The department claimed that this was necessary but the union negotiated a clause requiring that all out-of-turn work be compensated at time and one-half unless a man is placed on the shift for more than fourteen days. It is clear from talking to management personnel that this kind of clause has indeed infringed on the traditional prerogatives of the chief as have call-back and call-in. However, no one in this or any other department complained to us that they had been hamstrung. Rather the feeling we got was one of being "inconvenienced." A couple of departments who found their overtime budgets pressed by the demands of the contract were able to get supplementary funds as the occasion demanded.

In the case of standby we found that most abuses were covered by the call-back and call-in procedures. The chief had ceased requiring excessive standby at home and the amount of excessive call-ins for parades, riots, and special events had also been decreased; as management found money to be a scarcer resource, they began to husband it more carefully. In one department there was a cash penalty for standby and a group of detectives were able to collect a sizable back-pay settlement because an overzealous detective sergeant had ordered them to standby for over three months after the order prohibiting standby was issued.

Court-Time Adjustments. In the past police officers were scheduled to go to court on off days at straight time pay or no pay at all. The unions have moved rapidly on this front in many cities. Most of the cities now provide some kind of premium pay, although the form may vary. Rochester has a four-hour minimum at straight time; Boston has time and one-half with a three-hour minimum; Cincinnati has straight time with a two-hour minimum (three hours for grand jury or common pleas court); this is an improvement from the previous situation in which an officer got a two-hour slip regardless of hours actually worked. One western city provides a three-hour guarantee at time and one-half. Department records indicate that most men actually come out ahead. Pittsburgh pays a $5.00 witness fee for each appearance as does Baltimore.

The question of court appearances has raised a managerial response in three of the cities in our sample. In Buffalo where an officer gets a four-hour minimum guarantee at straight-time rates, a city court judge warned that he would not permit the repeated appearances of officers due to continuances because it cost the city too much. In addition, the city judges voted to have police fill out a sworn statement when making misdemeanor arrests which could be forwarded with the prisoner, thus obviating the need for the officer's appearance.[12] In a city where the city pays time and one-half for actual time, the chief has worked out an agreement with the juvenile court in the county seat whereby arresting officers will not have to appear. He is also exploring with the union other ways to cut court-time costs. In a New England city the chief has two problems. The first is money, since the contract provides for a four-hour guarantee even in the case of continuances. The second is a provision that a man who spends *over* four hours in court in a given day cannot be called to work a second or third shift that day. In an attempt to deal with both problems, the chief plans to station a man with a two-way radio in court to call detectives as their cases are called.

In other cities the police have made efforts to talk with the presiding judge about schedule coordination but they have been rebuffed.[13] Court time has always been an abuse to police officers. Now that they are able to put a cost on the practice, the burden shifts to management. If experience follows the private-sector model, what started as penalty overtime should in due course come to be considered as a right, further complicating the management problem.

Night-Shift Differential. A second and/or third-shift pay differential (usually seven to fifteen cents per hour) is fairly common in the private sector. In the police service, however, it is a relatively new benefit. The experience in Boston is instructive. The department had worked under a three-shift schedule with shifts of 10, 6¾, and 7¼ hours respectively. When the union sought to negotiate three eight-hour shifts, they also requested a $15.00 per week night-shift differential to compensate the second and third-shift men for the loss in shorter hours. The city, in return got the right to establish a fourth shift.[14] In a New England city the union was offered an increase of $5.00 per month in the uniform allowance but asked for and received a $1.00 per week night-shift differential. The union had hoped this would open the door to future increases once the principle was established. So far, however, this has not happened. In San Francisco, the night-shift differential was included in the charter amendment which also asked for an end to firefighter parity. As indicated, the amendment lost 3 to 1.

While there have not yet been any changes in manpower allocation as a result of these differentials, we include the night-shift differential in this section to call attention to the potential impact of this benefit.

The Scope of Bargaining: Conditions of Work

These are the nondollar conditions of work over which there has been conflict in several of the jurisdictions visited. Each subject clearly has an impact on the chief's ability to manage. However, in each case there are two sides to the story. Our format in this section is to discuss the issue briefly and cite some examples of behavior from the field.

Manning

The Use of Civilians. Management would like to introduce civilians into jobs previously performed by sworn personnel in part because the sworn personnel are not really trained to handle these administrative and clerical tasks and in part because the patrolmen's new salaries have priced them out of the market for these jobs. Most unions in our sample opposed civilianization, although few were successful. Union reasons for opposition primarily focus on some variant of the need for security and confidentiality, the need for the arrest power (available only to sworn personnel) in order to gain respect, or the need for experience in the field to properly perform the function (as in handling the dispatcher's job). The most novel reason given by one major union president was that civilians don't always obey orders while sworn officers always do; and civilians always leave for lunch at noon whereas sworn officers stay until the work is done. The economics of the situation is such that civilianization will probably become more important in the future.

In two cities the unions allowed civilianization with only token opposition. In one of these cities the chief took approximately sixty sworn officers out of non-law-enforcement jobs (clerical, desk, parking) and put them on the street, replacing them with clerks, metermaids, and technicians. The union *did* object, however, when the chief wanted to eliminate the two men who manned the station-house desk, citing the contract which required two men. The chief cited the fact that the jobs previously performed by these men were being handled elsewhere. The stalemate was resolved when the chief had two city carpenters come in to physically remove the desk. In a second city the union has not objected to sworn officers being freed from routine jobs for street duty. Most of the civilians will be used to handle citizen calls in the communications room.

In Buffalo the department chose to abandon a plan for upgrading civilian-defense auxiliary police after union opposition. The union had proposed that the money to be used for upgrading be applied to overtime for current officers.[15] In a western city the chief has been reclassifying positions from sworn to civilian. While the union objects, the chief insists that reclassification is not a negotiable issue and the union has not challenged his position. In another city, management has had mixed success. Civilians were hired for station-house clerical jobs but the union did block the introduction of civilians into the fingerprint technician job on the grounds that the jobs involved a high degree of internal departmental security. The civil service commission agreed and refused reclassification. In Boston, the mayor proposed to hire fifty civilian traffic directors and fifty civilian clerks. The city council supported the union in defeating the civilian traffic director plan so the mayor went to the state legislature to get a bill allowing him to bypass the council in reclassification cases. The union beat him again. The council did, however, allow the mayor to fund the fifty civilian clerks. In a midwestern city, the chief proposed a plan to give traffic enforcement duties to civilians: a traffic control officer—I would handle parking violations and a uniformed TCO-II would direct traffic. The personnel board approved the plan over union opposition but the union managed to kill the plan in the council.

A hopeful sign—in the sense of promoting the development of professionalism in the leadership of police agencies—is the number of departments in our sample in which management brought in civilians in top line and staff jobs without significant union opposition—New York City, New Haven, Hartford, Baltimore, and Dayton. This is consistent with our observation in Chapter 6 that the potential for professionalization is probably greatest at the management level.

One-Man Versus Two-Man Squad Cars. The number of men in a squad car is one of the most emotional issues we encountered. Management wants the freedom to assign one-man cars and two-man cars on the basis of its perception of the data on crime by areas and shifts; the unions want to maximize patrolman safety under street conditions they perceive as tantamount to wartime. In our sample we saw both aspects of the issue: cities where the union was attempting to pressure a move from one-man to two-man cars and cities where management was attempting to move from two-man cars to one-man cars.

In three of our cities there was an increase in two-man cars. Recently one New England city made fourteen of the thirty-four cars on the 6 P.M. to 2 A.M. shift two-man cars. These are the fourteen cars in the high-crime area and the move was probably the result of perceived need and union pressure; however, it was a unilateral management decision. Similarly, in a California city, where in 1970 the city went to all two-man cars on the swing shift where the union had been calling for two-man cars, there was a demonstrated need but the decision was made by management. In Boston where patrol cars had been 70 percent two-man, Mayor White gave the union 100 percent two-man cars prior to the gubernatorial primary in which the union subsequently endorsed him.

In three other cities, the movement was away from two-man cars toward single patrol. In one western city, even though a couple of officers had been injured in one-man cars over the eighteen months preceding our visit, and even though the union was pressuring for two-man cars, management unilaterally changed the ratio of one-man/two-man from 30/70 to 50/50. When the union objected, management indicated it was not the union's decision to make. In a midwestern city, the union has pressured for no more one-man cars and presented a general grievance to the chief. The result is a freeze on the *status quo*; one-man cars stay but there is no increase. In an eastern city an elaborate walkie-talkie communications system has staved off union pressure for two-man cars. The union has basically accepted manpower deployment as a management function.

In New York City the two-man car is a current center of contention. The commissioner has an arbitration award supporting his right to determine manning. However, the union is vehemently opposed and will not agree to one-man cars even in so-called safe districts. A letter accompanying the current contract says that the *status quo* shall be maintained through the current contract. In Cincinnati the city and union cooperated in seeking a mutually acceptable solution to the manning problem. When a Cincinnati police officer was shot, police wives and then the FOP demanded two-man cars. The union president appeared on TV and radio and before the city council. From the council he got a commitment for 300 new patrolmen (although he never got the men) to provide the manpower necessary to have two-man cars. To avoid the heavy overtime costs incurred by the two-man cars and to restore management flexibility in manning, the department proposed personal two-way radios in exchange for a return to one-man cars. The union president went along with the chief and arranged a meeting at which the chief was able to explain the change to the men. The agreement was accepted.

Promotions, Plainclothes, and Detectives

We discuss these three topics together because in the context of the police service any job change that takes a man out of the uniformed patrolman's function is considered a desirable move. The basic issue with respect to plainclothes and detective assignments is management's desire for flexibility weighed against the patrolmen's demand for job security. In the area of promotions, no consistent pattern has emerged. In some cases the unions wanted seniority to count more heavily, in other cases they wanted seniority to count less. Most unions in our sample, in fact, never got beyond the talk stage in the area of promotions.

Detective can be an assignment or a rank. If a rank, then a man would take an examination and achieve tenure if promoted to detective. Where detective is an assignment the chief retains the right to move men back into uniform. Plainclothesman is an assignment for patrolmen who will be called upon to do undercover work. It, too, is a job in which the chief exerts complete control on tenure. In Boston the union and management negotiated a clause which provides that any plainclothesman who does detective work for one year will automatically get a detective rating and an eight-dollar-per-week raise. In New York the commissioner has decided to treat plainclothesmen as detective trainees. It is also in New York where the issue of detective tenure has been most hotly debated. In 1970 the Detectives Endowment Association was able to get a bill through the city council giving detectives tenure after six years. Once tenure was obtained a detective could be removed only after a departmental hearing. The Mayor vetoed the bill and the union was unable to override the veto. As mentioned earlier, the Detectives' Endowment Association was able to guarantee a pension at the highest detective level attained by getting a bill passed in Albany.

A midwestern city serves as an example of labor-management cooperation in working out a potential problem. The chief wanted to make detective an assignment rather than a rank; he was concerned that once a man had achieved the civil service rank of detective by passing an examination he would be beyond the "reach" of the chief even if he were to "retire mentally on the job." The chief proposed the creation of a police specialist who could be returned to uniform at the chief's discretion. The union argued that this would open the door to favoritism, increase insecurity by bouncing people up and down from patrolman to detective and back, and increase the financial risk for an officer investing in civilian clothes for detective duty. The parties met and conferred and agreed to the creation of a specialist category which would be filled through competitive examination. Once a man became a specialist he could be shifted from plainclothes to uniform at the chief's discretion; however, his pay would stay at the specialist rate. As part of the agreement several bureaus formerly staffed by patrolmen also were upgraded to the specialist rank, presumably increasing the level of competency in each.

While the unions in our sample have been more vocal than active regarding promotions to rank, in Pittsburgh the union became concerned with the departmental practice of appointing acting inspectors from among the captains and lieutenants on the grounds that the promotions were more "permanent" than "acting," thus blocking promotions for those aspiring to the rank of lieutenant or captain (since vacancies in these ranks were not created as long as men held temporary promotions). Challenging the appointment of nineteen lieutenants and captains to the temporary rank of inspector, the union received a favorable verdict from the civil service commission. However, on advice of the city counsel the civil service commission reversed its finding and the union lost its appeals to the common pleas court and superior court.[16] In Seattle the union opposed a charter amendment that would replace the "rule of 3" in civil service promotion decisions with a "rule of 5 or 25 percent—whichever is greater." The union said it would mean the death of civil service and the return of politics to promotion decisions. They purchased radio, TV, and newspaper ads to fight the amendment but the amendment passed and later the union admitted that civil service had not died.

In a second West Coast city the chief informs the civil service commission when an examination is required and also informs them of the number of positions to be filled. The union lobbies with both the chief (over the timing and number of openings) and the civil service commission (over content, sources of questions, and the time it takes for the results to be returned after the examination). In Dayton the union filed suit to enforce the state law that says efficiency ratings should be 5 percent of the civil service examination; the city had been using efficiency ratings as 20 percent of the grade. Finally, in another midwest city, management proposed a combination of education and time in grade in order to take promotion exams. Whereas previously one might have taken the lieutenants exam after three years in grade, the new requirement was a combination of post-high-school education and time in grade equal to five. A lieutenant challenged the new rule and the city's solicitor declared it illegal. The union supported the city and the rule.

Seniority

Here we are concerned primarily with seniority as a decision variable in job and shift assignments. As is true in the private sector, seniority is seen by the men as a factor guaranteeing equal opportunity and a hedge against favoritism, while management views it as an infringement on their flexibility. The issue is the question of the senior-qualified man versus the "best" man.

In one city the union wanted a seniority provision to govern assignments to the 6 P.M. to 2 A.M. shift. The union claimed that the city had previously used 6 to 2 as a punitive assignment; the city now makes all shift assignments on the basis of seniority. In another city seniority on a *de facto* if not *de jure* basis now counts 50 percent toward job assignments and 100 percent in shift assignments. In an eastern city there has been *de facto* use of seniority in transfers and assignments. During our visit the union was attempting to get 100 percent seniority written into the contract on the grounds that it is impossible to accurately differentiate among officers when assigning them to different jobs, and that therefore seniority is the only fair way to make assignments. The city has refused on the grounds that a contract clause would prevent them from considering other relevant factors if they felt this was necessary. In one New England city the union pushed for seniority after complaining about the prevalence of politics in selecting people who would move from nights to days. They also sought seniority for promotion to details as well as to the juvenile, detective, and criminal identification bureaus. The latter issue is currently in arbitration. The chief would prefer a merit plan for promotions and shift changes but could not describe the harm seniority has caused. In another New England city the chief opposed the seniority clause in principle but when pressed could only fall back to the distinction between the "best" man and an "able" man. The union contends that the "best" man always involved politics and favoritism. In Pittsburgh the union had a bill introduced in the state legislature which provided that all transfers, assignments, and so forth would have to be made on the basis of seniority. The mayor strongly opposed the move, wrote letters to legislators, appeared at hearings and was able to get the bill killed in committee.[17] The union had offered to compromise but the mayor held out and won.

In Detroit the situation is somewhat confused. The union contract says that "seniority shall be a major factor in filling job openings provided that the employee is fully qualified otherwise." It also says that the "department shall not be jeopardized through artificial constraints resulting from the application of strict seniority." The contract further excludes seniority from applying to some of the specialized units and bureaus. In practice most assignments are made on the basis of seniority. However, the department does have the freedom to move less senior people on the strength of special talent or ability. While it has not tried to exercise the full strength of the contract language by mass personnel movements disregarding seniority, the department along with the union is testing the clause in a series of grievance arbitration cases. Finally, the Omaha contract provides for shift assignment by seniority. Men bid for shifts on February 1 and September 1 each year. Job assignments on each shift are solely a management prerogative. The chief and the union have been flexible in determining the application of the language, especially in cases dealing with specialized bureaus and the assignment of lieutenants, so that the clause does not seem to have worked unbearable hardships.

In summary the experience with seniority clauses in our sample seems to indicate that while the application of seniority to job and shift assignments in many cases is a significant change in procedure, no one has effectively shown that seniority is an obstacle to effective resource allocation. While police officials claim seniority precludes optimal allocation, we found no evidence to suggest that allocation was optimal in the absence of seniority.

Arbitrary Transfers

Transfers have been used in police agencies as a form of discipline or an indication of displeasure. The men objecting to this behavior have in some cases attempted to regulate the conditions under which disciplinary transfers can be made. Management on the other hand argues that sometimes transfers are essential for the good of the service. As examples, they offer the case of a white officer in the ghetto who if he is not transferred will kill someone or be killed or cause another officer's death. Or they cite the case of the man who may be on the take but against whom they cannot get conclusive proof. They will transfer him to break up the situation.

In Pittsburgh four white officers were transferred for overzealous police work in a ghetto situation. To protest the transfers the union engaged in a three-day "blue flu" which by the third day had infected one-quarter of the force. The issue was resolved when the parties held a public hearing before the city council and agreed to submit the issue to binding arbitration.[18] It is anticlimactic to mention that the arbitrator upheld the city's right to make the transfers.

Contract language in an eastern city specifies that a transferred officer must, on request, be given a specific reason in writing since "for the good of the service" would not be an acceptable reason. While on the surface this would seem to hamstring management, it takes on a different meaning when one considers the specific abuse the language was meant to correct: a previous change in political parties in the city government had led to a wholesale transfer of men within the department. The purpose of the clause was to eliminate this behavior. The fact that the language may also have important side effects is, of course, an important problem and one of which negotiators should be aware as they consider similar problems and remedies.

Moonlighting and Paid Details

Moonlighting, or the holding of a second job by sworn officers was not an issue in all the jurisdictions we visited, but it does illustrate a situation where collective bargaining can lead to a creative solution to a mutual need. Many departments are faced with demands for service they cannot meet because of resource scarcities. The men, on the other hand, often feel that the salary from the regular job is not sufficient to provide the style of life to which they would prefer to grow accustomed. One bridge between these two concerns is for off-duty police officers to perform police-type duty in their off hours at a comparable hourly wage. Police agencies frequently receive calls for uniformed officers to chaperone parties, to direct traffic at shopping centers, sports events, or construction sites, or to serve as private supplemental police for particular neighborhoods in the community. In New York City, police officers moonlight as cab drivers. In San Francisco a few police officers moonlight as bank tellers. The reported effect of this added presence has been to reduce robberies in both categories in the respective cities.

There are a number of problems connected with the department providing uniformed officers on a moonlighting basis. Some involve the city's liability in case of accident or death or civil suit against the officer from an incident which occurs during moonlighting. Other problems concern the nature of jobs and the number of hours of moonlighting permitted. Usually jobs are prohibited which would increase the probability of contact with undesirable elements in the community such as those persons engaged in vice or gambling. For this reason bartending is almost always excluded. The hours question is one of how many hours a man can work a second job without infringing on his ability to perform in his primary job.

Some unions (Providence, Cranston, Boston, New Haven) have negotiated a paid detail contract clause. Whereas previously moonlighting opportunities had been assigned on a favoritism basis, the clauses provide for sign-up lists, allocation of opportunities by seniority, minimum pay rates, and other conditions. As we indicated above, this is an emerging area and one where the liability problem may cause spottiness in the diffusion of the pattern. But it does represent an example of how the bargaining process has provided an integrative solution to a mutual problem.

Name Tags

One of the issues achieving prominence during the civil disturbances of the late 1960s was the question of name tags on uniforms. Protesters claimed that when police officers violated their civil rights they had no way of identifying the perpetrator because the badges and other identifying insignia had been removed. The officers countered that the badges had been removed to prevent their being used against the police as weapons. The men resisted sewn on name tags because they said this would open the door to harassment of their families by protesters who read the names off the tags during demonstrations. In Seattle the city painted badge numbers on the riot helmets and sewed them on overalls. While the men objected, the union took no action. In Detroit the union opposed the order to wear name tags on the grounds that they had not been consulted and that this was a violation of the maintenance of conditions clause in the contract. The issue went to arbitration with the city claiming the issue was not arbitrable. The arbitrator ruled it was arbitrable, ordered the department to confer with the union but said that the department did have the right to require name tags be worn. As a result, the tags are now worn.

We already mentioned in Chapter 5 the situation involving the Boston union and name tags but it bears repeating here. At a 1969 disturbance at Harvard

University, the Boston police removed their badges claiming that the stick pins could be used to jab them. Mayor White proposed sewing on name tags and the commissioner agreed. The union objected, claiming that this would lead to harassment of their families. The commissioner ordered the tags sewed on and arranged for union tailors to come to headquarters to sew them on. The police threw up a picket line and the union tailors refused to cross. The police-union attorney filed a grievance and the department agreed to hold off until the grievance was resolved.[19] The union lost the grievance and took it to arbitration. Simultaneously the union attorney introduced a local option permissive bill in the legislature which would, if adopted by a city, ban the wearing of name tags if identifying numbers were worn. The union got the bill through but the governor sent it back for redrafting. Finally, the governor signed it and the union got the bill passed in the city council. The arbitrator finally came down with his award supporting the city but by this time the issue was moot and the men do not wear name tags.

Sick Leave

Sick leave is not so much an issue over the generosity of the benefit as it is over the lengths to which a police agency will go to control abuses of the sick-leave privilege. In general, management is concerned that there are abuses of sick leave while the men object to the fact that management sends supervisors to their homes to verify illnesses. In three cities in our sample, however, management crackdowns led to quite significant decreases in sick-leave days taken. In one city, management made its move when it found that an excessive number of sick days were being taken on Friday and Saturday evenings. There is, of course, a potentially expensive interrelatedness between residency requirements and policing sick leave; for example, in New York City many of the men reside in the suburbs, and the sergeants who check on those claiming to be sick must travel long distances. The significant factor in this discussion, however, is that while the unions do object strenuously, they have taken no actions that would infringe on management's prerogatives in this area.

Uniform Changes

We include this issue less for content than as an example of an area where union-management cooperation has sometimes proved useful. Consider the following range of experiences: In one city the chief appointed a uniform committee composed of rank only. The men passed around a petition demanding that the chief rescind his plans for change. The black officers' association was also opposed because no black was on the panel. There was also talk of a no-confidence petition against the chief if he did not rescind his plans. Union leaders were able to head off this mini-revolt but they did inform the chief of their concern with his action. The result was the formation of a new broadly representative committee to advise him on the desirability of uniform changes and an extension of the deadline from July 1971 to July 1972. In Boston the mayor wanted the men to wear light blue shirts. When the union voiced objections on the grounds that these shirts made better targets for snipers, the issue was dropped. In two other cities, the unions would like to be represented on the uniform committee but presently are not. In Los Angeles the union representative is a nonvoting member of the committee but the scope of the committee's activities extends to weapons, questions of who pays for what, and so on, as well as the nature of the uniform. In Cincinnati the union president is a voting member of the committee.

Reorganization and Management Studies

In several cities in our sample major changes in procedure or complete reorganization were attempted. In some cases it was with the union's cooperation and in other situations over their opposition. In a third subset, the unions were opposed but the opposition was ineffective. We cite three examples of positive departmental-union cooperation. In one New England city, the new mayor in conjunction with the police union, but over the opposition of police management, brought in the Public Administration Service for a management survey; with the cooperation of the union and despite the opposition of some departmental leaders, the changes recommended by PAS were implemented. In a California city, the new chief introduced a large number of changes, including a new workweek of four ten-hour days but only after extensive consultation with the union and with his command staff. Almost all of these changes were implemented smoothly. A third example of cooperation would be the implementation of the Jacobs Plan in Los Angeles.

In three other cities, the unions have been neither supportive nor effectively deterrent. In Baltimore the IACP management survey led to the appointment of a new commissioner with broad sweeping powers to institute change. The two unions have not been pleased with all the changes instituted, but neither have they been effective in keeping change from occurring. The same is true of the situation in New York where sweeping changes are being instituted at the management level. While the line organizations have objected strenuously to some of these changes, they have not yet succeeded in stopping any of them. In a third city where the changes were largely in program style—the delivery of a new kind of law-enforcement service—the union has not been able to kill any programs, but it has managed to slow down implementation.

Two unions were quite active in opposing sweeping IACP recommendations for change in their departments and were at least partially successful in their attempts to frustrate change. The Pittsburgh FOP attempted to deprecate the IACP survey team's qualifications and engaged in several attempts to thwart proposals for changes such as merging traffic and patrol into one operations bureau, creation of a community-relations unit, creation of an inspection bureau with an internal-affairs division, the removal of vice control from detectives to inspection, and the creation of a master patrolman classification.[20] With the exception of the last, the city was able to implement each of the other changes over FOP objections. A West Coast union pursued much the same tactics against an IACP report which called for nearly 600 changes. In this case, the union was able to frustrate both consolidation of precincts and the implementation of a master patrolman concept.

Discipline, Grievance Procedures
and Civil Rights

It is important to recall that there is a major difference between the private sector and the police service with respect to discipline. In the private sector discipline can be imposed by the supervisor and the employee may grieve the disciplinary punishment through the regular grievance procedure—in most instances, all the way to neutral binding arbitration. In the police service grievances, if handled at all, are handled independently from the disciplinary procedure. Grievances may be handled formally or informally depending on the size or structure of the department. In many departments "the chief's door is always open" constitutes the entire grievance procedure. Discipline, however, proceeds through a trial board, the chief's office and perhaps the civil service commission, the police and fire commission, or the courts.

The role of the union has been to press for regularizing discipline procedures, minimizing *ad hoc* decision-making on punishment and eliminating certain kinds of punishment such as working days off, long suspensions with no right of appeal, and the use of penalty tours. In this section we will look at some examples of union influence on the regularization of discipline processes and union attitudes toward providing a defense. Subsequently, we will discuss grievance procedures.

Discipline—Procedures. The union pressure for civil rights for officers is intimately related to their concern with regularizing discipline procedures. The basic union complaint is that men charged with departmental or civilian infractions are denied the basic rights guaranteed by the constitution to felons and other persons accused of crimes, particularly the right to counsel and the right to remain silent. Some of the unions in our sample have moved directly to attain these rights; others have attained them *de facto* if not *de jure*; and still others have made institutional arrangements that protect them without raising the rights issue directly.

Since 1968 Boston, Buffalo, and New York City have contracted "bill of rights" guaranteeing Miranda rights to officers: the right to counsel at interrogations and hearings and a guarantee that what is said in the investigation will not be used against the accused officer in a criminal proceeding. In another city, the FOP sought to include a bill of rights in the contract; the city balked at the contract suggestion but agreed to a letter of intent. Detroit has no formal bill of rights but there exists a *de facto* working agreement that accords Miranda rights and provides that men will not have their testimony used against them in court. In San Francisco and Pittsburgh the unions have pushed requests for a bill of rights, with the San Francisco Police Officers' Association achieving success and Pittsburgh still seeking it.

In two cities the police commissioners decide punishment by choice of the men and the union, even though formal machinery exists outside this arrangement. In one eastern city, for example, internal investigation carries on its investigation; the man's commanding officer recommends punishment and the commissioner punishes. A man cannot be suspended unless he agrees. If he does not agree, formal charges can be brought in a trial board. The men, as indicated above, tend to prefer the commissioner to the trial board.

In another city a 1971 crime commission report characterized discipline in the department as practically nonexistent and inconsistent when applied. The new union leadership has expressed a desire to participate in the development of a fair and consistent system of discipline within the department. In an eastern city, union pressure for a fairer disciplinary system led to the formation of a new trial board system in January, 1971. The board consists of five officers, three of whom are lieutenants or higher picked by the city and two of whom are from among the bargaining unit members—patrolmen, detectives, and sergeants—and picked by the union. The accused has a right to union counsel or his own legal counsel. In Buffalo, the union contract spells out the discipline and discharge procedure. Internal investigation gathers information to determine if a man should be formally charged. If he is charged he can have an informal hearing with the commissioner. A man is also entitled to a formal hearing but most men prefer the informal hearing. The contract explicitly limits the punishments which may be imposed: reprimand, fine up to $100, suspension up to two months, demotion, dismissal. Everything else is proscribed.

Trial boards in Detroit have become much more legalistic since the advent of the union. In presence are not only the union attorney and an assistant corporation counsel, but also a neutral legal scholar from one of the city's law schools to advise the chairman of the trial board. The union can appeal the severity of a board decision but not the issue of guilt or innocence; nor are punishment transfers used prior to a trial board ruling and the rulings themselves are more consistent. Widely varying penalties for the same offense have been eliminated.

In 1963 the union in Pittsburgh was able to lobby a bill through the legislature which drastically modified the trial board system in order to correct abuses that had existed. Unfortunately, the new system has also brought problems, at least from management's point of view, since not much discipline is handed out.[21] Under this new system an accused officer puts the names of twenty-five officers in a hat (presumably his friends); the department puts the names of twenty-five lieutenants in the hat. Seven names are drawn and the accused strikes two and the department strikes two—the remaining three issue a final and binding decision. The city is most upset with the results of this procedure and has unsuccessfully attempted to get the legislature to repeal the bill; unsuccessfully tried to get an arbitrator to rule the system invalid, and at the time of our visit was in court trying to get the system declared invalid.

Discipline—Union Policy on Defense. Unlike unions in the private sector, police unions do not automatically defend an accused member. Not only does policy vary by city, it is not consistent across organizations affiliated with the same national organizations. The biggest distinction is between charges raised internally by department investigators and civilian complaints. A second distinction made is between an accused who is "clean" and an accused who is "dirty." We illustrate with the following examples.

In New York City the sergeants' union will take an accused member through his criminal trial; the PBA, detectives, lieutenants, and captains will take a man through the grand jury. In Detroit the DPOA represents the accused through internal investigation, trial board, and court. The same is true in Baltimore, Dayton, Cleveland (CPPA; the FOP will represent a man or pay his own attorney up to $1,500 maximum), Oakland, Vallejo, and Hartford. In Oakland and Hartford, appeals are not automatic but are subject to the decision of the union attorney.

In one eastern city the FOP will defend a man on departmental charges but not civilian complaints; in a midwestern city a man will be defended by the FOP on all civilian complaints but only on request will the union consider a defense against departmental charges. When a request is received the union investigates and if the union finds the accused innocent, the seventeen-man executive board is polled to see if he will be allowed to use the union attorney. The union would prefer not to defend on departmental charges because it puts them in an adversary relationship with one of their own. In a third FOP city, the union will conduct a hearing before its legal aid committee—if the accused is found not guilty, the union will defend him.

Police agencies often will let a man resign rather than face charges. This will allow both the man and the department to get by without further tarnishing their respective reputations. Unfortunately, it also undermines citizen trust in the department and lowers the cost of getting caught for certain types of wrongdoing. Another secondary but important effect is that sometimes an innocent man will be forced into a resignation. One union is attempting to negotiate an agreement that men to whom the chief offers this option shall have twenty-four hours to reconsider after signing the resignation papers.

Grievance Procedures. A grievance can be a violation of the contract, a violation of established practice, a violation of rules or regulations, or a violation of a man's rights. The typical private-sector grievance procedure is characterized by union representation for the accused; steps that carry the grievance to higher levels in the organization; time limits on management and the union; and some final and binding step, usually arbitration by an outside, neutral third party. Grievance procedures of this type are spreading among police agencies but as yet are not particularly widespread.

It is our feeling that two factors explain this relative paucity. The first is the large number of informal procedures usually under the rubric of "the chief's door is always open if you've got a problem" (or the chief's door is at least open to the union president). The second reason is closely related. In the vast majority of departments, superior officers have no reason to accept any responsibility for grievance-handling since they know that the chief will ultimately make the final decision. In part, this is a symptom of the failure to prepare officers promoted to supervisory positions to accept the responsibilities of those positions and, in part, the failure of the system to teach the chief and his immediate subordinates to meaningfully delegate authority. All of this notwithstanding, multistep grievance procedures leading to final and binding arbitration are now found in Boston, Buffalo, Cranston, Dayton, Detroit, Hartford, New Haven, Omaha, Providence, and Rochester. In Seattle and Baltimore the chief is the final step in the procedure. In New York City there are regular monthly meetings between the line organizations and the department's personnel officers. In Philadelphia there have been weekly grievance meetings between the commissioner and the FOP since the inception of the organization in the 1930s.

Miscellaneous Other Issues

Earlier we indicated that in discussing the impact of unions on the potential for professionalization we could not divorce this from the impact on the chief's ability to manage. This is also true of the relationship between the issues in this chapter and those we will raise in the next chapter—the impact on law-enforcement policy formulation. However, in addition to these issues, our interviews produced a large number of other issues that individual unions raised in their department, issues not necessarily found elsewhere. We mention a few here just to give the reader a feel for what these might be. It is important to remember that labor-management relations are quite pragmatic and situational. A manager should never be surprised at what the union might bring up next.

In one city the FOP has filed suit to let women take the civil service examination; in a second city the union has stymied the design of new police headquarters building; in Buffalo the union was able to stall but not ultimately eliminate the introduction of off-duty marked cars for patrolmen. In that same city, the union took the city to the U.S. Supreme Court on the issue of whether men charged with a civilian complaint had to appear in a lineup. In Seattle the union has taken the city to superior court over the matter of polygraphs and their use in internal investigations.

In three cities the administrations wanted to change the color of squad cars. In one the union said no and won; in a second the union said no and the chief said "that's tough"—the chief won. In the third case the union was consulted in advance and approved.

Summary

We began this chapter with the question "to what extent has the union interfered with the ability of the chief to allocate resources within the department." Our data on the issues of bargaining suggest several tentative conclusions. First, the demands of police unions seem to be consistent with the traditional demands of trade unions representing other production and maintenance workers with respect to wages, hours, and conditions of work. For all their talk of professionalization, the police are conceptually indistinguishable from steelworkers or auto workers in their on-the-job concerns, a finding consistent with Kleingartner's analysis of the unionization of professional employees in bureaucratic organizations generally.[22] We would argue from this that the real impact of the union has been to force shared decision-making in the allocation of resources, whether the resources discussed are monetary (more wages and fringe benefits instead of using those same dollars for new programs or equipment) or human resources (all of the hours provisions and working conditions which impinge on the chief's absolute freedom to assign men as he sees fit).

A second pattern that emerges is the importance of distinguishing what the union says it is going to do from what it actually does; of distinguishing what the union attempts from what the union accomplishes; and of distinguishing the anticipated effect of a union-induced change from the actual impact of that change. The union may demand 100 percent enforcement of the law, but the men faced with department sanctions do not respond to the union's call; the union may oppose sewn on name tags, but they are placed on the uniforms anyhow; the union may win a seniority clause, but the actual effect is negligible relative to the image of chaos anticipated prior to the change. This analysis is not to suggest that union threats and demands may not delay change or even frustrate change from being proposed; our study design did not allow us to develop accurate data on these types of situations. However, this analysis does suggest that there is some position between hysteria (resulting from a failure to distinguish accomplishment from attempt) and whitewash (refusing to consider the frustrating impact of strong unions on inexperienced management) which represents a realistic appraisal of the union's impact.

This leads to our third and fourth points. Much of the negative impact of unions has occurred because of union exploitation of the multilateral bargaining opportunities in the public sector and the failure of management to rationalize the process by limiting the arena for gains to the bargaining table. Numerous examples were cited where the union was able to whipsaw management by moving from the bargaining table to the city council to the state legislature and back again. Finally, there must be a strong management across the bargaining table from the union demanding *quid pro quo*, seeking innovative solutions to mutual problems, and opposing demands which would impose intolerable burdens. We found no evidence of this kind of two-party bargaining on any broad scale; rather we found only selected cases in selected relationships where this degree of sophistication had been achieved.

We spoke earlier of the primary impact of unions as forcing joint decision-making particularly in the traditional areas of wages, overtime, protection against call-in, call-back, standby, and abuse of court-time requirements. Whatever the short-run consequences of higher costs and less flexibility may be, we see the long-run impact of this shared decision-making as forcing management to come to grips with the fact that the human resources of the department are not a free commodity but rather a scarce commodity and as forcing management to deal with the managerial problem of allocating these scarce resources among competing ends. We cited examples where men are called out less frequently or hours assigned more rationally or court time scheduled more rationally only after overtime, call-in, call-back, and court time were paid at an overtime rate in cash. As long as overtime was straight-time compensatory time off there was little incentive for management to treat the human resources of the department as anything but a relatively free commodity.[23] We see this change in the economics of the situation as the major long-run impact of the union on the chief's ability to manage.

There were several examples where the union was able to frustrate management goals by resort to the referendum and legislative and elective politics over issues as varied as wages, the introduction of a fourth shift, unbalanced shifts, new shift hours, name tags, and departmental reorganization. However, where there was some rationalization of the bargaining process and a reasonably sophisticated management bargaining team, the bargaining process was used to generate mutually satisfactory or integrative bargains: the trade-off in one city of union cooperation in establishing a fourth shift in exchange for the implemenation of eight-hour shifts; the trade-off between a shorter workweek and the right to use civilian employees in jobs previously performed by sworn personnel; and the cooperation of union and management in one midwestern city where detective tenure was exchanged for the new specialist rating and one-man cars were instituted along with a new communications system allowing the man to be in constant contact with headquarters.[24]

The Brookings Studies

Any discussion of the impact of unions on the ability of management to manage must acknowledge an intellectual debt to Slichter, Healy, and Livernash's 1960 study, *The Impact of Collective Bargaining on Management* cited earlier. Looking at the collective-bargaining landscape some fifteen to twenty years after the turbulent labor relations decade of the late 1930s and the early 1940s, the authors attempted to relate what had occurred to some of the dire projections that had grown out of the unrest surrounding the birth of industrial unionism. More recently, another Brookings study has attempted to replicate this effort in the public sector. David Stanley looks at the impact of unions *during* the period that they are in the process of organizing and attempts to place their impact in some kind of perspective vis-à-vis the criteria established a decade earlier by Slichter, Healy and Livernash.[25] We conclude this chapter with a brief review of the findings in each of these studies so that the reader may judge for himself the extent to which the findings of this study and these other studies are consistent with one another.

Unions in the private sector, the authors of ICBM found, have narrowed the scope of management discretion, fostered the development of management by policy, and necessitated organizational changes whose net effect was to centralize labor relations policy-making. The narrowing of management discretion has come about through contract language, contract administration and grievance arbitration as in the establishment of rules for lay off, transfer, promotion; through requirements that management be fair or reasonable or act with just cause; and sometimes through language prohibiting certain types of conduct such as excessive overtime.[26] The trend toward development of management by policy is largely a function of the costs imposed by the union on *ad hoc* decision-making in personnel matters—lost arbitration cases, whipsawing, and so forth:

If one single statement were sought to describe the effect of unions on policy-making, it would be: "They have encouraged investigation and reflection." Some unions are in fact only a slight check on management; other unions run the shop. But whether the union influence is weak or strong, it always tends to force management to consider the probable consequences of its proposed decisions and to adjust those decisions accordingly.[27]

To carry out this "investigation and reflection," management developed labor-relations staffs and organizations to coordinate their activities. While the authors found a great deal of variance with respect to the locus of decision-making in multiplant firms, the net impact of unions was to centralize decision-making on policy matters in industrial relations.[28]

With respect to the nature of the relationship, Slichter, Healy, and Livernash found that as of 1960 there was a limited but significant growth of formal cooperation, a decline in the number of relationships with intense conflict, and a growing adjustment of the parties to the new relationship. The authors also noted an increase in management willingness to take a strike to eliminate inefficiencies brought on by earlier excessive yielding to union pressures (however, hindsight has shown us that this is a cyclical phenomenon related to management's ability to pass on costs).[29]

Compare these 1960 findings in the private sector with the following conclusions reached by Stanley after studying nineteen relationships in the public sector in the late 1960s. In response to the rhetorical question, "What is happening to government achievements under union pressures?" Stanley answers "Not much." For example, he says on the one hand "unions can impair efficiency in a strongly unionized department if they accelerate cost increases and if they insist on work rules and conditions that hinder the flexible use of management techniques. On the other hand, unions may improve program effectiveness by demanding that the organization be adequately staffed, by pressing for equal levels of service throughout the city or by insisting on a sound safety program."[30]

Mainly "what is happening" to local government is that both legislative bodies and chief executives are *more preoccupied with union matters* and are *more limited in their discretion to manage.*[31]

In support of decreased discretion, Stanley cites the fact that unions now engage in bilateral decision-making on budgets, that unions have a voice in grievance procedures and the administration of grievances, and that unions become involved in job classification, work assignments, program policies, and to a limited extent the tenure of public officials.[32] In general, however,

recent history suggests that the [financial] gains of the unions have not been excessive. There will be efforts in the future to get more, and both the political and procedural restraints will be burdened, but disastrous outcomes are hardly likely.[33]

The unions, says Stanley, do not want to take over management completely, rather they want an adversary against whom they can press demands: "Management needs to show strength."[34] He points out that management must organize and staff itself to deal with employee relations and do everything possible to maintain fundamental management prerogatives.[35] "Public officials often miss opportunities to bargain hard and merely use a defensive strategy of responding to union demands. In some units they could bargain for increased productivity, improved work quality, or work rules conducive to efficiency."[36] Stanley concludes:

The increase of unionism in local governments has helped employees to keep up with the rest of the economy and has added to their protection against arbitrary or inconsistent treatment. They have clearly won the right to organize, to negotiate, and to secure structured consideration of grievances and they undoubtedly have the right to strike, *de facto*. But there seems to be little prospect that the transaction will become overbalanced against management, given the continued functioning of the American political system and the exercises by management officials of a reasonable mix of resolution, ability to listen, decisiveness, labor relations knowledge, and good will.[37]

We feel that our findings and the findings of these two studies are consistent on the following points: the unions have narrowed management discretion, they have fostered the development of management by policy, they have protected employees against arbitrary or inconsistent treatment, and they have shown that management had better begin diverting greater intellectual and organizational resources toward dealing with this new power center in its midst. Like Slichter, Healy, and Livernash, we too found the beginnings of cooperative relationships and a decline in the number of relationships with intense conflict. In Chapter 10 we will amplify on these conclusions and make some recommendations for policy development. In this next chapter we look at the impact of unions on the formulation of law-enforcement policy in the community.

8

Police-Union Impact on the Formulation of Law-Enforcement Policy

What constitutes the formulation of law-enforcement policy can be a difficult question. A department has many policies: a policy concerning prostitution; a policy concerning the use of sick leave; even a policy concerning the frequency with which squad cars will be washed. In this list it is easy to distinguish the first, which is a law enforcement policy issue, from the other two, which are administrative policies. However, how does one classify policies coming under the broad rubric of "manning?" We discussed "manning" under the heading "ability to manage," but the use of civilians, the number of men in a squad car, and the number of cars on the street are also an important part of law-enforcement policy. Conversely, the question of the type and number of weapons carried by policemen and the conditions under which they may be used are discussed under "law enforcement policy" but they are clearly germane to the chief's ability to manage.

Other law-enforcement policy issues are not as readily discerned because they are discussed in contexts which draw attention away from the underlying law-enforcement policy implications. Thus earlier in the book we discussed the question of entry standards and minority recruitment in the context of the professionalization issue. We might also have discussed these in the context of their impact on law enforcement policy—the extent to which the minority community perceives efforts to exclude blacks from the department as an unobtrusive measure of the department's hostility toward them. In short, while public attention is focused on particular disputes, each of which involves some aspect of control and authority, the broader policy issues tend not to get raised. In this next section we attempt to point up some of these broader policy questions.

Law-Enforcement Policy Issues[1]

How Will the Law Be Enforced

Police services are delivered within the context of broad policy guidelines. The precise policies to be followed are subject to a great deal of discretion. The basic thrust of union efforts has been to place limits on managerial discretion.

In the case of civil disturbances, for example, management may choose to follow a policy of containment rather than risking life on both sides by attempting to extinguish the disturbance. In several cities where this policy was pursued the unions objected strenuously. In New York City PBA President John Cassesse's call for "100 percent enforcement of the law" in August 1968 was issued in the context of police dissatisfaction with the containment policies of city officials established during the Martin Luther King riots in April 1968 and continued into the following summer,[2] as was a similar statement by former Boston Police Patrolmen's Association President Richard MacEachern a few days later.[3] Similarly, a group of Baltimore policemen, through a publicized letter to their AFSCME local, criticized the department's preparedness for, and handling of, the King riots,[4] and during the riots the Police Wives Association publicly castigated the "weak-kneed" policy used in containing the disturbances.

The most explicit union activity in this area occurred in Pittsburgh where the FOP lodge published formal investigatory reports after two civil disturbances. The first followed the King riot, and strongly criticized the department's lack of preparedness and the containment nature of the city's response.[5] The second report dealt with a June 1970 disturbance which followed the slaying of a black youth by an elderly white woman. In this report the union severely criticized the city's permissiveness and appeasement of the "hoodlum element."[6]

Sometimes law-enforcement policy can be affected by benefits secured strictly for "bread and butter" reasons. In the previous chapter, for example, we mentioned that unions in many cities have secured financial compensation for off-duty court appearances, some of it at premium rates. Thus, at the time of our field visit, Boston patrolmen earned approximately $22.50 for each off-duty court appearance (time-and-one-half pay with a three-hour minimum). One conceivable law-enforcement impact of this benefit is that officers, especially those on evening and night duty, may see a financial incentive to make arrests which necessitate a court appearance the next day. This phenomenon has been given a name—"bounty hunting," making arrests primarily to increase earnings. We pursued this issue in three cities, where management interviewees admitted that when premium pay for court appearances was first established there may have been a few bounty hunters but that such men were transferred to other positions. Management interviewees minimized the phenomenon, saying that aggregate arrest figures (which we did not examine) showed no significant increase in arrests after court-time premium pay was established. However, street patrolmen in two of the cities were emphatic that bounty hunters did exist.

The question of how the law is to be enforced can be influenced in other ways. A department which does not engage in active minority recruitment or which uses entry standards as a barrier to minority hiring conveys a clear message to the minority communities on how that department views those communities.

Another factor that can be quite important is the union's stance on residency. The question of whether a police officer need reside in the city of his employment is an important law-enforcement policy issue with emotional overtones. The men argue that given their middle-income economic status they should be free to live in the suburbs where the streets are safe and the schools sound. Cities, on the other hand, argue that residing implies a commitment to the city and to its improvement, that public employees should reside in the tax district, and that the men should be available for call-in, call-back, and standby. Norton Long raises another interesting perspective: with the center-city population becoming more dependent over time, the nonresident police, teachers, and other civil servants come to represent emissaries from the mother country to the colony or from the government to the Indians on the reservation.[7] This latter perspective is often overlooked.

Whenever the residency issue arose in our sample, it was usually because of union attempts to eliminate it. For example, the New York City PBA has lobbied extensively in Albany for the right to live outside the city, and successive pieces of state legislation now give city policemen the right to live in several suburban counties. Cleveland officers removed the residency requirement through a charter amendment. In contrast, unions in several other cities were unsuccessful in attempts to eliminate residency requirements. Police organizations in Chicago lost a lawsuit, and the Milwaukee union failed with a law suit and at the bargaining table. Cincinnati tried a city-council resolution and a lawsuit and lost both times.[8] In Detroit the patrolmen's union fought a lengthy court battle against the requirement but lost. The Seattle union objected to the mayor's decree that new policemen must live within the city limits (though those already on the force could maintain their suburban residency), but at the time of our visit had not been able to change the situation. In one city the union actually did oppose the elimination of a residency requirement.[9]

In summary, a few unions have been able to eliminate residency requirements, and a few unions may have contributed to the phenomenon of bounty hunting through securing a premium for off-duty court appearances. Several unions have objected to management's containment policies for handling civil disturbances, but nowhere did we find that management had changed its riot policies in response to union criticisms. However, these union demands for a "hard line" are a clear statement to the community of how the rank-and-file views its law-enforcement duties, and they are a clear statement to police and city officials who may be considering adopting other policies or techniques which de-emphasize the use of force.

The Use of Force

The armament carried by officers and the conditions under which weapons or physical force is used are an important element of the law-enforcement policy of the community and, like the issue of how the law is to be enforced, has an impact on the way in which the community perceives the department's intentions toward them. Among the issues raised are the number of weapons carried, the use of private weapons, the presence of long guns, the conditions under which an officer may fire his weapon, and whether the rifles and shotguns should be carried in the trunk, in the front of the car, or taken from the car routinely.

Consistent with their "hard line" on the handling of civil disorders, police unions have pressed for heavy armaments and minimal restrictions on the police right to use force, especially fatal force. In seven cities in this sample the use of force was an overt issue, usually with the police unions opposing actual or proposed restrictions on their coercive license. The Cleveland unions, for example, were successful after the 1968 Glenville shootout in pressuring the department for new armaments. Interviewees in two other midwestern cities told of men on patrol carrying unauthorized long guns in addition to their authorized sidearms. In the Hartford gun-guideline example cited in Chapter 3, the union's hard bargaining (not to be confused with collective bargaining), lobbying, and display of public support was instrumental in persuading the city council to vote against the adoption of gun-use restrictions. The San Francisco union was able to persuade the chief and the police commission to change a proposed set of gun guidelines so that an officer involved in an on-duty homicide is not automatically suspended pending an investigation.[10] In Seattle the union negotiated a contract clause providing that no officer can be required over his objection to work without a gun.

In contrast the Oakland union has protested in vain against the chief's gun-use restrictions (which are much tighter than the "fleeing felon" standard in the state law). A union in a western city pressed unsuccessfully for the right of each officer to carry the weapon of his choice. In an eastern city the union lobbied the city council for the right to carry shotguns in squad cars, but the chief was able to muster sufficient opposition to have the union voted down. In a midwestern city the union unsuccessfully made public demands for, and lobbied with the chief for, a shotgun for each man in a squad car (instead of the existing one per car) and for the reinstitution of a formerly eliminated dog patrol. Finally, after the 1971 murders of two New York City patrolmen the PBA called for shotguns in every patrol car. Though this demand was rejected, the department did begin training in shotgun handling for many members of the force. The union has again raised the issue in 1973.[11]

Many of the police demands for increased armaments and the authority to use them can be traced to their belief that patrol conditions in many central cities are tantamount to wartime. Support for this belief comes from the increasing rate of assaults on police officers and the increasing numbers of policemen killed during the 1960s and early 1970s. For instance, in 1960 28 police officers were killed in the line of duty as a result of felonious assault; in 1970, 100 officers were killed; and in 1971 the figure increased to 126.[12] Many of the rank and file see the use of heavier force as a self-protection issue.

The direct impact of union efforts in some departments has been to minimize the restrictions placed on an officer's use of firearms and to help obtain increased armaments. In other departments the unions have pushed in the same directions but have had no observable impact. Successful or not, the union's demands for heavier armaments and minimal restrictions on their use are additional statements to the community, especially the minority segments of the community, of police intentions toward them.

Civilian Review of Police Behavior

The topic that has attracted the most publicity in the area of law-enforcement policy is union opposition to civilian review of citizen complaints against individual officers or groups of officers. The most celebrated instances are the Philadelphia and New York cases: in both cities the unions successfully thwarted civilian review. In New York City the defeat of Mayor Lindsay's proposal came as a result of a referendum in which the union succeeded in killing civilian review but actually increased the volume of complaints to the departmental review board as a result of its publicity campaign broadcasting the existence of such a board. In Philadelphia the civilian review board was dropped by the mayor even after a favorable state supreme court verdict reversing two lower courts who had sustained a union challenge to the legitimacy of the board. We have also described how the Rochester union's court battle against the review board in that city contributed to the board's demise.

In Boston in 1968 the patrolmen's union worked with several city-council members to scrap the police portion of Mayor Kevin White's proposed Model Cities program, including a civilian complaint board. In Buffalo the union lobbied vigorously against a proposal before the city council to give that city's Commission on Human Relations subpoena power when investigating charges of police misconduct, and the council defeated the proposal. In Baltimore in 1970 the two unions campaigned vigorously against a Baltimore Urban Coalition proposal for a civilian review board, and the issue was abandoned by its proponents in the face of this opposition.[13] After the Pittsburgh Commission on Human Relations investigated and recommended that several policemen be disciplined for their behavior in a series of incidents, the Pittsburgh FOP lodge castigated the commission, announced that policemen would refuse to cooperate with it, and asked the mayor to investigate it.[14]

The Detroit patrolmen's union has engaged in a running battle with the Michigan Civil Rights Commission ever since the 1967 riot (the commission is a state agency empowered to investigate civil-rights complaints and publicize their findings). The union filed a suit against the commission late in 1968, and in 1970 the two organizations reached an out-of-court agreement to modify the manner in which the commission investigates, processes, and publicizes citizen complaints against policemen (the settlement primarily affords policemen more opportunities to participate in the proceedings and keeps them informed of developments with their case). The union has opposed local political candidates who favor civilian review boards and strongly criticized a proposed city ombudsman plan, seeing it as civilian review under another name.[15] The Seattle union publicly denounced that city's Human Rights Commission as a *de facto* civilian review board for its investigations into charges of police misconduct. Interviewees in three other cities said that their respective police unions actively lobbied with city officials to prevent the creation of civilian review boards.

The direct impact of union activities in many of these cities seems clear: civilian review boards that existed have been defeated, and new proposals to establish review boards have been killed before they were implemented. In other cities the impact may have been more indirect. Union condemnation of human relations and civil rights commissions may not have produced any structural changes, but the expressions of police opposition to any kind of civilian review of police behavior have informed community leaders of the difficulties of instituting formalized review procedures. In all, civilian review was an issue in eleven of our twenty-two cities.

Citizen Complaints and the Identification of Police Officers

Like civilian review of complaints against officer behavior, facilitation of complaints and identification are a manifestation of an adversary relationship between police and the community.[16] The policy issue raised is the extent to which the department will facilitate the taking of complaints and the identification of officers.

In an eastern city the union objected to a department plan to have officers earn community goodwill by interviewing five citizens each week, with a key portion of the interview consisting of the officer explaining to the citizen how to file a complaint against the police. The union dropped its objection when the interview program produced evidence of substantial public support for the police. In Omaha the union criticized the department's new citizen complaint procedure, which the chief said was adopted at the request of a local citizens' committee. The union objected to the fact that complaints could be made by telephone, saying that all complaints should be made in person and the officer being complained about should have the opportunity to confront the citizen as he made the complaint.[17]

In Boston, Detroit, and Seattle the identification question surfaced as a name-tag issue. In Seattle the union agreed to name tags on shirts and identifying numbers on riot helmets and overalls, the latter after many citizens complained of police brutality and the inability to identify police offenders during campus and antigovernment demonstrations. As we discussed earlier the Detroit patrolmen's union used the grievance-arbitration procedure to stall but not prevent the introduction of name tags, and the Boston patrolmen's union was able to prevent name tags via the judicious combination of picketing police headquarters, using the grievance-arbitration procedure, lobbying with the state legislature and governor's office, and lobbying with the city council.

In Buffalo the identification issue surfaced as an identification lineup of all the police on a particular shift in order that the black victims of alleged excessive police zeal be afforded an opportunity to identify the assailants. As explained in Chapter 5, the union used a federal court suit to delay for more than a year the implementation of the lineups, thus reducing the chances for accurate identification.

These specific issues again point up the distinction between the direct and indirect impact of union efforts. Only in Boston did the union score a total victory, though in Buffalo and Detroit the unions were able to delay implementation of identification mechanisms. However, the union position in these cases conveyed to the community a clear picture of rank-and-file police attitudes toward the handling of citizen complaints and identification of police misconduct.

The Functioning of the Criminal Justice System

In theory the various aspects of the criminal justice system function independently: the police effect arrests, the prosecutor decides if a formal charge is warranted and prosecutes the case, the judge presides over the trial and passes sentence, the legislature defines criminal activity and determines a range of penalties, and a parole board may determine what portion of a particular sentence will actually be served. While in practice these are not necessarily independent events, still the question arises as to whether such interdependence as does exist should be formalized through police union activities such as court-watching, union endorsements in campaigns for prosecutor and judge, or union endorsements in campaigns for mayor and governor where the candidates go on record as to the types of individuals who will be nominated to civilian review boards, parole boards, and other agencies having jurisdiction in the criminal justice area.

Police unions in our sample were quite concerned about judicial handling and disposition of criminal cases. Police unions in five cities threatened to engage in *court-watching* (stationing an observer in court to record the disposition of criminal cases), and these statements were invariably couched in coercive language castigating judicial leniency. The Detroit patrolmen's union, through its wives' auxiliary, actually engaged in court-watching for six months. The Seattle union publicly threatened to implement a court-watching program but backed off after receiving substantial adverse criticism. One midwestern union collected data for six months but never used it. The Seattle and Baltimore unions endorsed judicial candidates because of their ideological sympathy with the police.[18] In Pittsburgh the police delayed the appointment of a black magistrate in whom the union had taken a vote of no-confidence, and the union publicly castigated some magistrates for releasing on own recognizance and nominal bonds certain categories of criminal suspects. The union president warned that the union will watch all magistrates to see if they follow the magisterial code section on bail-setting and will charge them with misconduct if they violate the code.[19]

In this sample's most far-reaching union attempt to affect a local judiciary, the Detroit patrolmen's union pushed for the impeachment of Recorder's Court Judge George Crockett after he released a large group of blacks involved in a shoot-out with police (see Chapter 5): they purchased newspaper advertising condemning his action, picketed the local criminal courts building to protest his action, gathered citizen signatures on petitions calling for his ouster, and filed charges against him with the Michigan Judicial Tenure Commission. While these efforts failed to have the judge removed from office, union interviewees felt that the union's efforts put the local judiciary on notice that the police will not tolerate such behavior in the future.[20]

Union spokesmen in four cities said their organizations have lobbied to influence the substance of criminal statutes or changes in the penal code. For example, the Baltimore unions successfully lobbied against a city proposal to increase the upper age limit for juvenile offenders from sixteen to eighteen. The former president of the union in another city said he actively lobbied on behalf of certain criminal statutes in the state capitol. Electoral processes may also be used to influence law-enforcement matters. The California Supreme Court declared the state's death penalty unconstitutional in early 1972; the response among several police groups (and others) was to launch an initiative effort which resulted in a death penalty constitutional amendment on the November 1972 ballot. In Pittsburgh in 1971 a "law and order" district attorney who enjoyed good relations with the police and who was up for reelection refused to prosecute thirty-four policemen who fraudulently collected $41,000 in witness fees.[21] In an example from outside our sample, the Eugene (Oregon) Police Patrolmen's Association endorsed and gave a large contribution to the successful challenger to the incumbent district attorney in the November 1972 election.

It is difficult to pinpoint any direct impact of union efforts to influence the operation of the criminal justice system. One may feel, as we do, that the independence of the components of the criminal justice system is reduced when judges and district attorneys are elected with the aid of police-union support or when the police lobby to influence criminal statutes, but we cannot accurately describe the effects of this alleged reduced independence upon the handling and disposition of criminal cases. Similarly, several police unions have made threatening noises about "judicial leniency," but it is difficult to show how these union statements and activities have affected judicial handling of criminal cases.

In contrast, we can discern some indirect impact. By their statements and activities, the police organizations have informed the community that the police favor strict bonding, prosecuting, and sentencing practices and in general a "get tough" approach to the handling of criminal cases. On the one hand, these postures are supported by those segments of the community who are concerned about "law and order" and "crime in the streets." On the other hand, other segments of the community may see these police postures as being directed against them.

Other Issues

We encountered a host of other law-enforcement-related issues and police-union involvement in them. In New York City the PBA opposed the creation, funding, and subpoena powers of the Knapp Commission and its investigations into police corruption. In Seattle the union went to court to block a new chief's use of polygraphs (lie detectors) in internal investigations of police corruption. The Seattle union also informally negotiated changes in the coroner's inquest system used when a civilian is killed by a police officer. The Boston patrolmen's union lobbied in the city council and state legislature to block a mayoral proposal to give traffic control duties to civilians, and the Buffalo union was instrumental in convincing city officials to abandon a 1968 plan to upgrade 475 civil defense auxiliary policemen to limited duty status (i.e., they would carry radios and nightsticks but would not have firearms or arrest powers).[22] The Buffalo union also opposed the establishment of minority-oriented, community-peace-officer plan and stalled (but did not prevent) the introduction of a program whereby 61 officers would have off-duty use of squad cars in exchange for answering calls in their vicinity. In Rochester the union established a "truth squad" to monitor police-related news in the city papers (this effort was abandoned after one month),[23] attempted unsuccessfully to convince the state conference of police unions that officers should stop informing arrestees of their Miranda rights,[24] and attempted unsuccessfully to have a children's book that pictured police officers as pigs in blue uniforms removed from the public library.[25]

Police unions have also engaged directly in electoral politics on behalf of local candidates whom they perceived as ideologically compatible with rank-and-file law-enforcement interests. Some of the more publicized examples include police-union endorsement of or sympathy with such mayoral candidates as Sam Yorty in Los Angeles, Charles Stenvig in Minneapolis, Roman Gribbs in Detroit, Frank Rizzo in Philadelphia, and Louise Day Hicks in Boston. Police unions have also opposed candidates from whom they felt ideologically estranged: in Cleveland the unions were bitterly opposed to Mayor Carl Stokes; the New York

City PBA was one of the few municipal unions that did not support Mayor John Lindsay's reelection efforts in 1969. Police unions have also supported city councilmen with whom they are ideologically compatible, including former police-union president Wayne Larkin's successful bid for a seat on the Seattle City Council. It is difficult to discern any direct impacts of these union electoral involvements, but an important indirect impact has been to increase the saliency of the "law and order" issue.

Summary

Because the individual issues over which conflict occurs in the area of law-enforcement policy tend to be viewed in isolation as single occurrences, often the underlying issues of control and authority are not articulated. In this chapter we have attempted to relate the specific incidents to the larger policy context in which they might be viewed. Two major themes have emerged from this investigation. First, while the unions may not have been particularly successful in their frontal attacks on various aspects of law-enforcement policy, we should not overlook the impact of their actions on the minority communities and on the willingness of political officials to act in future situations. Second, as the reader reviews in his mind the types of actions undertaken by the unions, it becomes obvious that it was not the collective-bargaining process but rather the political arena which the unions exploited in their attempts to influence law-enforcement policy. We consider each of these themes briefly.

Direct vs. Indirect Impact

As one considers the direct victories by unions in the law-enforcement policy area, he is struck by the fact they revolve around either one issue (civilian review) or two cities (Seattle and Boston). The list of unsuccessful efforts is much more impressive: the handling of civil disturbances, the judicial disposition of criminal cases, greater armament and more freedom to use it, the election of "law and order" politicians on any grand scale, influence on hiring standards, and so forth. For example, consider the efforts of the Detroit patrolmen's union: through its wives auxiliary it engaged in court-watching for six months; it attempted but failed to impeach a local black judge; it stalled the introduction of name tags (and flap holsters) until arbitrators ruled in support of the city's right to require them; it filed a lawsuit against a civil rights commission to force it to change its method of operation involving citizen complaints against the police; it spoke out against civilian review, including political candidates who supported the concept; pressed for heavier armaments for street patrolmen; and it repeatedly espoused a "hard line" on law-enforcement issues. While the union scored no direct victories, the totality of its statements and actions created a clear picture about where it stood on civilian control, citizen identification, judicial disposition of criminal cases, and the use of force. Similar examples could be cited from other cities.

It is the overall impression left by the union's totality of behavior from which we draw our concern about the indirect impact of the union's efforts to influence the formulation of law-enforcement policy. While we cannot measure these results, we are concerned with the potential impact of overall union activity in causing city and police executives not to undertake certain programs and policies in anticipation of the union's reaction and the political costs attendant to the struggle—even if management believes it will ultimately prevail.

Secondly, we are concerned with the impact of the union's totality of behavior on police-community relations. Union positions on law-enforcement policy issues are frequently "hard line" or "get tough"—remove restrictions on the use of force, crack down on offenders, extinguish riots rather than contain them—and oriented toward maximizing rank-and-file discretion in the performance of their duties and insulating on-the-job behavior from nonpolice review—opposition to civilian review, complaint systems, and identification.[26] While unions may have valid reasons for opposing civilian review and while each officer accused of a departmental or civilian indiscretion deserves a vigorous defense, the fact is that these union positions are perceived as hostile signs in the black community. Although the measurement of citizen attitudes toward police-union law-enforcement efforts was not within the scope of this study, our data (newspaper files and interview comments, especially from black officer association representatives) suggest that these union efforts had some negative impact on police minority-community relations in at least eleven cities: Boston, Buffalo, Cleveland, Detroit, Hartford, New York City, Omaha, Philadelphia, Pittsburgh, Rochester, and Seattle.

We caution strongly against ignoring these secondary consequences of union actions in the policy area, and we especially caution against underestimating the impact of a union on law-enforcement policy because the union has had few direct successes.

Collective Bargaining and Political Action

Police union concern with proposals for civilian review boards and gun guidelines, with citizen complaint procedures and identification lineups, with judicial disposition of criminal cases, with managerial handling of civil disturbances, and with investigations of police corruption reflects very real rank-and-file police concern with actual or proposed changes in police working conditions. However, this concern usually cannot be translated into specific bargaining demands because these issues are not decided at the bargaining table. In contrast to the issues examined in the previous chapter, most of which were resolved at the bargaining table, the resolution of the issues discussed in this chapter will remain political issues to be fought out in various political arenas.

In fact, the major factor that distinguishes the impact of police unions on law-enforcement policy formulation from their impact on the ability to manage is that the former would have occurred in the absence of collective-bargaining rights whereas much of the latter would not. Moreover, the changing constitutional climate with respect to the First Amendment rights of public employees, including free speech and participation in elective politics, has created an environment in which the already politicized police employee organizations have extended the range of their activities.[27]

Thus the testimonial dinner for a criminal court judge in Milwaukee, the New York City campaign against the civilian review board, and the visit of Vice-President Agnew to the prayer breakfast of a New York City police employee organization to praise the police and condemn opponents of law and order all would have occurred in the absence of collective bargaining. Similarly the activities of the line organizations in New York City in their attempts to block the Knapp Commission hearings into corruption (the attempts to block creation, funding, and subpoena power) all took place in the courts and the press outside the context of collective bargaining.

Public policy with respect to free speech and political action is unclear. For years, the celebrated dictum of Mr. Justice Holmes had been predominant: "The petitioner may have a constitutional right to talk politics, but he has no constitutional right to be a policeman."[28] This has been interpreted as limiting the rights of police officers to make critical public statements on policy issues and as limiting their participation in elective politics—the latter because of possible misuse of their unique power and station in the society. However, as we shall see, this position has recently been modified with respect to public-policy statements.

The ambivalence of public policy with respect to political participation is best seen in the sometimes tacit, sometimes overt encouragement by police executives of participation by employee organizations in legislative and elective political activity discussed in Chapters 4 and 5—larger appropriations for city government, salaries, retirement systems, and welfare benefits. Given this unofficial sanction and a functioning political organization, and given the leverage inherent in the public concern with law and order (also discussed in Chapter 4), it is not surprising that police employee organizations took advantage of their new constituency to move into elective political action and public statements on issues of law-enforcement policy even though local regulations may have prohibited both.

This expanded activity with respect to public statements was reinforced by the changing constitutional climate during the 1960s. In a line of cases from *New York Times Co. v. Sullivan* [376 U.S. 254 (1964)], through *Pickering v. Board of Education*, [88 S.Ct. 1731 (1968)], the Court moved from a virtual prohibition of public employee rights to the exercise of critical speech to a standard which has been interpreted as allowing critical statements so long as they do not include knowing falsity, disclosure of confidential information, falsehoods which would impair the operation of the agency, destruction of an effective superior-subordinate relationship, or adversely affect work relationships in the agency.[29]

An example of the extent to which we have moved from the Holmes' statement can be seen in the Maryland case, *Eugene C. Brukiewa v. Police Commissioner of Baltimore City*, [257 Maryland 36, 263 A. 2d 210 (1970)]. Brukiewa, the president of the Baltimore police union, had made comments critical of the department and the commissioner on a local television program. He was suspended by the department's disciplinary board, which ruled that he had violated two departmental regulations relating to discussion of departmental business in public and criticism of superiors. A Baltimore City Court upheld the suspension on the grounds that the regulations cited were clear and unambiguous. The state appeals court overruled the city court on the grounds that the state did not show that the appellant's statements hurt or imperiled the discipline or operation of the police department and were, therefore, within his right to make under the First Amendment and the decisions of the Supreme Court.

Most of the activities discussed in this chapter were a function of the unions' exercise of their political prerogatives. Whether these activities were legal or illegal is irrelevant; the fact that the unions are free to engage in such activities and the concomitant lack of official sanctions levied against them must be viewed as tacit approval consistent with the evolving climate just discussed. Finally, because of the numerous actors who participate in law-enforcement policy debates and the formulation of policy (judges, prosecutors, human-rights commissions, leaders from various segments of the community, elected officials, police management, police rank and file, etc.) and the fact that law-enforcement issues are decided in a variety of forums (the state legislature, the city council, the mayor's office, courtrooms and judicial chambers, the prosecutor's office, the station house, etc.), we suggest that most of the issues discussed in this chapter will remain political issues to be fought out in the political arena and are not likely to become included within the scope of collective bargaining in the short run.

9 Black Officer Organizations

In Chapter 2 we briefly mentioned our investigations of black officer associations. We found that these organizations exist in almost every city we visited which has more than twenty-five to thirty black policemen. While we were unable to interview the leaders of all these organizations in our sample cities, we were able to talk with association representatives in twelve cities: Baltimore, Chicago, Cincinnati, Cleveland, Dayton, Detroit, New Haven, New York, Oakland, Philadelphia, Pittsburgh, and San Francisco.[1]

Like the militant police unions discussed in Chapter 2, militant black officers associations followed two lines of development—the transformation of existing organizations and the formation of new militant organizations. Some, like the New York City Guardians, founded in 1949, evolved from social-fraternal organizations of black policemen into "racial rights" organizations; while providing recreational activities was still a function of these organizations in 1971, it had taken a secondary position to the organizations' efforts to push the racial grievances of black officers and black citizens. Other associations were founded in recent years explicitly to deal with racially based grievances. For instance, the Oakland Black Officers Association was founded in 1970 because of several black officers' concern with what they perceived as overt racist attitudes and behaviors by white policemen toward black policemen and black citizens. We turn now to a more detailed examination of these organizations.

Areas of Concern

The black police associations in our study had two main areas of interest and activity: the relations between black policemen and white policemen (including department management) and relationships between the police department and the black community.

Departmental Discrimination

The associations' primary area of concern focuses on intradepartmental matters, specifically on what they perceive as discriminatory departmental work practices and racist conduct of white policemen toward black officers. Black complaints here include lack of promotional opportunities (vertical segregation), prohibition of blacks from holding certain jobs or being in certain bureaus (horizontal segregation), unjust discipline, and prejudicial treatment of black officers by white officers. Some samples illustrate:

—Black police in four of the cities complained that black officers were either denied fair promotional opportunities or else unofficially segregated within the department into generally undesirable jobs. In Hartford, for example, the Guardians complained that blacks were not appointed to "inside jobs"—the vice squad, detective and burglary squads, headquarters jobs, and so forth, but instead were assigned almost solely to patrol duty in the city's highest crime area (the local black ghetto).

—In several cities, black police complained that there has been inadequate recruitment of black police applicants.

—Black police in four cities related incidents which demonstrated white police racial prejudice toward black police: Wallace stickers and "nigger" jokes in locker rooms, fist-fights, black-white brawls, and instances of drawing their guns on each other. Black police felt that the racial animosity of some white policemen caused these incidents.

The Hartford situation exemplifies an interesting paradox and policy issue: a black community desire for black policemen in the black community versus black police officer desires for equal treatment.

—Prior to August 1969, Hartford police management purposefully assigned the bulk of the city's black policemen to patrol duty in the black areas of the city. This was done primarily in response to demands by black community spokesmen that black policemen could interact better with black citizens and thus reduce police-community animosity. However, the black policemen involved, represented by the Connecticut Guardians, had a different perspective.[2] They believed that their concentration in Hartford's North End constituted de facto departmental segregation. The fact that patrol assignments in the high crime North End were among the most difficult and dangerous jobs in the department added fuel to their complaints. They demanded that blacks be assigned throughout the department, that blacks be given a chance to exercise leadership, that blacks be given increased formal training opportunities, and that more black police be recruited.

These grievances were not resolved until after a series of mass sick calls by a large portion of the black policemen. The controversy was settled when the Guardians agreed to process their grievances through the majority union's negotiated grievance procedure and the department agreed to assign black policemen throughout the department. Ironically, in this case, black police desires were accommodated over black community desires.[3]

Police-Community Relations

All of the black-officer association representatives we interviewed mentioned that their organizations have attempted to improve relations between the police department and the black community. Specific community-relations efforts include: engaging in recruiting efforts to increase the number of black policemen; protesting police mistreatment of prisoners (primarily black prisoners); offering assistance to black citizens in filing complaints against policemen; forming alliances with black activist groups in the city; giving speeches to black community groups; sponsoring athletic, social, and recreational programs for black youth; and in general, trying to reduce citizen distrust of police and to create a better police image in the black community. Again, some samples illustrate:

—The Guardians in New York City have been very active in trying to increase the number of black policemen. The organization pushed to get a police cadet program established (most of the cadets were black or Puerto Rican); established a tutoring program to help the cadets pass the civil-service entrance examination; successfully asked the city to extend the duration of civil-service entry lists in order to reach the black applicants clustered in the bottom half of the lists; and was instrumental in the establishment of departmental Candidates Review Board, formed to review the cases of rejected applicants (primarily minority applicants rejected by primarily white background investigators). Black associations in Oakland and Cincinnati also have actively engaged in recruitment efforts.

—The New Haven Silver Shield is a member of the city's Black Coalition, an umbrella-type organization of the city's black community groups. The Silver Shield members frequently appear before local black youth groups.

—In the words of its president, the Afro-American Patrolmen's League in Chicago considers itself primarily a community service organization. As such, it has established a citizen complaint referral service, conducted voter registration drives, and attempted to block millions of federal dollars going to the police department on the grounds that its hiring, assignments, and promotion policies discriminate against blacks.

As these and the previous examples illustrate, there is no neat dividing line between efforts to combat in-house discrimination and efforts to improve police-community relations: successful intradepartmental efforts to get black officers promoted or assigned to important decision-making positions may improve community relations, while efforts to increase the recruitment of police officers from the black community may mean an increased voice for blacks in internal departmental affairs.

Nor are these options of equal importance to each association; most in fact emphasize internal concerns over community concerns (even though some organizations such as the AAPL in Chicago and the Pittsburgh Guardians appear to focus most of their efforts toward establishing better police-black community relations). This is not unexpected since discriminatory practices directed against members are of a more immediate and tangible nature than poor police practices involving nonmember citizens, and since it appears easier to obtain a satisfactory resolution of specific intradepartmental grievances than to somehow improve the general state of relations between hundreds of policemen and thousands of citizens: in many cities an order from the top has opened assignments and promotional opportunities to blacks; similar orders have not been as effective in changing the relations between officers and the black community.

Activities

Black officer associations engage in a variety of activities to press their claims. In our sample the most common influence methods appear to be lobbying with the chief's office, litigation, lobbying with city officials, and publicizing issues of concern.

Black associations go to the chief or other department executives when they are concerned with intradepartmental issues, just as do the white-dominated unions, usually with issues focusing upon discriminatory treatment of black officers by white officers. However, more frequently the associations make use of the courts. In some cases the target may be the union, as in 1966 when the New York City Guardians sued the PBA to prevent it from using black PBA members' dues money to finance the union's referendum campaign against Mayor Lindsay's civilian review board. In Detroit the Michigan Guardians financed a suit to have the commissioner reinstate a black lieutenant transferred from his precinct to break up a dispute between the patrolmen's union and the lieutenant. Some associations have gone to the city administration for assistance: the New York City Guardians lobbied with Lindsay administration officials over items such as extending the civil-service entry lists, and the Officers for Justice in San Francisco lobbied with the city council and the civil service commission to change the height and weight entrance standards so that more minority persons would be eligible to become policemen.

The black associations have a wide range of interests, but they do not engage in as wide a range of activities as do the unions. Most noticeably, they do not engage in collective bargaining, although some of them function as *de facto* grievance representatives in order to press their members' racial grievances. We found only one instance (Hartford) of an association-sponsored disruption of service, probably because most of the associations realize that job actions would not significantly reduce the amount of police services delivered to the citizenry. Nor do the associations appear to be important factors in electoral contests, probably because they are relatively small organizations.[4] However, from the stand point of publicity they are active on a range of issues. Furthermore, their activities and statements seem to generate more newspaper coverage than their relatively small size would warrant. In part this is a function of the newsworthiness of police and civil-rights issues, and in part a function of the degree of militancy with which they press their claims.

Degree of Militancy

Our evidence suggests that the degree of militancy a black association exhibits in its activities (including its public statements) is a function of three main factors: the perceived hostility of the work environment, leader preferences, and the balance of internal political power between the voices of caution and confrontation.

Perceived Hostility

By far the most important factors are the organization's and particularly the leaders' perceptions of the hostility of the work environment. In turn, the two most salient portions of the work environment are the racial attitudes and actions of the department's managerial hierarchy (especially the chief) and the majority union (as expressed by the statements and actions of the union leaders). For example:

> —Black association interviewees in two cities emphasized that whenever they have a grievance, they always go to the chief and attempt to solve their problems in his office. The leaders of both groups believe that the respective chiefs were receptive to their problems and would work to resolve their grievances. Thus these groups followed the approach of gathering all the facts necessary to document their grievances (evidence of overt racial prejudice among white officers, need for increased black recruitment efforts, need for increased black promotional opportunities, need for a haircut code in tune with the changing societal grooming standards, etc.), presenting this evidence to the chief, and expressing their desire for his cooperation in resolving these problems. These groups did not make threatening public statements or engage in job actions because the leaders believed a behind-the-scenes accommodationist approach was the most successful.

Of the twelve cities, our impressions were that black association leaders in five cities believed that they would have more success on internal departmental grievances if they worked with the chief's office rather than adopting a publicly antagonistic policy.

Black association leaders in three cities appear to see a basically hostile work environment, and thus they have adopted a more aggressive or militant public posture. Black groups in these cities do not expect assistance from either the managerial hierarchy or the majority union in resolving their problems. Thus one of their approaches seems to be to adopt a militant public image with the apparent goal of obtaining community and/or political support.

An important factor in black association assessments of the degree of hostility in the work environment is their perceptions of the racial attitudes of the majority union.

—Black interviewees in four cities said that the respective majority unions did not adequately represent the interests of black police officers. They note that the leaderships of the majority unions are almost entirely white and some of them pointed to a refusal or unwillingness of the unions to take action on behalf of black officers involved in disputes or grievances. The Guardians in New York City have attempted to function as a union by formally representing their members in the department's disciplinary procedure. The majority Patrolmen's Benevolent Association has objected, saying that this undermines their exclusive representative status.[5]

Leader Preferences

The degree and extent of public militancy is in part a function of association leader preferences. Some leaders, for a variety of personal reasons, prefer to achieve association goals by quietly working within "the system" and not rocking the boat. For instance, the president of the black police association in a midwestern city is a middle-aged lieutenant who admits that he is a "conservative" among black association leaders. He prefers an accommodationist approach with department and city officials. Other leaders seem to prefer a more confrontationist posture, apparently on the belief that confrontation achieves more results than accommodation. Of course, much of any leader's preferences may be a function of his perceptions of the hostility of the work environment.

Internal Politics

A third explanatory factor is the balance of political power within the association between militantly oriented members and the more conservative ones. Newspaper accounts suggest that a militant pressure group within the Connecticut Guardians was largely responsible for the August 1969 mass sick calls by Hartford's black policemen aimed at eliminating departmental discrimination.[6] Black association spokesmen in three other cities where the leadership might be labeled "moderate" admitted that militant factions existed in the respective organizations, and these factions pushed for the associations to take a more militantly confrontationist approach in obtaining their goals. Just as the 1968 "100 percent enforcement of the law" controversy between New York City PBA President John Cassesse and Mayor Lindsay was at least partly a result of Cassesse attempting to "get out in front of" the strong conservative pressure which had recently developed within his union, so is it possible that the general emergence of more militant postures among black officer associations is a response to the internal pressures created by a portion of the membership.

Black-White Intradepartmental Relations

Our evidence suggests that relations between black and white policemen in many departments are poor. This conclusion is based upon examining specific incidents of black-white police conflict and asking black and white interviewees to describe the state of race relations in their departments. We read about or were told about a multitude of incidents exemplifying racial hostility, ranging from locker room "nigger jokes" to a racial brawl at a police picnic to incidents which ended with drawn guns. The responses to our questions regarding the quality of race relations ranged from "abominable" through "poor" or "strained" or "no worse than in any other big city, and maybe a little better," to "good" (only white interviewees said "good"). This section examines some of the reasons for the state of police race relations, focusing on the role of black officer associations and the changing racial attitudes of black policemen.

White Police Racial Prejudice

The published literature on race relations and the police leads to the conclusion that prejudice against blacks is quite common among white police officers.[7] This prejudice may have increased in recent years as blacks have struggled to assert their right to an equal role in American society and as blacks have been less and less willing to tolerate police abuse.[8] In any case, racial prejudice among many white policemen tends to be deep-rooted enough to include black policemen. Every one of our black officer interviewees related examples of racial abuse by white colleagues.[9] As Nicholas Alex notes, a black officer "is not quite a policeman to his [white] working companions because he is stereotyped as a member of an 'inferior' racial category."[10]

Black Police Response

Why have relations between black and white policemen become publicly worse in recent years? First, there are many more black policemen than there used to be, thus increasing the frequency of black-white police interaction. Second, the same black push for equality which has caused many more blacks to be hired as policemen has also resulted in a vastly different attitude among those blacks hired. Since most police departments have an upper entry level age limit of thirty to thirty-five, the relatively large numbers of blacks hired in recent years are young men. Compared to their elder brothers, their racial abuse tolerance level is very low. Black officer interviewees in several cities told us that in the old days the blacks on police forces tolerated a great deal of personal abuse in addition to more or less officially sanctioned discriminatory work practices (assigning blacks solely to the black community, no integrated work teams, etc.). These interviewees went on to tell us that those days are gone forever. Black police have no illusions about the existence of racial prejudice among white colleagues, but they, particularly the younger ones, appear determined to fight back (sometimes literally) at instances of racial injustice. The following situation represents the most vivid example of this feeling we encountered:

> —One of the authors went to a black officer association meeting in a large city. One of the prime topics of conversation were recent incidents where white officers had abused black officers (giving them traffic tickets, pointing guns at them, in one case firing a shot at a black officer, using racially abusive language, with most of these incidents occurring with off-duty or plainclothes black policemen). The leader of the militant faction of the association got up and gave an impassioned speech asking that all the brothers bury the hatchet over whatever differences they have and unite to fight abuse from white policemen. His main theme was that they (the audience and himself) were policemen eight hours a day, but to the white policemen they were still "niggers" twenty-four hours a day. To emphasize his point that he was not ever going to be pushed around by any white policemen, he stepped from behind the lecturn and pulled up his loose-fitting shirt to reveal two service revolvers attached to his belt. His speech received the loudest applause of the evening.

White Reaction

The emergence of this militant "I won't take it" feeling among black policemen has made many white policemen fearful, distrustful, and antagonistic toward many black policemen. In some cases, this white reaction has gone as far as to see some black policemen as traitors to the police service. The white policemen who hold these views are correct in the sense that most of their black colleagues probably do not share the majority pattern of prejudicial feelings and discriminatory actions toward minority group citizens. Both the "I won't take it" feeling and the negative white reaction were vividly illustrated by an incident in Hartford:

> —In Hartford in November 1970, a black policeman slugged a white officer whom the black officer thought was abusing a Puerto Rican girl while arresting her. The Guardians issued a statement which warned that black officers will physically restrain white officers who exercise brutality toward citizens. This incident provoked a strong negative reaction among the white officers, including the managerial hierarchy. We were told that as a result of this incident many white policemen looked upon the black officers as adversaries rather than as colleagues.[11]

The crux of the intrapolice race-relations issue appears to be a fundamental change in black police consciousness. We were told that two decades or so ago, black policemen tended to act as if they felt they were policemen first and black men second. Today, black officers emphasize that they are black men first and policemen second. The much more aggressive activities of the black associations, compared to their activities as recently as seven or eight years ago, clearly manifest this fundamental change in black police consciousness.

Union-Association Relations

As one might conclude from the foregoing discussion, relations between the majority, white-dominated unions and the black officer associations are strained. A white interviewee in one city characterized relations between the union and the black association as a "stand-off—we've got our guns pointed at each other, and each is waiting for the other to make the next move." White policemen appear to be resentful of the black officer associations because these groups have emerged as the vehicles for institutionalized black protest. In addition, many white union leaders and police executives said that black associations are unnecessary because the union fulfills the representation function.

In fact, one of the most important reasons for poor relations is union fears that the black associations may be attempting to usurp their representation role.

—Oakland Police Officers Association officials were apprehensive at the emergence of the Oakland Black Officers Association in 1970, fearing that the OBOA was establishing itself as a rival union. These fears dissipated as it became apparent that the OBOA was concerned with racial grievances and had no intentions of challenging the union's exclusive bargaining representative status.

—Similarly, the New York City Patrolmen's Benevolent Association has become upset at administrative permission for the Guardians to represent their members on certain types of grievances, claiming that such practices violates the PBA's exclusive representative status.

—In another city, we heard some speculation that one of the reasons the union was concerned with obtaining the agency shop, especially since at the time they had more than 95 percent membership, was union leader fears of a rival black union in the department (the city is almost 50 percent black, and black officers are being recruited at a very fast rate).

However, we discovered that in most cities black officers are content to let the union fulfill its traditional role of bargaining for economic and noneconomic benefits and pushing traditional grievances (overtime, seniority rights, transfer, discipline, etc.) while the black officer association concerns itself with the racial grievances of its members and with improving police-black community relations. Consequently, the two groups in most jurisdictions are engaged in noncompeting functions (though they may oppose each other on particular issues). These relatively separate objectives are reflected by association representatives' statements that a majority of the black policemen in their cities are union members. Black policemen are as concerned about economic benefits and traditional grievance representation as are white officers, and several black interviewees explicitly stated their satisfaction with the benefits the union has achieved for them. On the other hand, most black interviewees stated that white union officers could not represent the racial interests of black policemen, since the union officers' constituency is overwhelmingly white. In most of the cities in this sample, blacks constituted such a small percentage of the force (usually in the 5 to 15 percent range), that black officers had no chance of electorally capturing union leadership positions; thus the need for black associations.

The fact that black officers have some needs satisfied by the union and some by the association has resulted in dual union and association memberships for the majority of black officers in most of the twelve departmen s we s u. In no city did any black association interviewee claim that all th policemen were association members, and in some cities it appeared that only a minority of the black officers belonged. In three cities (Omaha, Pitsburgh, and San Francisco) there had been concerted withdrawal of black members from the majority union.

National Amalgamation Efforts

National ties among local black officer associations follow the same loose pattern we saw among majority unions, and for the same basic reason. Any particular black association operates in a local market. It is concerned with the racial grievances of members in a particular local public agency and with police-black community relations in a particular city.[12]

At the time of our field study, the National Council of Police Societies (NCOPS) was the largest organizational amalgamation of local black associations. It included as members associations in New Haven, Hartford, New York, Philadelphia, and other eastern cities. Another multicity organization was the Midwest Regional Council of Police. This group included associations in Pittsburgh, Detroit, Buffalo, Cincinnati, and Cleveland. These organizations hold occasional meetings to exchange information on their activities and to obtain publicity for their efforts. Each is now a zone of the National Black Police Association chartered in Chicago in 1972 with Moses Baldwin of the Detroit Guardians as its first president.

Another organization founded in 1971 was the National Conference on Minority Police. According to one of its founders, local black associations from a variety of cities met three times in 1971 attempting to establish the Conference as an informational and educational organization. As of October 1971, the Conference was attempting to establish a subscription-participant newsletter whose main purpose would be to obtain national publicity for black police grievances in particular cities. It was still functioning as an educational organization when this book went to press.

It was apparent from our conversations with black officer representatives in 1971 that there had been a wide variety of opinions regarding efforts to form national organizations. Representatives in small cities complained of being in organizations dominated by large city associations. Some representatives disagreed with the degree of militancy, or lack of it, expressed by associations in other cities. Some representatives thought that the primary efforts of local and national organizations should be directed toward changing public attitudes about the police, while others emphasized intradepartmental grievances. Several interviewees were vague about the activities of their own local associations and current (as of mid-1971) efforts to form national organizations. While originally we had concluded that because of personal differences, limited financial resources, and especially the localized nature of black association operations it might be some time before a viable national black organization became solidly established, we do note that the National Black Police Association has apparently bridged many of these difficulties and brought all of these organizations together in a national organization dedicated to information sharing, education, and strategy formulation.

Summary

Just as we found a wide variety of behaviors among majority unions and their managerial adversaries, so did we find much variety among black officer associations and their impact upon the department. Some organizations are publicly very militant, others present a conservative image. Some devote their primary efforts toward improving police-black community relations, others emphasize work-related racial grievances of their members. It seems fair to say that all of these associations have aroused some apprehension, fear, anger, or resentment among many white policemen and union leaders.

We see the emergence of active black officer associations as a positive phenomenon. The fact that many of these organizations have come into existence in recent years attests to the increasing number of black policemen. The fact that black policemen no longer tolerate racial abuse is a healthy development. This emergence of militant racial feeling has caused a lot of black-white friction among policemen in the short run, and the incidents we mentioned earlier are a visible manifestation of this friction. However, in the long run this increased and active black presence should contribute to better police-black community relations, to improved police services to the black community, and to improved personnel practices within police departments.

10 An Overview of Impact

The rapid rise of militant police unionism in the middle and late 1960s caught most practitioners and observers by surprise. Contrasting this new militancy with the void which had preceded it, several observers were led to make dire predictions concerning the inordinate power which would accrue to police unions through the bargaining process and the potential abuse of this power in undermining the traditional role of the chief and in influencing the formulation of law-enforcement policy in the community. These predictions, discussed in Chapter 1, were the basis of our inquiry into the labor-relations process as it has evolved in twenty-two municipalities across the country. In this chapter we will review our findings in regard to these predictions, especially as they relate to the power of unions and the bargaining process, the role of the chief and the bargaining process, and the bargaining process and law-enforcement policy.

Bargaining Power and the Bargaining Process

In the absence of fundamental reforms in police-agency personnel policy, it is likely that police unionism will be the wave of the future and that power struggles will continue to develop not only with regard to wages, hours, and conditions of work, but also with respect to law-and-order politics and the relationship of the police to the minority community. This struggle will occur within the context of the labor-relations process, a process which we have defined broadly as not only traditional collective bargaining between employer and employee representatives but also the whole range of elective and legislative political activity which police employee organizations have utilized in pursuing their goals.

The argument is made that bilateral collective bargaining with a political overlay gives the police union an inordinate amount of power relative to the city: not only may the union engage in bargaining, it may leverage its bargaining table power with political power or engage in political activity independent of collective bargaining to achieve goals denied them at the bargaining table. Further, the union may use political activity to affect issues which are not subject to determination through the collective-bargaining process. Examples of each of these kinds of behavior were discussed in Chapters 4, 5, and 7. It would be an error, however, to attribute the worst things people fear to the advent of collective bargaining because in the absence of public employee unionism and

177

collective bargaining, police employee organizations would still utilize the whole range of political activity to achieve goals relating to law-enforcement policy, the relationship to the minority community, and wages, hours, and conditions of work. In this section we look at the current power relationship, the need for redress or a balancing of power, and the potential inherent in the collective-bargaining process for achieving such a balance.

Rationalizing the Bargaining Process

Collective bargaining and the legislative and electoral political processes are not alternatives. The structural diversification of management decision-making authority will always provide an incentive for the union to exploit as many access points as feasible in order to maximize its gains. The changing constitutional climate regarding freedom of speech and participation in political activity merely accelerates this propensity.

In order to rationalize the bargaining process, two things are required: elimination of union access to other city decision-makers during the bargaining process and agreement by other branches of government to deny the union access on bargainable issues after the bargaining process is completed. The integrity of the labor-relations process depends on all issues being aired simultaneously in one arena so that various *quid pro quo* can be worked out which leave each party relatively satisfied for the duration of the resultant agreement. If the union can maximize in each of several arenas (working conditions in the department; wages and hours with the city negotiator or mayor; pensions in the state legislature; early retirement in the city council), the city executive loses control over large segments of his budget. To change the labor-relations process, either the law will have to be restructured, the city will have to convince all of the parties on the management side that the costs of responding to union political pressure are greater than the benefits (assuming they are), or the union will have to be convinced that there is a greater payoff from working within a bilateral process.

Although laws which exclude the union from participation in the legislative and electoral political processes could theoretically be drafted, it is highly unlikely that they would be held constitutional, and even if they were it is even more unlikely that they could or would be enforced. Another possibility would be to draft a law or to get a voluntary agreement which restructured the labor-relations process by centralizing all bargaining authority in a single officer of the government thus eliminating several access points at which the union might exercise political leverage.

This second alternative, rationalization on the management side by joint agreement among the several branches of government in the municipality, did work in one city in our sample where the city manager forced bargaining out of the council into a bargaining committee composed of department heads. However, in this case the nine-man city council was elected at large and the union's electoral power was somewhat diffused. In a city with a larger council elected by districts, it is less likely that such voluntary rationalization could occur, especially if the union had a good track record in electoral politics. An exception to this is Milwaukee where a larger council elected by districts has ceded full responsibility to the city's office of labor relations and denied the unions subsequent access. However, in this case the chief negotiator is a former councilman of long standing who carries a great deal of personal respect and prestige. Even if such voluntary arrangements could be worked out, however, this would still only account for rationalization on a horizontal level and not vertically—the union would still be free to go to the people by referendum or to the state legislature for special benefits. Thus the third alternative—voluntary union-management cooperation in rationalizing the bargaining process—seems to hold the greatest promise.

Earlier in this report we discussed situations where the union put a referendum before the people—and the city opposed them; where the city put a referendum before the people and the union opposed them; where the union introduced bills in the state legislature and the city opposed them; where the city went to the legislature and the union opposed them; where the union attempted to seek changes in employment conditions through the city council and the city opposed them; where the city went to the council and the union opposed them; and where the union sought to bargain over certain issues and the city was able to have these issues declared nonnegotiable. In part this conflict comes about because the union is attempting to exploit as many avenues as possible in seeking to maximize its gains. On the other hand, in the case of charter amendments and in some cases pensions, there is a necessity for either referenda or the enactment of laws at the state level before any changes can be implemented through bargaining. It is on this necessity for changes beyond the bargaining table in order to affect bargaining agreements and on the high cost of adversary proceedings in numerous arenas that a case for voluntary cooperation can be built.

The concept of agreed legislation is one in which all of the interest groups in a potential conflict situation negotiate a mutually acceptable proposal prior to submitting it to a legislative body. Whereas in the normal legislative process a bill would be submitted and each of the interest groups would lobby at cross purposes attempting to get their version adopted, in the agreed legislation process each of the affected interest groups would lobby in favor of the bill which had been mutually agreed upon in advance. In terms of police collective bargaining it would be mutually advantageous if those contract changes which could only be achieved through statutory changes or referenda were first negotiated at the bargaining table and then brought to the appropriate legislative or electoral body as agreed legislation.

Antecedents of agreed legislation can be found in instances of union-management cooperation which have occurred outside of the bargaining process. For example, a rough analogy can be made to the support by some private-sector unions for management's congressional lobbying efforts on behalf of protectionist tariffs, higher subsidies, and more ship bottoms. And in Chapters 4 and 5 we discussed examples of union efforts to increase the city's ability to pay by lobbying for approval of the mayor's budget, lobbying for legislation to enable the city to levy a sales tax, and campaigning for the passage of a city-payroll tax referendum. Finally, the concept of agreed legislation is technically indistinguishable from the current practice in all public-sector collective bargaining of union and executive management jointly lobbying for city-council enactment of necessary legislation to implement mutually acceptable contract terms. The distinction between agreed legislation and this current practice is that agreed legislation envisions a much broader scope.

A second aspect of voluntary cooperation involves the creative nature of the bargaining process itself. Several private-sector examples of this kind of cooperative behavior are often cited—the West and East Coast containerization agreements in longshoring; the Kaiser steel productivity increase sharing agreement; the Armour automation agreement easing job severance for displaced employees. In this study we have cited similar examples where integrative solutions were reached benefiting the police and the city: the trade-off between a shorter workweek and increased use of civilians; shift changes exchanged for night differential pay; introduction of a new rank to replace the loss of detective tenure. All of these examples require that everything be centered on one bargaining table.

Taking both of these concepts together—the creative potential inherent in the bargaining process and the concept of agreed legislation—we can begin to sketch out the incentives for voluntary cooperation. In agreeing to bring all employment issues to one bargaining table and foreswearing subsequent political forays in search of a better deal, the union gives up a great deal of power, especially in those arenas and on those issues where it has been successful. However, it gains in three ways. First, putting all issues on one table opens the door to wide ranging and innovative *quid pro quo* since management will be less wary about having to give in at the bargaining table and then giving in again in the city council and in the state legislature. Second, through the process of agreed legislation the union not only saves money on the lobbying process, but with the city as a partner the union will have greater access and greater credibility on some issues. Third, one of the costs of multilateral bargaining to the union leader is the fact that his rank and file expect him to continually exploit the multiple access points and to deliver. There is no finality to the bargaining process. Rationalizing the bargaining process would take some of this constant pressure off of the leadership. The reader should note, however, that voluntary cooperation does not require that the union cease attempting to leverage bargaining table power *during* the bargaining process.

Management gains a great deal from voluntary cooperation by bringing all issues to one table and eliminating the uncertainty of subsequent union forays. In exchange for this the city has to recognize that it must deal openly with the union and that the cost of a package under voluntary cooperation is apt to be greater than under the previous arrangement. However, this is subject to three qualifications. First, while the initial "cost" (in dollars and in managerial flexibility) of the package may be greater, the total cost over the course of the contract may not be greater—there is no "other shoe" to be dropped from time to time. Second, whether costs are greater or less, at least they can be more accurately anticipated. Third, management gains a measure of control over its own labor-relations process. It can effect *quid pro quo* and exert control over the shape of the package.

Whether these incentives are adequate to effect cooperation remains to be seen. On the one hand, union-management relationships historically have been adversary relationships, with the two sides relating primarily in a distributive or win-lose manner. The union attempts to maximize economic benefits and control over personnel decisions; management attempts to minimize labor costs and maximize managerial discretion and organizational efficiency. Thus the reader rightfully may have serious doubts about the feasibility of this kind of cooperative venture.

On the other hand, municipal executives and police unions presently are faced with a fragmented decision-making structure which imposes costs on both sides. Thus there is an incentive for cooperation of the kind we have discussed. The prime attraction of voluntary cooperation is that unlike legislation mandating a single employer representative or a management-only rationalization scheme which would be difficult to achieve and enforce, it would be a program built on *mutual* advantage and therefore liable to be more durable and more effective than the other two alternatives. Voluntary cooperation does not require an assumption that the adversary nature of the labor-management relationship will disappear; rather, the union and the city will continue to seek their own goals during the bargaining process. It is after agreement has been reached that the parties will jointly seek implementation of those items which require legislative or popular approval.

The Role of the Chief and the Bargaining Process

In Chapter 1 we noted some of the concerns expressed by chiefs of police and the public about the extent to which police unions would undermine the chief's "traditional" authority.

The "Traditional" Authority of
the Chief

In personnel matters the chief of police traditionally has been an autocrat. His power to discipline, discharge, suspend, punish, and reward in an industry patterned after the military model and in which there is no lateral entry led to a substantial degree of control in personnel matters. As we have seen, the chief has lost much of this traditional control; however, the high turnover and declining average age in most departments, the tight labor markets of the late 1960s, and the other environmental factors discussed in Chapter 2 giving rise to militant police unionism were probably as much to account for the undermining of this traditional power as were the unions themselves.

Simultaneously there has been an interest in the community since the early 1960s in reconsidering the locus of policy-making for the police. The reform movements of the 1930s "isolated" the police department from political interference and at least created the impression that the traditional authority of the chief included the formulation of law-enforcement policy for the community. The civil unrest of the 1960s and the police response has created an awareness of the locus of decision-making power and some public concern that it be taken from the police agency and put in the hands of elected officials (and conversely, some public concern that it not).

In both cases—personnel matters and policy formulation—the traditional authority of the chief has clearly been undermined and in both cases the union has emerged as a new power center in the determination of policy. However, it is important to view the union as just that—a powerful new interest group in the policy determination process.

Chamberlain and Cullen present a useful definition of the management function that gets around the sticky question of management rights and management prerogatives. They view the managerial process as the balancing of competing interest groups within an organization so as to achieve the goals of the organization while still meeting the needs of these groups.[1] A private-sector analogy would be a comparison between two firms, one of which does not have to go to capital markets for its cash requirements and the other which does. The former management (such as Ford Motor Company prior to 1955) is free to run its company without reporting either to the government or to stockholders. Its profits and other operating data are a secret. The firm that issues stock or goes to a banker must report operating results to the government and to its stockholders or open its books to the banker and accept certain kinds of restrictions. The latter firm does not go out of business, it simply adjusts its style to accommodate these new power centers. Similarly, when a firm becomes unionized, it adjusts its style to deal with the new power center in its midst by attempting to make only those concessions that are in the long-run best interests of the firm while meeting the economic and institutional needs of the union.

This is a useful concept to adopt in responding to the question "to what extent has the union undermined the 'traditional' authority of the chief?" In this context we can respond that the "traditional" authority has been heavily undermined in both the policy area and the personnel area, but the flow of events has probably been at least as responsible for this as has the union. The role of the union has been twofold: to negotiate a new set of operating rules which move the system toward a new equilibrium position (management by policy, protection of employees against arbitrary or inconsistent treatment, and the institutionalization of the mechanism of collective bargaining for continuing power-based interactions) and to inject into law-enforcement policy debates the voice of the rank and file police officer who must work within the boundaries established by these policy decisions. The chief retains the right to manage subject to these new procedural constraints.

The Role of the Chief in Bargaining

If we assume that the city will attempt to rationalize the bargaining process and move all agenda items to a central bargaining table, what should be the role of the chief. This is a difficult question because much of the answer depends on the role of the chief in his agency.

Traditionally the chief has been under a great deal of pressure to support the wage demands of the union, not only because he rose through the ranks or because his salary is tied by formula to the patrolman's rate but primarily because the men have taken this as a loyalty test: does he support us or them? To fulfill his managerial role and to refuse to support the union is seen as a severe blow to morale. The chief's position on working conditions is less ambiguous. Here he sees clearly the direct challenge to his traditional authority and is usually quite conservative in his approach to change.

As managerial training for police executives becomes more widespread and sophisticated and as the unions come to accept an adversary relationship between certain departmental command personnel and the rank and file, the chief will have an important role to play in collective bargaining. Most important, he will have to insist on a seat in the policy council of the management bargaining team for himself or his representative. Second, he will have to emphasize the program and capital requirements of his budget so his entire resources are not absorbed in personnel expenses. He will have to emphasize those things which he wants recaptured from earlier less sophisticated bargaining days and what he is willing to pay to buy back each of these earlier indiscretions. He will have to advise on what *new* clauses he wants in the contract such as productivity, lateral entry, education requirements, and so forth. He will need to review union proposals for their potential impact on the operation of the department and review management counterproposals as well. In short, he must insist on an active role in the bargaining process in order to maintain his ability to manage in the "new order."

The Bargaining Process and
Law-Enforcement Policy

One of the major problems in policing today is "how to be responsive to the majority interest in the community while protecting the rights of minorities." It is in the context of this question that the issues raised in Chapter 8 have real meaning: the enforcement of the law, the functioning of the criminal justice system, the use of force, the civilian review of police behavior, and the facilitation of citizen identification of police officers.

In our discussion of these issues, or more correctly the manifestations of these issues, we saw how the union, regardless of motivation, was essentially a conservative, reactionary force. We discussed the implications of the impressions these union actions create among members of the minority community, especially their perceptions of police attitudes toward them.

As we have emphasized, this behavior by police employee organizations would not cease if both unionism and collective bargaining were to be outlawed tomorrow. Rather, police employee organizations would continue to utilize the media, the courts, the legislative process and electoral politics (both issue- and candidate-oriented) to achieve these same goals. We argue that the addition of collective bargaining to these other channels of communication and action may serve to enhance rather than restrict the rights of the minority over the long run.

Some of the encouraging steps we perceive in the protection of minority rights are the rise of black officer associations and the types of activities discussed in Chapter 9; the fact that racial grievances can be filed in an established grievance procedure (perhaps leading to final binding neutral arbitration); and the fact that regularized discipline procedures protect blacks and whites. As more minority group members become police officers and as blacks gain increased political power in our major urban areas, these institutionalized procedures will gain even more significance. The machinery now being established and utilized for the purposes of the incumbent majority will continue to be utilized for the purposes of the future majority, even as the nature of that majority changes over time.

A Final Word

The reader will note that in this final chapter we have shifted the emphasis from police unions to the bargaining process, for it is the character of the bargaining process which will in the long run determine the nature of labor-management relations in the police service.

The primary impact of police unions has been to create the outlines of a new system of governance in the police service. This new system not only entails shared decision-making power and review of management personnel decisions, it has also formally removed the sole responsibility for the formulation of personnel policy from the chief's hands to a central labor-relations office. Labor relations is going to become an increasingly important function in the management of police agencies. It remains to be seen how long it will take police managers to accept this fact and to prepare accordingly for this aspect of the "new order."

Notes

Notes

Chapter 1
Introduction

1. Joseph Eszterhas, "Police Unions Are Reaching for More," *Cleveland Plain Dealer*, 24 August 1969.

2. New York: Simon and Shuster, 1969, Ballantine Books Edition, p. 271.

3. Hervey Juris and Kay Hutchison, "The Legal Status of Municipal Police Employee Organizations," *Industrial and Labor Relations Review* 23, 3 (April 1970): 352-66. This emphasis on pathology also dominates William Bopp, *The Police Rebellion: A Quest for Blue Power* (Springfield, Illinois: Charles C. Thomas, Publisher, 1971). For contrast, see John Burpo, *The Police Labor Movement* (Springfield, Illinois: Charles C. Thomas, Publisher, 1972) an interesting first attempt at considering the relationship in more abstract terms.

4. As Juris has stated elsewhere—"The Implications of Police Unionism," *Law and Society Review* 6, 2 (November 1971): 231-45—had it not been for the influence of the 1919 Boston Police Strike, we might not be so far behind in our research in this area. Unfortunately the effect of that strike was to direct attention away from the police employee organizations as they existed toward speculative research as to the potential dangers of police unionism affiliated with the AFL-CIO. The 1944 International Association of Chiefs of Police monograph *Police Unions and Other Police Organizations* and the 1958 revised edition of *Police Unions* saw the challenge as coming solely from affiliated organizations and failed to anticipate the challenge from the local police-only independents. By 1969, however, a special group was able to report to the IACP Convention that while unions were still to be avoided, the chief had better be aware that their own personnel practices were possibly out of line and that unless these practices were remedied the rank and file would turn to employee organizations to engage the chief in collective bargaining in a search for mutually determined remedies. (International Association of Chiefs of Police, "Report of the Special Committee on Police Employee Organizations" [typescript], 1969.)

5. Juris and Hutchison, "Legal Status."

6. Where we had no specific name for the chief labor relations executive, the questionnaire was sent to the mayor/manager's office. We had a specific name for each chief and each union leader.

7. Most of the material in this paragraph comes from Orley Ashenfelter and John Pencavel, "American Trade Union Growth: 1900-1960," *Quarterly Journal of Economics* 83, 3 (August 1969): 434-48.

8. An "international" union is one which has either Canadian, Canal Zone, or Puerto Rican members in addition to its U.S. members.

9. Examples of affiliated unions would include the American Federation of State, County, and Municipal Employees (AFSCME), the Service Employees

International Union (SEIU), and the National Association of Government Employees (NAGE), all of which are public-sector unions who organize police officers; some private-sector affiliates would be the Steelworkers (USW), the Machinists (IAM), and the Electricians (IBEW). Examples of currently independent unions would include the Auto Workers (UAW), the Teamsters (IBT), and the United Mine Workers (UMW). The vast majority of police unions are unaffiliated.

10. This has since been updated by President Nixon in Executive Order 11491.

Chapter 2
Police Employee Organizations

1. Much of the information in this section comes from Don Berney, "Law and Order Politics: A History and Role Analysis of Police Officer Organizations" (unpublished Ph.D. dissertation, University of Washington, 1971); and Philip Kienast, "Police and Fire Fighter Organizations" (Ph.D. dissertation, in progress, Michigan State University, 1971).

2. Berney, "Law and Order Politics," citing Emma Schweppe, *The Firemen's and Patrolmen's Unions in the City of New York* (New York: King's Crown Press, 1948), p. 49.

3. Kienast, "Police," ch. 4, p. 3.

4. Berney, "Law and Order Politics," p. 76.

5. Ibid., pp. 68-76; Kienast, "Police," ch. 4, pp. 1-3. For literature on the PBA see Berney, "Law and Order Politics," chs. 2, 3, 5; Kienast, "Police," ch. 4; Schweppe, *Firemen's and Patrolmen's Unions*; J.P. Gifford, "The Political Relations of the Patrolmen's Benevolent Association in New York City" (unpublished Ph.D. dissertation, Columbia University, 1970).

6. Berney, "Law and Order Politics," p. 77; Kienast, "Police," ch. 4, p. 4.

7. Berney, "Law and Order Politics," p. 78 citing Schweppe, *Firemen's and Patrolmen's Unions*, p. 25; Sterling Spero, *Government as Employer* (New York: Remsen Press, 1948), p. 256. Spero has a lengthy chapter on police unionism.

8. Berney gives a 25-page account; see also Richard L. Lyons, "The Boston Police Strike of 1919," *The New England Quarterly*, 20, 2 (June 1947); Claude M. Fuess, *Calvin Coolidge: The Man From Vermont* (Boston: Little, Brown, & Co., 1940).

9. Francis Russell, "The Strike That Made a President," *American Heritage*, 14, 6 (October 1963); see also the sources in the previous footnote.

10. While the strike hindered the development of active police collective self-improvement efforts for several decades, it had an immediate salutary effect on police economic benefits. Officials in many cities, including Boston, raised police salaries in order to prevent additional walkouts. An historical anecdote:

The current (1971) Boston patrolmen's union president's father-in-law was one of the policemen fired in the 1919 strike.

11. Spero, *Government*, p. 281.

12. It is interesting to compare these early organizational efforts of the two public safety groups. The early police-union movement was destroyed by the Boston strike. However, the early fire-union movement successfully survived thirty work stoppages during 1918-19 (Ibid., p. 231) and went on to encompass almost all of the nation's urban firemen in the International Association of Fire Fighters. Perhaps the difference is that no big wave of fires broke out in these cities.

13. A New Haven, Connecticut policeman told us that when he came on the force in 1945, the old timers then still talked in very disparaging tones about the Boston strike in particular and police unions in general.

14. International Association of Chiefs of Police, *Police Unions* (Washington, D.C.: IACP, 1958). See also a later article in the industry's trade journal, Robert Sheehan, "Lest We Forget," *Police*, pt 1 (September-October, 1959) and pt 2 (November-December 1959).

15. Berney, "Law and Order Politics," pp. 109-16; Kienast, "Police," ch. 4, pp. 8-9.

16. Berney, "Law and Order Politics," p. 118.

17. Ibid., p. 131.

18. Ibid., p. 140.

19. Kienast, "Police," ch. 4, pp. 10-12.

20. Berney, "Law and Order Politics," p. 142.

21. Kienast, "Police," ch. 4, pp. 12-13; included at this initial meeting were representatives from associations in New York City, Detroit, Los Angeles, Chicago, Houston, Milwaukee, San Francisco, Washington, D.C., and state associations in New York, New Jersey, and California. See Berney, "Law and Order Politics," p. 143.

22. Kienast, "Police," ch. 4, p. 14, citing the NCPA constitution.

23. Ibid., ch. 4, p. 14; Berney, "Law and Order Politics," pp. 144-45.

24. Kienast, "Police," ch. 5. In 1968 there were approximately 315,000 municipal policemen. In 1969 the combined membership of ICPA, FOP, AFSCME, and other affiliated locals exceeded 240,000. This does not include unaffiliated organizations. While these figures are not definitive, they lend support to the choice of the term "widespread."

25. Name was changed from National to International Conference of Police Associations in 1965 when the organization added Canadian affiliates.

26. A readable account of police dissatisfaction, including support for George Wallace, is in A. James Reichley, "The Way to Cool the Police Rebellion," *Fortune*, 78, 7 (December 1968): 109-14.

27. Kienast, "Police," ch. 4, pp. 16-17.

28. Two such examples are found in the *Government Employees Relations*

Report, no. 365 (September 7, 1970), B-14; *Wall Street Journal*, 19 January 1971, p. 1.

29. One hundred twenty-seven work stoppages occurred in the protective services (police and fire) from 1966 through 1969, compared to 16 for 1958-65 (Berney, "Law and Order Politics," p. 170), citing Sheila White, "Work Stoppages of Government Employees," *Monthly Labor Review*, 92, 12 (December 1969): 30 and the Labor Management Relations Service, *Public Employee Strikes: Causes and Effects*, no. 7 (no date). A *Government Employee Relations Report* index count revealed 13 police work stoppages between May 1970 and January 1971.

30. As one police union leader told us, "all we want is for everybody to quit taking swipes at us." In addition to our field interviews, other written sources contain repeated references to the increased hostility directed toward the police, particularly from black militants and white radicals. See Skolnick, *The Politics of Protest*, ch. 7; Reichley, "Cool the Police Rebellion"; Berney, "Law and Order Politics," ch. 4; Kienast, "Police," ch. 4; William Bopp, *Police Rebellion*.

31. One union leader told us we should emphasize the police feeling about the lack of high-level support, as it was one of the most important issues affecting his members. As a further example, much of the history of poor relations between New York Mayor Lindsay and the New York City PBA started with Lindsay's establishment of a civilian review board.

32. As we will see in chapters 3 and 4, the emergence of law and order as a political issue gives the police and police unions more potential political power. Thus the law-and-order problem may act as a two-edged sword.

33. Fred P. Graham, *The Self-Inflicted Wound* (New York: Macmillan Company, 1970), ch. 4.

34. *Hartford Courant*, 3 May 1970.

35. The "crime problem" also includes elements of public dissatisfaction with noisy and disorderly expressions of discontent by dissenting students and minority groups.

36. Berney, "Law and Order Politics," p. 157; 18.1 percent increase for police versus 23 percent for federal employees and 35 percent for local transit employees. In 1966 the average maximum patrolman pay in cities over 100,000 was $7,327; U.S. Department of Labor, Bureau of Labor Statistics, *Current Wage Developments*, No. 284 (September, 1971), p. 59.

37. In several large cities top patrolman pay is in the $12,500-$14,500 range.

38. Of the seven work stoppages which occurred in six different cities prior to field visits, five were conducted in the pursuit of economic benefits (Vallejo, Detroit, Rochester, New York City [2]), one was noneconomic (Pittsburgh), and the classification of one depends upon which side's version is accepted (Milwaukee). A *Government Employee Relations Report* check of ten other strikes in 1970-71 reveals eight strikes for economic benefits and two recognition strikes. While many work stoppages were triggered by a noneconomic procedural incident (e.g., an adverse court ruling, a city council refusal to ratify a tentative agreement), the issues in dispute were primarily economic.

39. *Wall Street Journal*, 19 January 1971, p. 1; Skolnick, *Politics of Protest*, ch. 7.

40. New York City interview information.

41. I.R. Andrews, "Wage Inequity and Job Performance: An Experimental Study," *Journal of Applied Psychology* 51 (1967): 39-45; J.S. Adams and W.E. Rosenbaum, "The Relationship of Worker Productivity to Cognitive Dissonance About Inequities," *Journal of Applied Psychology* 46 (1962): 161-64; E.E. Lawler and P.W. O'Gara, "Effects of Inequity Produced by Underpayment on Work Output, Work Quality, and Attitudes Toward the Work," *Journal of Applied Psychology* 51 (1967): 403-410; and A. Friedman and P. Goodman, "Wage Inequity, Self-Qualifications, and Productivity," *Organizational Behavior and Human Performance* 2 (1967): 406-417.

42. Marc Karson, "The Psychology of Trade Union Membership," *Mental Hygiene* 41, 1 (January 1957). See also E. Wight Bakke, *Why Workers Join Unions* (New Haven, Connecticut: Yale University, Labor and Management Center, Reprint no. 1, 1946).

43. The CPPA was founded when a group of patrolmen felt that the FOP was not sufficiently strong in denouncing Mayor Carl Stokes for removing white policemen from the Glenville ghetto after a 1968 shoot-out with black militants in which three policemen and four citizens were killed.

44. *New York Times*, 8 August 1968, p. 18.

45. *New York Times*, 16 August 1968, pp. 1, 38. Soon after the formation of LEG, Cassesse issued a statement calling upon his members to enforce the law "100 percent" even in the face of a direct order to ignore a violation of the law. Mayor Lindsay and then Police Commissioner Leary countered that Patrolman Cassesse did not make departmental policy, and the rhetorical dispute faded after Cassesse issued "guidelines" to his members which consisted of little more than quotations from departmental rules.

46. Cassesse resigned the presidency of the New York City PBA in mid-1969.

47. To avoid the conflict in names, the Cassesse group later changed its name to the National Union of Police Officers (NUPO).

48. Judgments about the nature of organizational activities expressed in this subsection are based on newspaper clippings and interview information and are naturally somewhat impressionistic and subjective.

49. *Wall Street Journal*, 29 July 1969, p. 1.

50. Local control similar to that in policing has existed with other groups of unionized employees working in localized product markets. The best private-sector examples are the building-trades unions in the construction industry (which is moving to more regionalized labor relations); and most other municipal employee unions which, like police unions, operate in a localized industry.

51. This cost-benefit explanation is not totally sufficient. In addition, both the NUPO and IBPO are relatively new organizations and must usually contend with and overcome existing organizational arrangements in their organizing efforts. Similarly, the local cost-benefit thesis does not totally explain AFSCME's failure to enroll large numbers of policemen, since most of its

members also work for municipalities. AFSCME is overwhelmingly a union of civilians, and policemen have been such a small minority in the organization that they have not been able to make their voice heard. Further, interview comments portrayed most policemen as desiring representation by police-only organizations, which reflects their perceptions of the unique nature of the law enforcement industry and its concomitant employment problems. Finally, AFSCME's active involvement in civil rights efforts (which reflects its substantial black membership) has not struck a sympathetic response among police officers.

52. Oakland Police Officers Association, *Call Box* 1, no. 7 (July 1972): 2. This includes Canadian organizations representing more than 5000 policemen.

53. Some of the 1972 goals for example, included a Policemen's Bill of Rights, a national police fair labor standards act, and exemption from income taxes of policemen's first $5,000 of earnings.

54. Kienast, "Police," ch. 5, p. 1.

55. This lack of return on a substantial investment was the main reason given for disaffiliation by the three unions in our sample which formerly were AFSCME locals—Seattle, Omaha, Hartford.

56. After our field visit, Oakland affiliated with the ICPA and the membership voted to drop the PORAC affiliation. Oakland Police Officers Association, *Call Box* 1, nos. 4 and 5 (April and May 1972).

57. From union spokesmen's comments in several departments, it appears that the national organization's primary value is to keep local leaders informed of police-union developments in other cities. This information can be very helpful when preparing for contract or grievance negotiations or for a court case in which the union is involved.

58. Two other bargaining statute options which were included in our questionnaire but did not apply to any of the cities in our field study are: "permissive"—a city may bargain if it wishes—and "prohibited"—state law forbids municipal collective bargaining.

59. Leonard Sayles and George Strauss, *The Local Union* (New York: Harper and Row, 1953); Arnold Tannenbaum and Robert Kahn, *Participation in Union Locals* (Evanston: Row, Peterson and Co., 1958); Theodore Purcell, *The Worker Speaks His Mind on Company and Union* (Cambridge: Harvard University Press, 1953); Arnold Rose, *Union Solidarity: The Internal Cohesion of a Labor Union* (Minneapolis: University of Minnesota Press, 1952); Joel Seidman, et al., *The Worker Views His Union* (Chicago: University of Chicago Press, 1958); Jack Barbash, *American Unions: Structure, Government, and Politics* (New York: Random House, 1967).

Chapter 3
The Nature of Police Labor Relations

1. Neil Chamberlain and Donald Cullen, *The Labor Sector*, 2nd ed. (New York: McGraw-Hill, 1971), p. 204. There are approximately 140,000 separate

union-management contracts in the United States.

2. The relationship may also be seen in political, sociological and psychological contexts. However, it is assumed that the economic context is the more immediate constraint.

Similarly, employees have a bundle of needs, not all of which are economic. However, it is widely accepted that most people's economic needs (for food, clothing, shelter, etc.) take precedence over their social, ego, or self-fulfillment needs. For a widely used "needs hierarchy" see Abraham Maslow, *Motivation and Personality* (New York: Harper and Row, 1954).

3. H. Gregg Lewis, *Unionism and Relative Wages in the United States* (Chicago: University of Chicago Press, 1963).

4. See Albert Rees, *The Economics of Trade Unions* (Chicago: University of Chicago Press, 1962), ch. 3; Harold Levinson, *Determining Forces in Collective Wage Bargaining* (New York: Wiley, 1966), ch. 1; and John Dunlop, *Wage Determination under Trade Unions* (New York: Augustus Kelley, 1950). In their analysis of municipal unionism, Wellington and Winter present the paradigm of the limits of private-sector collective bargaining, and these limits are expressed primarily in the form of a wage-employment trade-off. See Wellington and Winter, *The Unions and the Cities*, ch. 1.

5. See John Dunlop, *Industrial Relations Systems* (New York: Holt, Rinehart, and Winston, 1958), ch. 1.

6. The validity of this bilateral paradigm is reduced if direct wage and price controls become a permanent feature of the American economy.

7. Robert A. Dahl, "The Concept of Power," *Behavioral Science* 2, no. 3 (July 1957): 203.

8. "The view of bargaining power as an effective force behind the whole collective bargaining relationship and the process of intergroup agreement is the one adopted here." Neil Chamberlain and James Kuhn, *Collective Bargaining*, 2nd ed. (New York: McGraw Hill, 1965), p. 170.

9. This analysis of bargaining power is from Chamberlain and Kuhn, *Collective Bargaining*, ch. 7. It is similar to the more summary definition offered by another author: "Bargaining power is viewed as the ability to get advantageous terms in the transaction," with the transaction defined "as the exchange of goods (or satisfaction) between parties." This definition deals only with "selfish transactions, in which each party tries to receive more in return for less." Alfred Kuhn, "Bargaining Power in Transactions: A Basic Model of Interpersonal Relationships," *American Journal of Economics* 23, no. 1 (January 1964): 49-63.

10. This discussion of Marshall is taken from Albert Rees, *The Economics of Trade Unions*, pp. 70-73; citing Alfred Marshall, *Principles of Economics*, 8th ed. (New York: Macmillan, 1920), pp. 383-86.

11. Albert Rees, *Economics of Trade Unions*, ch. 2.

12. "The most significant difference . . . is that labor relations has an economic foundation in industry but a political base in government." David T. Stanley, *Managing Local Government under Union Pressure* (Washington, D.C.: Brookings, 1971), p. 19.

13. In the private sector, selection to the ranks of top management is usually (but not always) based on these administrative abilities.

14. For those services that have a direct cost-price connection or readily available private-sector alternatives such as public transit, an increase in price may very definitely cause a loss of customers.

15. Another example comes from New York City, where Alice Cook's study suggests that "public labor relations are fundamentally determined and carried out under the laws of politics and that the consequent settlements are political acts." Alice Cook. "Public Employee Bargaining in New York City," *Industrial Relations* 9, no. 3 (May 1970): 267.

16. Kenneth McLennan and Michael H. Moskow, "Multilateral Bargaining in the Public Sector," Industrial Relations Research Association, *Proceedings of the Twenty-first Annual Meeting* (Madison: Industrial Relations Research Association, 1969), pp. 31-40. (Hereafter referred to as IRRA.) Moskow and McLennan developed this definition in the context of urban community involvement in schoolboard-teacher union bargaining.

17. Thomas Kochan, "Internal Conflict and Multilateral Bargaining," (Industrial Relations Research Institute, University of Wisconsin, 1971), pp. 17-18.

18. For a detailed discussion of this fragmentation of managerial control over personnel issues, see John F. Burton, Jr., "Local Government Bargaining and Management Structure," *Industrial Relations* 11, no. 2 (May 1972): 123-40.

19. Another way of expressing this dispersion of decision-making authority is to consider municipal government as lacking in the strict hierarchical authority structure of the type found in the private firm. For example, the mayor usually cannot tell the city council how to vote (though he may influence the outcome) nor can he tell a judge how to decide a case (unless, of course, the mayor has *de facto* control via political party hegemony).

20. We are indebted to George Strauss for his suggestion of this distinction.

21. Consequently, this kind of multilateral bargaining is very similar to Kochan's definition.

22. See McLennan and Moskow, "Multilateral Bargaining in the Public Sector." What is labeled here as community multilateral bargaining is very similar to the original McLennan-Moskow concept of multilateral bargaining.

23. This interest is more extensive and intensive than the public's interest in the outcome of the usual contract negotiation process.

24. Interview information; also the *Hartford Courant*, 2, 5, 6, 8, 9, 11 April and 15 December 1970.

25. Interview information; also Don Berney, "Law and Order Politics: A History and Role Analysis of Police Officer Organizations," ch. 5.

26. Police pay and fringes are regulated by the city charter. Increases in police fringe benefits must be approved by the voters, and informal negotiations among the union, city, and business community determined the substance of some of these charter amendments and the degree of support these measures would receive during the election campaign.

27. See Skolnick, *Politics of Protest*, pp. 279-80; and J.P. Gifford, "The Political Relations of the Patrolmen's Benevolent Association in the City of New York (1946-69)" (Ph.D. diss., Columbia University, 1970).

28. San Francisco police pay is pegged to the highest police pay in any other California city over 100,000 population. Cleveland police receive a salary 3 percent higher than the highest police pay in any other Ohio city over 50,000 population.

29. Los Angeles and San Francisco were in the process of establishing bargaining procedures, and a few months after the field visit the San Francisco union signed a noneconomic agreement with the city's police commission; Cleveland bargained with other city employees but not police and fire because the city claimed that the 3 percent charter provision in effect at the time constituted the city's total obligation to its public safety employees; and Baltimore had a collective-bargaining system for all city employee groups except the police.

30. Many state legislatures determine some of the employment conditions of municipal employees in various states. Where this is the case, the police unions must deal with more than one management organization.

Chapter 4
The Contextual Dimensions Affecting
Police-Union Power

1. This categorization is similar to a private-sector bargaining power distinction made by Kuhn: "In short, rather than divide between market forces and bargaining power forces, I think our analysis will be sharper if we divide between (1) those market *and* non-market forces which exist prior to or independent of negotiations, and (2) those market *and* non-market forces which are brought into play, by design or accident, as part of the tactical and strategic maneuvers of the parties during negotiations and/or strike." Alfred Kuhn, "Bargaining Power in Transactions: A Basic Model of Interpersonal Relationships," *American Journal of Economics* 23, no. 1 (January 1964): 62 (italics in original).

2. Murray Edelman, "Concepts of Power," *Proceedings of the 1958 Spring Meeting of the Industrial Relations Research Association*, in *Labor Law Journal* 9, no. 9 (September 1958): 623-28. Simon notes: "The point is that whatever (measurement) quantities we construct must reflect the characteristics of the phenomena we propose to measure with them. Ordinary cardinal (or even ordinal) numbers possess the property that they are completely ordered. If power relations are only partially ordered, then we shall certainly end up by talking nonsense about them if we insist that they should be represented by cardinal numbers, or that we should always be able to predict 'greater' or 'less' of them." Herbert A. Simon, "Notes on the Observation and Measurement of Political Power," *Journal of Politics* 15, no. 4 (November 1953): 514.

3. "... Either side's capacity to get agreement on its own terms depends upon its specific demand." George Hildebrand, "The Public Sector," in *Frontiers of Collective Bargaining*, John Dunlop and Neil Chamberlain, eds. (New York: Harper and Row, 1967), p. 151.

4. For example, see Rees, *The Economics of Trade Unions*, ch. 3.

5. One officer assigned to head recruitment in a major police agency which had not once been able to fill all its vacancies in the preceding twenty-two years pointed proudly to the civil service waiting list and said "when I was assigned to this position in 1969, I prayed for a recession. ..."

6. San Francisco Police Officers Association, *Notebook* 2, no. 4 (June 1971): 1.

7. The San Francisco charter says the police shall receive the highest pay of police in any other California city over 100,000; Oakland specifies that increases in police salaries shall be increased by at least as much as the percentage increase in local manufacturing wages; Cleveland's charter specifies that the police will receive 3 percent more than the highest paid police in any other Ohio city over 50,000 in population.

8. U.S. Department of Labor, Bureau of Labor Statistics, *Current Wage Developments*, no. 284 (September 1971): 60.

9. A large political science literature exists on community power structures and political influence, with the researchers' prime goal the determination of the degree of concentration of political power. For example, see Terry N. Clark, ed., *Community Structure and Decision-Making: Comparative Analysis* (San Francisco: Chandler, 1968).

10. For a scholarly account, see Edward Banfield, *Political Influence* (New York: Free Press, 1961). For a more popular account see Mike Royko, *Boss: Daley of Chicago* (New York: E.P. Dutton & Co., 1971).

11. See Wallace Sayre and Herbert Kaufman, *Governing New York City* (New York: Harcourt, Brace, and World, 1965).

12. See Theodore White, *The Making of the President 1968* (New York: Atheneum, 1969), ch. 7.

13. Hervey Juris, "Police Personnel Problems, Police Unions, and Participatory Management," *Proceedings of the 22nd Annual Winter Meeting* (Madison: IRRA, 1969), p. 318.

14. David Abbott, Louis Gold, and Edward Rogowsky, in *Police, Politics, and Race* (Cambridge: Harvard University Press, 1969), suggest that racial considerations ("white backlash") played a very important role in the board's lopsided defeat. Racial factors were also present in the Hartford gun-guidelines controversy and in the Seattle police vehement reaction to the coroner's inquest proceedings and verdict.

15. For further discussion and other examples see Skolnick, *Justice without Trial*, and *The Politics of Protest*; and Arthur Niederhoffer, *Behind the Shield: The Police in Urban Society* (Garden City, New York: Doubleday, 1967).

16. Berney, "Law and Order Politics," ch. 4.

17. *San Francisco Chronicle*, 16 September 1971.

18. For example, see Chamberlain and Kuhn, *Collective Bargaining*, pp. 282-83; and Orley Ashenfelter and John Pencavel, "American Trade Union Growth: 1900-1960," *Quarterly Journal of Economics* 83, no. 3 (August 1969): 434-48.

19. Arnold Weber, "Paradise Lost: or Whatever Happened to the Chicago Social Workers?" *Industrial and Labor Relations Review* 22, no. 3 (April 1969): 335.

20. In 1968 Eugene Brukiewa, president of the AFSCME police local in Baltimore, was suspended for publicly criticizing the department and the police commissioner. A state appeals court overturned his suspension: *Brukiewa v. Police Commissioner of Baltimore City*, 257 Maryland 36; 263 A. 2nd 210 (1970). In 1967 Joseph Stanek, president of the Pittsburgh FOP lodge, was suspended for six months for running for city council in violation of a city ordinance which prohibited policemen from being candidates for office. See the *Pittsburgh Press*, 16 March, 25 August, and 15 December 1967.

21. For a fuller discussion of the legal context of free speech, political activity, and the police, see ch. 8; also the *Wall Street Journal*, 30 October 1969, p. 1, for a discussion of police political activity in 1969 local elections.

22. See David T. Stanley and Carole L. Cooper, *Managing Local Government under Union Pressure* (© 1972 by Brookings Institution, Washington, D.C.), pp. 7-9. Stanley uses the label "less strong mayor" instead of "weak mayor."

23. Some readers may object to our including San Francisco in the strong mayor category. For instance, Stanley, *Managing Local Government*, p. 8; says that San Francisco "defies classification." However, the mayor is the city's dominant political figure; he appoints the city's three police commissioners, and he appears to be the single most important elected official with whom the police union interacts.

24. See the discussion in "The Influx of Young Policemen" section in chapter 2.

25. Chamberlain and Cullen, *The Labor Sector*, p. 211.

26. For similar findings from another field study which included nine of the same cities considered in this analysis, see Stanley, *Managing Local Government*, pp. 115-18.

27. For instance, Marine boot camp and fraternity initiation rites serve to develop cohesion among group members, in addition to satisfying other objectives.

28. Several authors have commented on the high degree of occupational solidarity or cohesiveness among policemen. See William Westley, *Violence and the Police: A Sociological Study of Custom, Law and Morality* (Cambridge: MIT Press, 1970), ch. 4; Niederhoffer, *Behind the Shield*; Skolnick, *The Politics of Protest*, ch. 7, and *Justice without Trial*, ch. 3; Kienast, "Police and Fire Fighter

Organizations," ch. 1; and Albert Reiss, *The Police and the Public* (New Haven: Yale University Press, 1971).

29. See Westley, *Violence*. Police management interviewees in several cities mentioned that this code of secrecy makes the imposition of internal discipline quite difficult.

30. David B. Truman, *The Governmental Process* (New York: Alfred A. Knopf, 1951), p. 159; and Robert A. Dahl, "A Critique of the Ruling Elite Model," *The American Political Science Review* 52, no. 2 (June 1958): 465.

31. This cohesiveness also helps explain why police and firefighters historically have been more highly organized than other groups of city employees. See Kienast, "Police and Fire Fighter Organizations," ch. 1.

32. The reader will recall from Table 2-1 that these two cities are covered by neither city nor state statutes regulating the labor-management relationship—no doubt a contributing factor to the fact that no exclusive representative has yet been selected in either city.

33. *Baltimore Sun*, 15 March 1968.

34. In the performance of these duties the police also provide a wide variety of social services. For several enlightened and enlightening discussions of the police function, see James Q. Wilson, *Varieties of Police Behavior* (Cambridge: Harvard University Press, 1968); American Bar Association, *Standards Relating to the Urban Police Function*, tentative draft (New York City: American Bar Association, 1972); Egon Bittner, *The Functions of the Police in Modern Society*, Public Health Service Publication no. 2059 (Washington: USGPO, 1970); and Albert Reiss, *The Police and the Public.*

35. See Skolnick, *Justice without Trial*, pp. 49-53.

36. J.P. Gifford, "The Political Relations of the Patrolmen's Benevolent Association in the City of New York (1946-69)" (Ph.D diss., Columbia University, 1970), pp. 315-16.

Chapter 5
The Manipulatable Dimensions of Union Power

1. Robert A. Dahl, *Modern Political Analysis* (Englewood Cliffs, New Jersey: Prentice-Hall, 1963), p. 43.

2. See Gifford, "The Political Relations of the Patrolmen's Benevolent Association in the City of New York (1946-69)," ch. 9. Of course, many other factors are important determinants of these PBA successes, especially the fact that the legislature does not have to fund PBA-sponsored economic legislation.

3. Dayton D. McKean, "Patterns of Politics," in *The 50 States and Their Local Governments*, James W. Fesler, ed. (New York: Knopf, 1967), p. 246: "A more fundamental difficulty with the term *lobbyist* is that it ignores what is an increasingly important part of the work of the representatives of groups: following the administration and the courts." See also Abraham Holtzman, *Interest Groups and Lobbying* (New York: Macmillan, 1966), ch. 5.

4. While police union litigation is very common, our field research did not uncover enough instances of judicial lobbying to warrant separate treatment. Influencing judicial elections is considered under the heading of electoral politics; only one example was found of a union filing an *amicus* brief (in support of the police commissioner's right to refuse to release internal police statements about their actions during a civil disturbance).

5. Interviewee comments about lobbying indicated that threats are rarely used. For a similar finding from a more intensive study of the lobbying process in state legislatures, see Harmon Ziegler and Michael Baer, *Lobbying: Interaction and Influence in American State Legislatures* (Belmont, California: Wadsworth), pp. 120-21.

6. The charter language is officially permissive, but the city has always interpreted it as "shall" rather than "may."

7. See the *San Francisco Chronicle*, 12 August 1969.

8. "A primary concern of all organized political interest groups in the United States is the character of opinions existing in the community. Group leaders, whatever else they may neglect, cannot afford to be ignorant of widely held attitudes bearing upon the standing and objectives of their organization." David B. Truman, *The Governmental Process*, 2nd ed. (New York: Knopf, 1971), p. 213.

9. An exception is the use of consumer boycotts in private-sector labor disputes. However, private-sector unions rely much more upon an actual or threatened withholding of service than upon consumer boycotts, and, as Rees has observed, these boycotts generally are a weak weapon. Albert Rees, *The Economics of Trade Unions*, pp. 42-43.

10. A union president in one city maintained a membership in the local press club and made a point of being personally acquainted with all the local newspaper and television reporters. He claimed he had never received a "bad press" on any issue in which his union had been involved.

11. During this impasse the Cranston IBPO local sponsored a local contest. The union publicly offered $250 to anyone who developed an idea that would get the mayor back to the bargaining table. The union generously announced that the mayor and his family were eligible to participate. The mayor was not amused.

12. This shoot-out, which Detroit police describe as an ambush by black militants, occurred at Detroit's New Bethel Baptist Church on the night of March 29, 1969. The police arrested 142 suspects and took them to the local station house, where several hours later Judge Crockett ordered their release. Crockett's actions soon became the most bitterly contested aspect of the entire sequence of events. For an analysis of the role of the news media in the incident, see Donald I. Warren, "Mass Media and Racial Crisis: A Study of the New Bethel Church Incident in Detroit," *Journal of Social Issues* 28, no. 1 (1972): 111-31.

13. The gathering of signatures may take place simply to amass some quantifiable but nonbinding measure of public support (as in Detroit, and

Milwaukee during the poststrike contract negotiations), or they may be conducted in order to place an initiative or referendum measure on the ballot (as in
the 1966 New York City PBA fight against the civilian review board and in a
1970 effort in San Francisco to place a fringe benefit charter amendment on the
ballot).

14. See the *Hartford Courant*, 11 April 1970.

15. The union-purchased advertisements appeared in the *Seattle Post-Intelli-
gencer*, 3 June 1970; and were subsequently condemned by the Seattle Crime
Prevention Advisory Commission as inflammatory and contributing "to the
current polarization and fragmentation of society. . . ." See Berney, "Law and
Order Politics," pp. 304-308.

16. See the *Detroit Free Press*, 15 April 1969. The *Free Press* refused the
Detroit Police Officers Association's advertisement because it was "inflammatory" (but printed an article about it). The *Detroit News* accepted it.

17. For some details of this exchange and the internal union repercussions,
see the *Boston Globe*, 5 and 13 September 1970.

18. For an analysis of this dispute, see A.H. Raskin, "Politics Up-Ends the
Bargaining Table," in the American Assembly, *Public Workers and Public
Unions*, Sam Zagoria, ed. (Englewood Cliffs, New Jersey: Prentice-Hall, 1972),
pp. 135-39.

19. See the *Boston Globe*, 30 June 1970.

20. The descriptions of these disruptions are taken primarily from interview
responses obtained during the field research. Additional information was
obtained from the Bureau of National Affairs, *Government Employee Relations
Report; The New York Times, The Rochester Times-Union* and *Rochester
Democrat and Chronicle, The Detroit Free Press*, and the *Pittsburgh Post-
Gazette.*

21. The union was seeking to force the city to implement a 3.5 to 3.0 pay
ratio with police sergeants to which the city had agreed two years previously.
Instead of ordering the city to implement the ratio, the court ruled that the city
had the right to a jury trial on the matter. At the time of the strike, the city's
liability totaled $2700 to each patrolman—$100 for each of the 27 months since
October, 1968 when the sergeants had received their pay raise—and the
patrolmen had been repeatedly assured by their union leaders that a judicial
victory was certain.

22. A *paid detail* is protective service work performed by a policeman on his
own time for extra money over and above his regular salary. Typical examples
include the security guard-type services delivered to industrial firms, sporting
events, construction sites, private parties, and so forth. In Boston paid detail
work is administered by the department, with management allocating the
available details among the patrolmen on the detail list. The hourly rate and
minimum number of hours are determined via collective bargaining with city
management and incorporated in the contract. In contrast, paid detail work in
several other cities is not departmentally administered, but is left up to
individual police officers and the contracting third parties.

23. See the *Boston Globe*, 8 January 1970.

24. See the *Hartford Courant*, 3, 4, 5, 6, 7, 9, 12, 13, 14, and 17 August 1969.

25. Even the two authors who are always cited when the right to strike in the public sector is discussed exclude the police (and fire) from this right. See John Burton and Charles Krider, "The Role and Consequences of Strikes by Public Employees," *Yale Law Journal* 69, no. 3 (January 1970): 418-40.

26. It can be argued that the death and destruction which accompanied the strikes in Boston and Montreal were a function of the failure of the city and the department to have any contingency plans. In the 1919 case this is understandable; in the Montreal situation it may be that the city was lulled into a false sense of security by the existence of a law mandating compulsory binding arbitration. In New York and Milwaukee where contingency plans were implemented, the same problems did not arise. A contributing factor may have been the fact that both strikes took place in the dead of winter, and one can only specualate what would have happened if these two strikes had occurred during an August heat wave. Vallejo's small size made it relatively easy for substitute law-enforcement personnel to provide a police presence. The other disruptions were partial strikes, and enough nonstrikers were available to maintain a police presence.

27. During the Detroit ticket strike there were estimates that the city had been collecting as much as $7 million yearly in traffic fines. [John A. Grimes, *Work Stoppages: A Tale of Three Cities* (Washington, D.C.: Labor-Management Relations Service, May 1970) no. 1, *Strengthening Local Government Through Better Labor Relations.*] Total city revenues for the 1966-67 fiscal year were $300 million (U.S. Department of Commerce, Bureau of the Census, *City Government Finances in 1966-67*, p. 30). If the one month ticket strike (ticket-writing dropped by about 80 percent) produced no tickets, the city would have lost about one-twelfth of $7 million in traffic fines or $583,000 or one-fifth of one percent of total city revenues for the year. To cite another example, New York City saved three days' pay for each day the January 1971 strikers did not work by applying the antistrike penalties of the state's public-sector collective-bargaining law.

Wellington and Winter also describe the noneconomic nature of a public-sector work stoppage: "The public employee strike is fundamentally different from the strike in the private sector; its sole purpose is to exert political pressure on municipal officials. They are deprived, not of revenues, but of the political support of those who are inconvenienced by a disruption of municipal services." Wellington and Winter, *The Unions and the Cities*, pp. 25-26.

28. See the *Trenton Evening Times*, 15, 16, 17, 18, and 28 February 1971. Many trucks did not cross the picket lines, but for those who wished to, it was easy to evade the picketed intersections.

29. For a detailed chronology of the Philadelphia affair, see Stephen Halpern, "The Role of Police Employee Organizations in the Determination of Police Accountability Procedures in Baltimore, Philadelphia and Buffalo,"

mimeo. (paper delivered at the meeting of the American Political Science Association, September 5-9, 1972).

30. The federal courts have a strict policy of noninvolvement in the determination of the substantive terms and conditions of employment. " . . . Allowing the Board [NLRB] to compel agreement when the parties themselves are unable to do so would violate the fundamental premise on which the [National Labor Relations] Act is based—private bargaining under governmental supervision of the procedure alone, without any official compulsion over the actual terms of the contract." *H.K. Porter Co. v. NLRB*, 397 U.S. 99, cited in Bureau of National Affairs, *Daily Labor Report*, no. 41 (March 1970): D-3.

31. Arbitration in Rhode Island, Pennsylvania, and Michigan is provided by state law; in Vallejo it is part of a recently revised (1970-71) city charter. Since our field research was completed, New York City, Oakland, and Wisconsin have established compulsory arbitration procedures which cover police negotiation disputes.

32. The limited evidence available suggests that the majority of fact-finder recommendations in the public sector are either accepted in toto or else become the basis for additional direct negotiations which lead to a settlement. See Michael Moskow, Joseph Loewenberg, and Edward Koziara, *Collective Bargaining in Public Employment* (New York: Random House, 1970), pp. 279-80, and Thomas Gilroy and Anthony Sinicropi, "Impasse Resolution in Public Employment: A Current Assessment," *Industrial and Labor Relations Review* 25, no. 4 (July 1972): 500-502.

33. We use this concept as it is used in Herbert A. Simon, "Notes on the Observation and Measurement of Political Power," *The Journal of Politics* 15, no. 4 (November 1953): 500-516.

34. Peter Bachrach and Morton Baratz, *Power and Poverty: Theory and Practice* (New York: Oxford University Press, 1970), p. 44. Their ideas first appeared in "Two Faces of Power," *The American Political Science Review* 56 (1962): 947-52; and "Decisions and Nondecisions: An Analytical Framework," *American Political Science Review* 57 (1963): 641-51.

35. "Our Critics . . . have made much of the point that B's nonaction, based upon his anticipation of A's reaction, is a 'non-event' which is, by nature, impossible of empirical verification." However, Bachrach and Baratz respond that "although absence of conflict may be a non-event, a decision which results in prevention of conflict *is* very much an event . . . ." Bachrach and Baratz, *Power and Poverty: Theory and Practice*, p. 46.

36. George Hildebrand, "The Public Sector," in *Frontiers of Collective Bargaining*, John Dunlop and Neil Chamberlain, eds. (New York: Harper and Row, 1967), p. 151.

37. While the overall incidence of parity is on the wane, it is still very much a factor in many of the large cities including most of the cities in our sample. In response to an item on our questionnaire, "Has parity ever existed in your city?"

43 police department respondents said "yes" and 5 said "no"; in response to the next question "Does parity presently exist?" 33 said "yes" and 13 said "no." See also David Lewin, "Wage Parity and the Supply of Police and Firemen," *Industrial Relations*, 12, 1 (February 1973): 77-85.

38. The Los Angeles Fire and Police Protective League still exists, but it has been reorganized into the Fire Chapter and the Police Chapter as a result of the city's implementation of a collective-bargaining system and the creation of separate bargaining units. In addition, the Fire Chapter has merged with Local 112 of the International Association of Fire Fighters, AFL-CIO.

39. The police sergeants union has filed unfair labor practice charges with the city's Office of Collective Bargaining, claiming that the contractual patrolman-sergeant pay ratio limited the sergeants' ability to bargain freely. Similarly, the Hartford police union filed a ULP charge with the Connecticut State Board of Labor Relations complaining that a "me-too" parity clause in firefighters' contract limited the police union's ability to bargain for itself.

40. Kienast, "Police," ch. 6.

Chapter 6
Police-Union Impact on the Potential
for Professionalization

1. Howard M. Vollmer and Donald L. Mills, eds., *Professionalization* (Englewood Cliffs, N.J.: Prentice-Hall, 1966), pp. vii-viii.

2. Ibid., p. 8.

3. O.W. Wilson, *Police Administration*, 2nd ed. (New York: McGraw-Hill Book Co., 1963).

4. Archie Kleingartner, *Professionalism and Salaried Worker Organization* (Madison, Wisconsin: Industrial Relations Research Institute, University of Wisconsin, 1967), p. 10.

5. Richard H. Hall, *Occupations and the Social Structure* (Englewood Cliffs, N.J.: Prentice-Hall, 1969), pp. 74-77, citing Ernest Greenwood, "Attributes of a Profession," *Social Work* 2, 3 (July 1957): 45-55.

6. Other authors have looked at the professionalization of the police. Arthur Niederhoffer, a sociologist and former New York City police officer, says that there is a concerted effort by many police officers to professionalize the police service (in our terms, they are engaged in the struggle for professional status) but that they have not made much headway. He sees the largest stumbling block as being the law-enforcement occupation's "traditionally low status in our culture. . . . There can be no profession where the public refuses to grant high status and prestige." A. Neiderhoffer, *Behind the Shield: The Police in Urban Society*, p. 21. Albert Reiss, a Yale sociologist says, on the other hand, that the police are professionals. Reiss defines the core of professionalism as the exercise of discretion with respect to clients and argues that the police exercise

the highest order of discretion—coercive authority over citizens. He then goes on to discuss how the bureaucracy limits this exercise of discretion and inhibits professionalization. A. Reiss, *The Police and the Public*, pp. 121-26. Susan White presents a proposal which encompasses the analysis used in this chapter as well as those used by Neiderhoffer and Reiss. Ms. White says that professionalization only has meaning in the context of the organization from which services are delivered and depends upon the development of an appropriate definition of the police function. She then develops a series of hypotheses relating function and organization. S. White, "A Perspective on Police Professionalization," *Law and Society Review*, Fall 1972, pp. 61-85.

7. Hervey Juris and Joseph Moag, working paper (in process) on the prerequisites for professionalization in the police service. The authors are indebted to Professor Moag for his comments on earlier drafts of this chapter.

8. James Q. Wilson, *Varieties of Police Behavior* (New York: McGraw-Hill Book Co., 1968).

9. American Bar Association Project on Standards for Criminal Justice, *Standards Relating to The Urban Police Function* (American Bar Association, 1972); Egon Bittner, *The Functions of the Police in Modern Society* (Washington, D.C.: National Institutes of Mental Health, Public Health Service Publication no. 2059, November 1970); President's Commission on Law Enforcement and Administration of Justice, *The Challenge of Crime in a Free Society* and *Task Force Report: The Police* (Washington, D.C.: U.S. Government Printing Office, 1967); Wilson, *Varieties of Police Behavior.*

10. Contrast the training for performance of the police function with the training for supervision, administration, and management in police agencies. In the latter case, there is generalization and focus on the managerial aspect of the function, and therefore formal training on an occupational level.

11. Charles B. Saunders, Jr., *Upgrading the American Police* (Washington, D.C.: Brookings Institution, 1970); John H. McNamara, "Uncertainties in Police Work: The Relevance of Police Recruits' Backgrounds and Training" in David J. Bordua, editor, *The Police: Six Sociological Essays* (New York: John Wiley and Sons, Inc., 1967); and Niederhoffer, *Behind the Shield.*

12. Hall, *Occupations*, p. 112.

13. Ibid., pp. 109-110 citing W. Richard Scott, "Reactions to Supervision In a Heteronomous Professional Organization," *Administrative Science Quarterly* 20, 1 (June 1965): 65-81.

14. Ibid., p. 109.

15. Ibid., pp. 109-110.

16. Ibid., p. 111.

17. An organization may be heteronomous with a lay board or heteronomous with a professional board. Our concern is with the nonprofessional board.

18. Hall, *Occupations*, p. 112.

19. George Kelling and Robert Kleismet, "Resistance to the Professionalization of the Police," *Police Chief* (May 1971): 35-36.

20. See Wilson, *Varieties of Police Behavior*; Reiss, *The Police and the Public*; and Bittner, *The Functions of the Police in Modern Society*.

21. Portland, Oregon (which was not in our sample) has recently concluded a contract which says no change may be made without the *prior approval* of the union.

22. President's Commission, *Challenge of Crime*.

23. Hervey Juris, "Police Personnel Problems, Police Unions, and Participatory Management," *The Proceedings of the 22nd Annual Meeting of the Industrial Relations Research Association* (Madison, Wisconsin: IRRA, 1969), pp. 311-20.

Chapter 7
Police-Union Impact on the Chief's
Ability to Manage

1. Sumner Slichter, James Healy, and Robert Livernash, *The Impact of Collective Bargaining on Management* (Washington, D.C.: Brookings Institution, 1960), pp. 954-57.

2. Because of the breadth of the material covered in this chapter, the reader may find it helpful to skim through the various subheadings throughout the chapter and to read the summary section carefully before coming back to reread the material. There is so much detail presented that it is difficult to maintain perspective. We believe the above suggestion will be helpful in overcoming this problem.

3. The police had been offered a compromise which both unions rejected: if each officer worked 13 hours less per month, the men would not be laid off. The unions preferred unemployment. However, in 1972, with a different mayor, faced with a 10 percent layoff or a 10 percent pay cut (to be repaid at retirement) the unions endorsed the deferred payment. See below for three more cases involving a wage-employment trade-off in the police service.

4. *Buffalo Evening News*, 15 August 1968.

5. The union then demanded working conditions parity with the fire fighters: beds in the precinct houses, color TV sets, elimination of the 20-hour moonlighting restriction. This was done tongue in cheek but resulted in many column inches of publicity.

6. *Seattle Times*, 10 December 1969.

7. The New York City fire/police officer pay ratio case was an extremely complex dispute involving the bargaining relationship, fact-finding, and law suits before it was ultimately resolved.

8. For a more detailed account of this complex dispute, see A.H. Raskin,

"Politics Up-Ends the Bargaining Table," American Assembly, *Public Workers and Public Unions*, Sam Zagoria, ed. (Englewood Cliffs, N.J.: Prentice-Hall, 1972), pp. 135-39.

9. See the *New Haven Register*, 14, 15, and 18 May 1969.

10. Consider the implications of having the least seasoned men on the street during the most demanding time period.

11. See the section below on night-shift differentials for a more comprehensive account of this situation.

12. See the *Buffalo Evening News*, 26 September and 11 October 1968.

13. Kelling and Kleismet refer to this in their article ("Resistance to Professionalization," *Police Chief*, May 1971) when they discuss the police officer as the one interested party to a criminal matter not considered when scheduling, continuances, and so forth are being discussed.

14. The union filed an interesting grievance challenging a management interpretation of this clause: the city was not including the shift premium in the checks of men injured or on sick leave. The union said they deserved the money because it was part of their regular pay. The arbitrator agreed.

15. See the *Buffalo Evening News*, 6 January and 19 February 1968.

16. See the *Pittsburgh Post-Gazette*, 25 January, 12 February, and 5 March 1969, and 15 April 1970.

17. See the *Pittsburgh Post-Gazette*, 24 June, 1 and 29 July, and 5 August 1970.

18. See the *Pittsburgh Post-Gazette*, 20, 21, 22, and 23 April 1970.

19. See the *Boston Globe*, 14 April, 16, 18, 19, and 20 June 1969.

20. See the *Pittsburgh Press*, 6 December 1966.

21. See an 18 November 1970 editorial in the *Pittsburgh Post-Gazette* arguing for the repeal of the trial board system.

22. Archie Kleingartner, *Professionalism and Salaried Worker Organization* (Madison, Wisconsin: Industrial Relations Research Institute, University of Wisconsin, 1967).

23. For example, a managerial interviewee in one large eastern city admitted that when overtime was costless the department regularly "overpoliced" parades and political demonstrations, and on occasion small demonstrations had more police than participants.

24. We know too little about the change process generally and almost nothing about change in police agencies. See Robert B. Duncan, "The Climate for Change in Three Police Departments: Some Implications for Action," *Fourth National Symposium on Law Enforcement Science and Technology* (Washington, D.C., May 2, 1972).

25. Stanley, *Managing Local Government*.

26. Slichter et al., *Impact of Collective Bargaining*, pp. 947-51.

27. Ibid., p. 952.

28. Ibid., pp. 952-54.

29. Ibid., pp. 957-60.

30. Stanley, *Managing Local Government*, pp. 138-39.

31. Ibid., p. 139.

32. Ibid., p. 140.

33. Ibid., p. 145.

34. Ibid., p. 145.

35. Ibid., pp. 148-49.

36. Ibid., pp. 150-51.

37. Ibid., pp. 151-52.

Chapter 8
Police-Union Impact
on the Formulation of Law-Enforcement
Policy

1. We are indebted to Herman Goldstein for his discussions with us on policy generally and especially for his comments on earlier drafts of this chapter.

2. *New York Times*, 13 August 1968, p. 1. It also represented an attempt by Cassesse to co-opt the conservative dissatisfaction in the PBA represented by the emergence of the Law Enforcement Group (examined in Chapter 2).

3. *Boston Globe*, 15 August 1968.

4. *Baltimore Sun*, 17 April 1968.

5. The union was bitterly critical of city officials' use of "red vest" patrols of ghetto youths used to help calm the situation, for the police maintained that many of these youths also engaged in lawless behavior.

6. Fraternal Order of Police, Fort Pitt Lodge No. 1, *A Report: The Manchester Incident, June 21, 1970* (Pittsburgh: Fraternal Order of Police, 1970), esp. pp. 86-91.

7. Norton Long, "The City as Reservation," *Public Interest* (Fall 1971), pp. 22-38.

8. The court found in favor of the police officer who resided outside the city but decided the case on such narrow grounds that it did not establish a precedent.

9. This occurred in Pittsburgh in 1968 when the city was having some difficulty finding qualified applicants. The union president proposed raising police pay instead. See *Pittsburgh Press*, 5 June 1968. A union leader in another city, which had a residency requirement but which interviewees said was about to be eliminated, was ambivalent about the requirement's expected demise. On the one hand, his members are strongly in favor of its elimination, so he was not in a position to push for its retention. On the other hand, he believed the union would have reduced municipal political clout if substantial numbers of policemen moved out of the city, thus making his job more difficult.

10. See the *San Francisco Chronicle*, 6 January 1972, p. 1.

11. For a presentation of the PBA's position, see the statement by PBA President Robert McKiernan on the "op-ed" page of the *New York Times*, 7 February 1973, p. 39.

12. Figures on the assaults on police officers and the number of officers killed are available in the annual Federal Bureau of Investigation, *Crime in the United States, Uniform Crime Reports* (Washington, D.C.: United States Government Printing Office).

13. For a more detailed account of union efforts in Buffalo, Baltimore, and Philadelphia, see Stephen Halpern, "The Role of Police Employee Organizations in the Determination of Police Accountability Procedures in Baltimore, Philadelphia, and Buffalo," mimeo, State University of New York at Buffalo, 1972.

14. See the *Pittsburgh Press*, 6, 10, 11 June 1969.

15. See *Detroit News*, 18 June 1971.

16. For two examinations of relations between the police and the civilian community, see Skolnick, *Justice without Trial*, ch. 3; and Reiss, *The Police and the Public*.

17. *Omaha World-Herald*, 25 July 1971.

18. In 1970 the Seattle union endorsed a state supreme court candidate and a local superior court candidate, and in 1970 the Baltimore AFSCME local endorsed a municipal court candidate. Of these three, only the Seattle superior court candidate won at the polls.

19. Descriptions of these Pittsburgh efforts can be found in Ralph Hallow, "The Mayor is 'Nobody's Boy,' " *Nation*, April 19, 1971, pp. 492-96; *Pittsburgh Post-Gazette*, 1, 22, and 26 October 1970.

20. The union president also claimed that these union-sponsored actions averted a strike by channeling rank-and-file energies into legitimate protest activities.

21. See the *Pittsburgh Post-Gazette*, 13 March and 22 September 1971. These policemen were disciplined by departmental trial boards for receiving the money.

22. *Buffalo Evening News*, 6 January and 19 February 1968.

23. *Rochester Democrat and Chronicle*, 12 September 1970.

24. *Rochester Democrat and Chronicle*, 18 April 1968.

25. *Rochester Democrat and Chronicle*, 18 January and 28 May 1971. The book in question was *Sylvester and the Magic Pebble* by William Steig.

26. What we referred to in Chapter 6 as the quest for professional status.

27. For a discussion of the political activities of social and fraternal organizations who were the predecessors of the current employee organizations, see Chapter 2.

28. *McAuliffe v. City of New Bedford*, 155 Mass. 216, 220, 29 N.E. 519 (1892).

29. From a legal point of view: "The First Amendment and Public Employees: *Times* Marches On," 57 *Georgetown Law Review* 134 (1968). From an operational point of view: Anthony Mondello, "The Federal Employee's Right to Speak," *Civil Service Journal* (January-March, 1970), pp. 16-21.

Chapter 9
Black Officer Organizations

1. Both of the authors are white. While black researchers might have achieved access in more cities, we believe we were treated with openness and candor. For a variety of reasons we were unable to talk with association leaders in Buffalo, Hartford, Los Angeles, and Omaha.

2. The Connecticut Guardians has members in Hartford and nearby cities.

3. See Nicholas Alex, *Black in Blue* (New York: Appleton-Century-Crofts, 1969), pp. 105-108 for a discussion of the same paradox in New York City.

4. The New York City Guardians is the largest black officer association we encountered, and it has approximately 2000 members. Compare that to the PBA's approximately 25,000 members. Similar ratios existed in other cities. The implications for relative political influence and financial resources to support organization activities are obvious.

5. This concern was expressed also by the chief in a large city who said that since the union was the exclusive representative he could not formally deal with the black officers group even if the union was not representing their interests. He felt that at best he could only entertain the complaints of individual blacks.

6. *Hartford Courant*, 22 and 26 July, 3, 4, 5, 6, 7 August 1969. We were unable to interview Guardian representatives in Hartford.

7. William A. Westley, *The Police: A Sociological Study of Law, Custom and Morality* (Cambridge, Mass.: The MIT Press, 1970); Jerome Skolnick, *Justice Without Trial* (New York: John Wiley & Sons, 1966); Arthur Niederhoffer, *Behind the Shield*; Burton Levy, "Cops in the Ghetto: A Problem of the Police System," *American Behavioral Scientist* (March-April, 1968): 31-34; W.E. Groves and Peter Rossi, "Police Perceptions of a Hostile Ghetto," *American Behavioral Scientist*, 13, 5 and 6 (May-June, July-August, 1970): 727-43; Albert Reiss, *Police and The Public* (New Haven: Yale University Press, 1971).

8. Manifestations of black hostility toward police include riots, attacks on policemen, abusive language, and noncooperation with police investigators.

9. See the *Wall Street Journal*, 4 September 1968, p. 1 for a story of the abuse suffered by one black policeman in Los Angeles.

10. Alex, *Black in Blue*, p. 14.

11. *Hartford Courant*, 20 November 1970.

12. We did note, however, that in a few cities (Hartford, Detroit, Pittsburgh, New Haven, Baltimore) the respective black associations include as members not only black policemen employed in the central city police department but also law-enforcement officers from neighboring city and county jurisdictions.

Chapter 10
An Overview of Impact

1. Neil Chamberlain and Donald Cullen, *The Labor Sector* (New York: McGraw-Hill Book Co., Inc., 1971), pp. 223-32.

Glossary

Glossary of Labor-Management Terms (With Particular Reference to the Police Service)

Advisory Arbitration

If in the course of negotiating a new (or first) agreement the parties find themselves unable to reach a mutually satisfactory arrangement, they may proceed to advisory arbitration. Advisory arbitration refers to the process whereby a neutral third party holds a hearing and recommends what the new terms and conditions of employment should be. His recommendations are *not* binding on either party.

Agency Shop

A type of union security clause whereby an employee within 31 days of employment must either join the employee organization or pay a service fee (usually equal to monthly dues).

Arbitration

See **Advisory Arbitration**
      Compulsory Arbitration
      Grievance Arbitration

Bargaining Unit

A particular group of employees which has been recognized by the city as an appropriate group to be represented by a single employee organization. There may be more than one bargaining unit in the agency: patrolmen, sergeants, lieutenants, and captains may each have a separate unit (i.e., each group bargains separately), they may all be in one unit (i.e., negotiate together) or any combination of groups may constitute separate units.

Blue Flu

A particular job action which consists of mass sick calls by members of the bargaining unit.

Card Check

A process whereby an employer may "recognize" an employee organization as the sole and exclusive bargaining agent for a particular bargaining unit. The employee organization presents the employer with cards signed by a majority of the employees in the unit indicating they wish to be represented by this

215

employee organization. After validating the signatures, the employer may either recognize the employee organization or call for a certification election.

Certified, Certification

Determination by the city, a state agency, or the chief that an employee organization which claims to be the majority representative for a bargaining unit does in fact represent a majority in that unit.

Collective Bargaining

The process in which representatives of the employees and representatives of the employer meet and confer and negotiate to determine to their mutual satisfaction the new terms and conditions of employment. The agreement is usually reduced to writing in the form of a contract, resolution, or ordinance.

Collective-Bargaining Agreement

The contract, resolution, or ordinance drawn up which specifies part or all of the terms and conditions of employment.

Compulsory Binding Arbitration

If in the course of negotiating a new (or first) agreement the parties find themselves unable to reach a mutually satisfactory arrangement, they may be required to proceed with compulsory arbitration. Compulsory arbitration differs from advisory arbitration in that (1) the parties *must* participate and (2) the decision of the neutral third party is *binding* on both sides.

Contract

One form of written agreement which may come out of collective bargaining (*see* Collective Bargaining).

Dues Check-Off

A union security clause whereby employee organization dues are automatically "checked off" by payroll deduction and remitted to the employee organization by the employer.

Exclusive Representative

See Sole and Exclusive Bargaining Agent

Fact-Finding

If in the course of negotiating a new (or first) agreement the parties find themselves unable to reach a mutually satisfactory arrangement, they may proceed to fact-finding. Fact-finding refers to the process whereby a neutral third party holds a hearing and after due consideration of the facts makes public his recommendations as to what the new terms and conditions of employment should be. His recommendations are *not* binding on either party. If this appears similar to the definition of advisory arbitration it is because they are virtually the same process. For all practical purposes the terms are interchangeable.

Grievance

An employee complaint that his rights have been violated. The complaint usually refers to a violation of the collective-bargaining agreement, a violation of an applicable ordinance or resolution, a violation of departmental rules, etc. How many of these violations will be subject to your grievance procedure will depend on how you define a grievance in the grievance procedure. Management may also file a grievance against an employee who has violated one of the above.

Grievance Arbitration

Often this is the final step in the grievance procedure. A neutral third party is appointed and he holds a private hearing and then issues a decision which is *binding* on the parties. Grievance arbitration differs from fact-finding, advisory arbitration, and compulsory arbitration in that these last three processes are concerned with the *negotiation* of *new* terms and conditions of employment while grievance arbitration is limited to the *interpretation* of *existing* agreements, laws, rules, etc.

Grievance Procedure

The process through which a grievance is adjudicated. The process usually consists of several steps which carry the grievance to higher and higher levels in the organization and possibly to an outside agent or agency for final resolution.

Impasse

When the employer and the employee organization have negotiated to a point where they have failed to reach a mutually satisfactory agreement and yet neither is willing to make any further concessions, as impasse is said to have occurred.

Informational Picketing

The term used to describe the picketing situation where the signs inform the public about the nature of the employees' grievance(s) against the employer and/or indicate that a labor dispute is in process.

Job Action

A phrase used to describe any of a variety of actions which involve a departure from normal work practices by a group of employees for the purpose of expressing their dissatisfaction over one or more issues in the employment relationship.

Maintenance of Membership

A type of union security clause whereby all those employees who are members of the employee organization at a certain time, and others who become members, must remain members for a specified length of time (usually the duration of the agreement or contract). New employees are not required to join, and at specified intervals those who are members may reconsider their membership decision.

Mediation

If in the process of negotiating a new (or first) agreement the parties are unable to reach a mutually satisfactory arrangement, they may go to mediation. Mediation is the process whereby a neutral third party is called in to meet with the employee and employer representatives together and individually in order to help find some common ground. The mediator always works in private; he exercises no power except moral persuasion and his own skills of explanation and exhortation. If he is unable to bring the parties together in an agreement he drops out of the picture.

Picketing

See **Informational Picketing**
    Recognition Picketing

Recognized, Recognition

The technical term indicating that management is willing to deal with a particular employee organization as the "recognized" bargaining unit. Less formal than certification.

Recognition Picketing

The term used to describe the picketing situation where the signs inform the public that the employer has refused to recognize the employee organization seeking to represent the employees.

Representation Election

An election supervised by an outside agency in which members of the bargaining unit vote by secret ballot to determine whether a particular employee organization will represent them for the purposes of collective bargaining.

Slow Down

A particular job action which consists of a deliberate reduction of output by a group of employees in an attempt to put pressure on the employer, e.g., refusing to issue traffic citations or issuing warnings in lieu of citations.

Sole and Exclusive Bargaining Agent

An employee organization which has been officially recognized as the sole and exclusive collective-bargaining representative of the men in the bargaining unit for which it sought representation rights.

Speed Up

A particular job action which consists of a deliberate increase in output in an attempt to put pressure on the employer, e.g., issuing an unusually large number of citations for dirty license plates or exceeding the speed limit by one mile per hour.

Strike

A particular job action which consists of a total withdrawal of services by part or all of the members of the bargaining unit.

Union

As we use it, union refers to *any and all* police employee organizations which seek to represent the men for the purpose of discussing matters relevant to the employment relationship—wages, hours, and other terms and conditions of work.

Union Security

See **Agency Shop**
    Dues Check-Off
    Maintenance of Membership
    Union Shop

Union Shop

A type of union security clause whereby all employees in a particular bargaining unit must join the employee organization. All new employees must also join (usually within 31 days of employment).

Wildcat

A job action or strike in which the men take the initiative themselves without any authorization from the leaders of the employee organization. Not only is the job action not in the hands of these established leaders, in fact the leaders may attempt to get the men to go back to work.

Index

Index

AFSCME, 11, 17, 18, 25, 27, 29, 30, 31, 38, 39, 96, 152
Abbott, David, 198
Adams, J.S., 193
Alex, Nicholas, 171, 211
Alioto, Joseph, 84
American Federation of Labor, 8, 16-17
American Federation of State, County, and Municipal Employees, see AFSCME
Andrews, I.R., 193
Arbitration, 92-94, 100; and see Dispute resolution procedures
Armour automation agreement, 180
Ashenfelter, Orley, 189, 199

Bachrach, Peter, 96, 204
Baer, Michael, 201
Bakke, E. Wight, 193
Baldwin, Moses, 174
Baltimore, Md., 37, 38, 50, 60, 63, 69, 120-21, 131, 133, 141, 144, 152, 155, 158, 163, 165, 197, 203, 210, 211; AFSCME, 90, 199, 210; IACP, 141; Urban Coalition, 155
Banfield, Edward, 198
Baratz, Morton, 96, 204
Barbash, Jack, 194
Bargaining power, see Collective bargaining
Berkeley, Cal., 59, 78, 120
Berney, Donald, 15, 16, 17, 18, 58, 190-92, 196, 199, 202
Bilateralism, 42
Bittner, Egon, 200, 206, 207
Black coalition, New Haven, 167
Black militancy, 21
Black officer organizations, 31, 113, 165-75
Blacks on police force 3, 4, 5, 88, 97, 165-75
Blacks, recruitment of, 111-113, 166, 167
"Blue flu," 70, 85, 86-87, 138
Bopp, William, 189, 192
Boston, Mass., 3, 37, 38, 58, 61, 66, 67, 71, 77, 84, 85, 87, 88, 89, 90, 91, 93, 94, 95, 100, 112, 126, 129, 130, 131, 134, 135, 139-40, 141, 143, 145, 152, 155, 156, 157, 159, 160, 161, 190-191, 202, 203; BPPA, 24, 30, 37-38, 84; police strike, 1919, 1, 16-17, 88, 189, 190
Brookings studies, 148-50
Brukiewa, Eugene C., 163, 199
Buffalo, N.Y., 28, 30, 37, 63, 67, 85, 90, 93, 94, 95, 99, 100, 111-12, 121, 122, 123, 125, 128, 131, 133, 143, 145, 146, 155, 157, 159, 161, 174, 203, 210, 211; Commission on Human Relations, 155; Erie Club, 15
Burpo, John, 189
Burton, John F., Jr., 196, 203

COPE, 10
California, 77, 78, 92, 99, 191; Alliance of Police Associations, 30; ICPA, 28; Supreme Court, 158; Peace Officers Research Association of, 26, 30
Call-back, 130
Call-in, 130
Candidates Review Board, 167
Cassesse, John, 25, 30, 38, 152, 170, 193, 209
"Catch-up" principle, 54
Cavanaugh, Jerome, 58
Chamberlain, Neil W., 43, 182, 194, 195, 198, 199, 204, 211
Chicago, Ill., 16, 17, 28, 56, 59, 100, 153, 165, 167, 191
Cincinnati, O., 60, 63, 83, 99, 100, 122, 128, 130, 131, 134, 141, 153, 165, 167, 174
Citizen complaints, 156-57
Civil rights, 142-45, 146
Civilian Complaint Review Board, NYC, 25
Civilian review, 155-56; and see Civilian review board controversy
Civilian review board controversy, 49, 69-70, 82-83, 155, 168
Civilianization, 132-33
Clark, Terry N., 198

223

About the Authors

Hervey A. Juris is an associate professor of industrial relations and urban affairs in the Graduate School of Management, Northwestern University. He received the A.B. from Princeton University and M.B.A. and Ph.D. from the Graduate School of Business, University of Chicago. He has published widely in scholarly journals in industrial relations and urban affairs and is currently doing research on the implications of the unionization of professionals in the public and private sectors.

Peter Feuille is assistant professor of management in the College of Business Administration, University of Oregon. He has taught previously at the University of California, Berkeley and at California State College, Hayward. He received the B.A. from Claremont Men's College and Ph.D. from the University of California, Berkeley. He has previously published in the area of public sector labor relations and is currently doing research on faculty attitudes toward university collective bargaining and on dispute resolution in public sector labor relations.